THE LAST STAND

OTHER BOOKS BY DAVID HARRIS

Our War (1996)

Dreams Die Hard (1993)

The League (1986)

The Last Scam (1981)

I Shoulda Been Home Yesterday (1976)

Goliath (1969)

THE LAST STAND

THE WAR BETWEEN WALL STREET
AND MAIN STREET OVER
CALIFORNIA'S ANCIENT REDWOODS

DAVID HARRIS

HEYDAY, BERKELEY, CALIFORNIA

The Library of Congress has cataloged the hardcover edition as follows:

Harris, David
The last stand : the war between Wall Street and Main Street over California's ancient redwoods / David Harris.
 p.cm
Includes index.
ISBN 0-87156-944-2
1. Pacific Lumber Company. 2. Consolidation and merger of corporations—United States. 3. Redwood industry—California—Humboldt
County. 4. Scotia (Calif.) 5. Environmentalists—California—Humboldt
County. 6. Earth First! (Organization). 1. Title.
338.7'63498'0979412—dc20   95-15384

Heyday paperback ISBN: 978-1-59714-441-4

Cover Photo: Mikolaj Walczuk
Cover Design: Ashley Ingram
Interior Design/Typesetting: Susan Ristow

Orders, inquiries, and correspondence should be addressed to:
 Heyday
 P.O. Box 9145, Berkeley, CA 94709
 (510) 549-3564, Fax (510) 549-1889
 www.heydaybooks.com

Printed in East Peoria, IL, by Versa Press, Inc.

10 9 8 7 6 5 4 3 2 1

For Lacey,
God rest her soul,
and my dad,
God rest his

Contents

Preface

The Pacific Lumber story was iconic when I first started reporting on it in 1986, and it has only become more so in the years
since. This struggle over a timber company, its workers, and its
forests in Northern California, captured the collision of late-
twentieth-century American enterprise with the rise of political
ecology and the decline of the laboring class. As such, it impacted
the shape and content of American society far beyond the borders
of Humboldt County and into the twenty-first century. *The Last
Stand*, first published in 1995, chronicles this backwoods drama
with big-picture scope and big-city implications, both past and
future, and is required reading for anyone interested in California, Wall Street, lumberjacks, or the environment. The events it
recounts still demand to be remembered and reexamined for the
lessons they have to teach us about who America is and how we
behave when resources are up for grabs.

This story is constructed of four overlapping elements, each with
its own characters and agenda, each at angles with the others. The
first of those elements is a species of tree, *Sequoia sempervirens*, the
coast redwood, found nowhere in the world but within forty miles
of the Pacific Ocean on California's western edge, between Monterey Bay and the Oregon border. No plant on the planet grows taller
than these redwoods, and few live longer. *Sequoia sempervierens*'s
natural lifespan commonly exceeds a thousand years, its mature
height can reach taller than three hundred feet, and its diameter
has been measured at a dozen feet or more. The species has been

around since the age of dinosaurs, and one clue to its longevity is *Sempervirens*'s unique biological character, which endows it with a remarkable capacity to resist pests and rot, whether alive and growing in the forest or felled and sawed into boards. In 1850, the new state of California contained some two million acres of untouched virgin coast redwood groves, ready to be plundered. By the time this story commenced in 1986, only one hundred thousand acres of those trees still survived under the protection of some eighty different public parks. Almost all of the other 1.9 million acres had been cut and milled into the deep red lumber yielded by only old-growth trees. At that point virtually the entire remaining inventory of unprotected ancient redwood timberlands belonged to the Pacific Lumber Company. Every other forestry company had long since logged the entirety of their old-growth. PL literally owned the last stand still standing.

Which, of course, made PL worth a lot of money. This story's second interlocking element centers on Wall Street, fresh to the era of ferocious corporate takeovers fueled by easy credit—a.k.a. junk bonds—issued at extremely high rates of interest and in sufficient quantities to allow investors to secretly acquire controlling interests in the stock of unwary corporations. In that frenzy of financial aggression, a Texas stock raider, Charles Hurwitz, turned his attention to Pacific Lumber, attracted by its unique assets and relative absence of indebtedness, and, using money borrowed with the backing of Michael Milken, a banker from the legendary Drexel Burnham Lambert firm who had earned himself the nickname "the King of Junk Bonds," Hurwitz seized control of PL. Upon assuming ownership, he described himself as a believer in the Golden Rule, which he explained as "Those who have the gold, rule." Once PL was his, he tripled, and sometimes quadrupled, the company's rate of harvest in its ancient forest, generating massive clear-cuts and a financial windfall that filled the coffers of Hurwitz's Texas parent company, all the while transforming Pacific Lumber into a North Coast symbol of avarice and indifference to anything other than maximizing short-term profit.

The great irony in this new age of Hurwitz was that PL and its workforce—the third element in this drama—had once been acclaimed for their conservative and personal approach to lumbering—the exact opposite of what happened during the Texas transformation. For the decades PL was privately held by the Murphy family, who had bought the company at the turn of the twentieth century, PL had never engaged in clear-cuts, instead practicing "selective cut," meaning they always left a few ancient trees behind to seed the next generation of forest and hold the hillside. Even more revolutionary, the Murphy PL only cut as many board feet per year as its lands grew. The bane of the timber industry had always been its tendency to cut itself out of work, and the Murphy family thought their approach would cure that ill. Their plan of limited cutting meant the company expected to be harvesting old-growth *sempervirens* well past the year 2040, with many more generations of their family working on PL lands, a virtually unheard of arrangement in the logging business. PL also nurtured its workers: most employees lived in Scotia, California's last surviving company town, grouped around its sawmill on the Eel River; the children of all employees had their college tuition paid by the company; all employees were served by the company hospital; all received sizeable Christmas bonuses; and all were covered by a generous pension plan. The trouble began when the Murphys started selling PL stock to the public, a move that opened the door to Charles Hurwitz, whose arrival with his self-suited Golden Rule cast a shadow over what had been a protected and paternalistic way of life. *The Last Stand* tracks the attempts of Humboldt County attorney Bill Bertain to defend the old PL and stymie Hurwitz's ongoing threat to that Murphy culture, retracing the turmoil that ensued as the company's workers lost the best friend they ever had and were forced to choose between a short-term boom and long-term security.

The fourth and final element in this story is an unlikely army with hair flowing over its shoulders, Birkenstocks on its feet, and an abiding commitment to saving what ancient forest there was left. If half of Humboldt County were loggers, the other half were hippies, and, enraged by Hurwitz's cutting frenzy out on the hill-sides, the hippies fought back with what tools they had, using forestry laws, public information campaigns, and civil disobedience to engage Hurwitz's PL in California's first statewide political conflict ever over what should happen to these last remaining enormous trees. Led by two organizers, Greg King and Darryl Cherney, and a self-taught legal genius known as "the Man Who Walks in the Woods"—Woods, for short—the hippies managed to slow down and then thwart Hurwitz when no one else could. Against all odds, this scruffy slice of counterculture focused public attention on the social values inherent in forestry practices and eventually wrote the most recent chapter in the saga of California's magnificent ancient *Sequoia sempervirens* by rescuing the last contiguous 7,500 acres of PL's old-growth forest for the state and federal park systems.

The chemistry generated in the interaction of those four elements still dogs us today as we try to find new ways to live with the nature that has nurtured us, while also utilizing the resources that have underwritten our prosperity up to this point. We have serious questions to answer about the future of civilization, and a number of them were framed in Humboldt County more than thirty years ago.

POSTSCRIPT

In January 2007, the Pacific Lumber Company filed for bankruptcy. By then, Charles Hurwitz had extracted an estimated $3 billion worth of PL's assets and "upstreamed" the proceeds back to his Texas corporation, where they were unreachable by PL's creditors. The bankrupt Pacific Lumber Company had almost $1 billion in outstanding debt.

The Takeover

1

At first, the phone call just brought Warren up short, like one of those cartoon collisions in which the front of the column screeches to a halt and the rest of the parade, helpless to control its momentum, stacks up against the leading edge like the pleats of an accordion—only in this instance, Warren Lawrence Murphy was rear-ended by a hundred years of Humboldt County history and five generations of his own ancestors, piling on as he stood there in the living room of his company house in the company's town, slack-jawed and at a loss for words. This was the beginning of the end, but Warren Lawrence Murphy hadn't a clue.

The day had been frantic since the 8:00 A.M. whistle blew, but nothing all that extraordinary had happened until now. Warren had hustled down to Mill A a half-dozen times, trying to untangle the new conveyors that refused to work right and then to hassle with the gang saw that kept fouling itself. Mill A had been back on line at full shift for almost a year since the rebuild, but it was still a nest of glitches and slowdowns and each fresh one meant John Campbell's tree stump of a neck would bristle and turn pink and Warren's backside would end up with singe marks all over it. Then, right before the lunch whistle, Maintenance located dry rot down in the kilns and, as if Warren wasn't already stretched like a five-pound line hooked to a fifty-pound fish, Campbell decided he wanted another set of numbers for the product flow around the proposed new power plant and he wanted those numbers yesterday and he didn't care what else his manager of lumber operations had on his plate, he wanted them in a bloody hurry, no excuses.

Frayed on all edges, Warren finally signed out of the office and went home about the time the evening fog bank reached Rio Dell on the far side of the Eel.

It was just your typical July day until the phone rang.

What'd you say? Warren mumbled into the receiver.

They want to buy it out, Enright repeated, a little exasperated at how thick Murphy was being. They want to buy the Pacific Lumber Company and they want you to front the deal.

Buy PL? Warren repeated the phrase to himself but it still didn't make sense. Buy PL? What could have gotten into those Texans' heads? Pacific Lumber wasn't the kind of company anybody could just walk in and buy. Not since the days of his great-great-grandfather, Simon Jones Murphy, anyway, and Simon had bought the company back when the only links between the county and the rest of the world were the fleet of lumber barques anchored in Humboldt Bay and the rutted wagon track that wound south through the Coast Range and washed out every winter, when the rain fell in sheets and the Eel turned surly. Buy PL? Warren's dad, Stanwood Albert Murphy, God rest his soul, would have gagged at the very notion, and he was the one who'd first listed Pacific Lumber on the New York Stock Exchange, fifteen years ago. "Buy PL?" Stan would have roared over a third martini down at the Scotia Inn. "Someone must be cuttin' your hair with a chain saw. You've lost your goddamn mind." And then he'd have led the bar in laughter, chuckling so hard his chin jiggled.

Buy PL?

That's right, Warren, buy PL, Enright repeated. You know, make a tender offer for the stock and the whole bit. You forgot what you learned in biz school already?

All of that corporate trading curriculum was indeed a dim memory to Warren. These days, almost a decade since his graduate student life at the University of San Diego, his thoughts were consumed with log scales, board feet, skid roads, Timber Harvest Plans, green chains, and head rigs, subjects with which no one at the School of Business concerned themselves. Warren's soft face creased as his mind sought recall.

But the company's not for sale, Warren said out loud.

Not for sale? Jesus, Warren, don't they get *The Wall Street Journal* up in Scotia? Everything's for sale these days. If its stock is traded, it's for sale. That's what's happenin', even to companies like PL. Haven't you ever heard of Ivan Boesky? Carl Icahn? Michael Milken? This is 1985. Corporate takeovers are America's biggest business.

Takeover? What did all that financial fast-lane stuff have to do with Humboldt County? Here, pop. 105,000, right next to the Pacific Ocean in California's upper left-hand corner, covering an area the size of all five New York City boroughs combined, well away from just about everything but the forest, folks pictured Wall Street as some kind of Disneyland for people too rich to sweat for a living—altogether foreign turf to the ramshackle sawmills and timber towns along the banks of the Eel, the Mattole, the Mad, and the Van Duzen.

Anyway, Enright was saying, these guys weren't like Boesky and the others. These were the Bass brothers, just about the classiest money in Texas. They weren't a bunch of raiders. They wanted a nice friendly takeover, they didn't want to have to fight the company in order to own it. The Basses didn't do business that way. That's why they want you. They want somebody to bird-dog this deal whose presence is a clear message of their good intentions. Who better than a Murphy? Your grandfather made the company the best in the business. Your mom's on the board. Hey, if your dad hadn't died so young . . .

His friend's words nudged Warren's mind off the present and back to Gobel's Mortuary in Fortuna, when he was a college freshman, living at the family's ranch on Larabee Creek up in the hills south of Scotia and working on a PL woods crew for the summer. He was walking through the crowd with his mom and his older brother, Woody, and his sister, Suzanne. The scene was all fuzzy around the edges but he remembered lots of mill hands wearing unfamiliar ties with crooked knots and loggers looking clumsy without their hobnailed boots and he remembered everyone's eyes were red as salmon eggs. People who never cried were crying and everywhere around him people sobbed at the mention of his father's name. There were so many of them the sheriff had to close off the street during the funeral and, as the mourners pulled back and made a path for the family to walk through, some stranger he couldn't place, standing over at the edge of his memory, said that losing Stan was the worst thing that had ever happened to Humboldt County. Worse even than the flood of 1964, he said.

Abruptly, Warren noticed his own silence. The receiver was just a dead weight against his ear and the conversation had stalled, so he cleared his throat and asked Enright just how the Basses had picked up PL's scent.

Enright said he didn't have a clue, but he allowed they probably weren't the only ones sniffing around. Wall Street's bargain hunters seemed to be hot on forest products companies these days, ever since Sir James Goldsmith bought Crown Zellerbach. All Enright knew was that Pacific Lumber's name came up in conversation with some Bass executives his company in Texas was dealing with and, when they revealed what the Basses were thinking about, he'd offered to try to hook them up with Warren, his old buddy from biz school.

As his friend talked, Murphy's mind continued to drift. Buy PL? Of course it wasn't his to sell—he only inherited a fraction of 1 percent of the stock, just like his brother Woody and his sister Suzanne—but it felt as if it was all his. There was no Murphy at the top of the company now, but Warren's ancestors' pictures were still all over the boardroom walls down in the San Francisco headquarters and, growing up, at the dinner table every night since they had been old enough to talk business, Stan had insisted that his children understand that the Pacific Lumber Company came first, that when the company said "jump," they were to ask "how high?" and if the company was under attack, they were to throw themselves on the barricades without hesitation. Warren was born to such fealty the way a Hindu was born to a caste. How could all that be sold? And how on earth could he be the one to sell it?

So what do you think, Warren? You game for it?

What?

What do you think? Enright repeated irritably. What shall I tell the Bass brothers?

I don't know, Warren hedged. I just don't know if I could . . .

Enright interrupted. This would be a big chance for Warren too, he admonished. Remember that. This isn't just about the Basses. Warren would come out of this in a position to run the whole shebang. Warren would be the Basses' timber man, sitting down in San Francisco making the thing work, just like his grandpa and his dad. And it'd happen right away, not another twenty years down the line. Right away.

Those words lifted the short hairs on the back of Warren Murphy's neck. His ambition had an easy-going facade, but, no one in the company doubted that he meant to be the next Murphy on the boardroom wall. He'd wanted that ever since Stan was laid in the ground, almost to the day—as though the termination of his father's insistence let him finally accept, for the first time in his life, that Pacific Lumber was indeed where he belonged, let him abandon his teenaged rebellion and swallow his destiny. After his dad was buried, Warren returned to his summer job out in the woods along Bear Creek, tying chokers for a crew that dropped and chopped thousand-year-old trees almost three hundred feet tall and, out there, the old guys, the ones who knew Stan personally, demanded to know what he was doing. He belonged down in the office, learning to take his daddy's place. The company needed a Murphy to run it, they said, that was just the way it was, and Woody, his brother, was a good ol' boy, but he didn't have what it took to wear Stan's shoes. And when Warren, tormented and grieving, couldn't find an answer that rang true to his own ear and to theirs, he just gave in and accepted his designation as Crown Prince.

So he dropped philosophy to study business, and, once out of school and back in Scotia, started learning Pacific Lumber, touring the company's bottom rungs from log deck to green chain to chop saw to order garden, mastering the collection of tasks PL paid hard-handed men $12 an hour to perform—always drawn along by the prospect of some day sitting on top of it all, in the same chair in which his father and grandfather had made their marks.

When, now, out of the blue, his old college buddy Enright dangled that dream right in front of his nose as though it might come true tomorrow, Warren, unable to say yes, couldn't say no either.

I'll run it up the flagpole, he told Enright. See what the guys over my head think.

With that, Enright said goodbye and the phone call was over.

But the subject wouldn't let go of Warren. He tried to shake it with a drink and a little television, but when he crawled into bed next to his wife, Sharon, and sought sleep, it was still there, stuck to

his brain as fast as a tick on a deer's ear. The thought of any change
in the Pacific Lumber Company character as set out some fifty years
ago by his grandfather, Albert Stanwood Murphy, made his stomach
clench. Thirteen years of hired managers since Stan died had left
old A.S.'s policies set in stone and that suited Warren just fine. On
the other hand, a change that brought another Murphy back to the
presidency really wasn't so much a change as a reaffirmation. Or so
Warren, tossing and turning deep into the night, was tempted to
suppose.

When he left his house the next morning, he went straight to the
office of John Campbell, Pacific Lumber's executive vice president
for forest products and its highest-ranking officer north of San
Francisco. John and Warren were friends, despite a ten-year difference in their ages and a lurking distrust in the back of Murphy's
head, mostly because of the screwing Campbell had given old man
Flinchpaugh in order to rise to his current post. But Campbell had
taken Warren along with him as he rose, so Warren had swallowed
his doubts and kept his mouth shut. John had the instincts of a
shark and he too planned to be president of PL some day. He was
not the kind of guy Warren wanted to end up on the wrong side of.

They want to what? Campbell exclaimed.

They want to buy the company, in a takeover, Warren repeated,
but they want it to be friendly and they want me to spearhead it
for them.

A laugh burst out of Campbell's mouth. Jesus H. Christ, he guf-
fawed, what the hell do they need you for?

Without waiting for an answer, Campbell punched the company's San Francisco headquarters number into his telephone. In
short order, he had Gene Elam, Pacific Lumber's president and
c.e.o. on the line. Addressing Elam, Campbell's voice sounded just a
bit more Australian and assumed the tone of a prize pupil talking to
his Sunday School teacher. He said he had something he thought
Gene ought to hear about and, switching on the speaker phone, announced that Warren Murphy was here with him.

Warren hid his feelings by borrowing a bit of Campbell's obse-
quiousness, but, in truth, he had little use for Elam, the company's
former accountant who'd never been initiated in the mysteries of
the woods and the mill. The only timber Elam had ever handled was
a pencil.

For his part, PL's president sat in San Francisco and listened to Warren's account of his phone call with growing impatience. He had enough serious business with which to deal and had no use for this kind of pointless, time-consuming rumor mongering. And he didn't want some junior executive who happened to be named Murphy blathering around, indulging his fantasies and mucking about in stock manipulation. The company's stock had enough trouble as it was.

Elam's response was brusque. Look, he said, you tell your friend we're not interested in anything he's talking about.

Not interested? Warren asked. He was incredulous that Elam didn't even want to look into it just to find out what was going on, if nothing else. You don't even want me to get more information about it?

Not in the least, Elam repeated. End of subject, end of conversation.

Back home that evening, Warren Murphy passed the news on to Enright and he never raised the issue with Campbell or Elam again. At the time, he concluded that it was all very interesting, the kind of off-the-wall incident that made a good story over a beer down at Mingo's Tavern in Rio Dell, but, otherwise, it was no big thing one way or another.

Months later, when Warren had to look back across the wreckage of his aspirations and let himself imagine what might have been, he couldn't get that phone call from Texas off his mind. If only he'd done more, he fretted, if only he'd taken it as a sign, a warning signal, if only . . .

By then, of course, events had accelerated and that momentary flirtation with the Bass brothers marked just the first step along the battered trail of his beloved company's undoing.

After that phone call from Texas, everything started coming apart.

2

The rest of Scotia, of course, hadn't a clue of what was coming either. Here, pop. 1,100, nestled in the crook of an elbow made by the Eel as it emerged onto the coastal flat, folks had little reason to be on the lookout. This was, after all, the backwoods. The latest fashion in everything except pickup trucks always arrived here two years late and news about anything besides working hours, deer season, sports, or the price of beefsteak usually got the short end of the stick. People here made a point of expecting more of the same from life and, almost invariably, got it.

The Pacific Lumber Company occupied the heart of that enduring sameness. Landlord, boss, and neighbor, the company woke everyone in the morning, worked them forty hours a week when they were able, and nursed them when they weren't. Pacific Lumber's garbage man hauled their trash, its carpenter fixed their squeaky screen doors and sagging shutters. They worshiped in its two churches, one Catholic and one Protestant, and sent their kids to its school, Stanwood A. Murphy Elementary. If they wanted a drink, they would buy one down on Main Street at Pacific Lumber's hotel, the Scotia Inn, or take the Albert S. Murphy bridge across the Eel to Rio Dell, pop. 2,300, and buy one over there. On the anniversary of the day he started at the company, every PL employee received a bonus that escalated each year and, at Christmas, PL distributed gifts to everyone's kids. If those kids wanted to go to college when they grew up, PL guaranteed them a scholarship at company expense.

The people who worked for Pacific Lumber rarely thought of it as a publicly traded investment. To them, it was a way of life that happened to issue stock.

And they expected the company to last forever, just the way it was. Pacific Lumber, the oldest log sawyer in California, and Scotia, the last company town left in the state, seemed to live outside the standard rules of time and capital. Change here was so rare that incidents of it could be easily distinguished on a short walking tour.

The old redwood boardwalks that had lined the shoulders of B Street, clattering under the feet of evening strollers, began giving way to concrete some time after the Great Depression. The community cookhouse disappeared around then as well and the company no longer sponsored gardening contests, so the array of flowers surrounding Scotia's bungalows wasn't nearly as striking as it had been in the late forties and early fifties. The company no longer staged its Labor Day picnic either. At it, the whole town used to gather next to the river, seated at a quarter mile's worth of tables, and devour a ton of barbequed beef, a ton of potato salad, nine thousand rolls, and three thousand bottles of beer, all on the company's tab. The old Green Goose whorehouse had been shut down in the 1920s and the building, just up the bank from the picnic grounds and below the log pond, was given over to a processing plant for Bertain's Laundry. The building burnt down one summer during World War II and, while the company fire department fought the blaze, Scotians remembered, young Charlie Moran, Stan Murphy's cousin and now a PL director, fell off the roof. The company immediately built a new plant for the laundry on the same spot where the Green Goose had once stood. On higher ground, Scotia's Main Street was still dominated by the Winema Theatre—handcrafted entirely from the prime redwood for which PL was famous and constructed to resemble a Bavarian lodge, complete with carved eaves and a portico supported by stripped and sanded logs—but the Winema, once a functioning movie house and host of local talent shows, was now used only for the occasional grammar school graduation or community meeting. The hospital, around the corner, just past the company offices, was once a full-service forty-bed facility but had been reduced over the years to a large-scale infirmary that sent serious patients to the newer county hospital ten miles north in Fortuna. The huge swimming hole the company used to dredge out behind a sand bar when summer shrank the Eel, fifty yards wide, to a depth of barely two feet, had been replaced by a standard tiled pool located in the town proper. Mill A, the size of a three-story airplane hangar with "Pacific Lumber Company" painted on its side, had been retooled to handle smaller Douglas Fir logs and now only Mill B, even larger, handled the mammoth old-growth redwood sections hauled down out of the Coast Range. U.S. Highway 101, Scotia's two-lane main drag until the 1960s, had become a four-lane freeway rerouted along the edge of town, on the high ground below the bluffs, obliterating some of Scotia's nicest houses, including the one in which Warren Murphy had been raised. Now, Scotia was just one more exit ramp, after Pepperwood and before Rio Dell.

Otherwise, the tiny town was pretty much the same as fifty years earlier, when old A. S. Murphy started making PL into the finest lumber company in the world.

Kelly Bettiga sometimes thought of PL's unending status quo the way he imagined an anthropologist might, usually as he sat over a piece of pie down at the Scotia Coffee Shop, when he'd tired of chit-chat with Ruby, the waitress, and still had a few minutes before he had to start his shift cleaning Mill A. Of course he'd never really studied the place with the methodology used by the social scientists he read for his courses up at Humboldt State University, but, as he liked to say, he was fuckin' third-generation PL and that counted for a lot. He'd been in and around this place all his life except for his hitch in the Navy, serving as the helmsman on an aircraft carrier standing to in the South China Sea, launching bombers at the Nam. Some day, when he finished his master's degree, he figured he'd get away from PL for good, but going to school during the day, working nights, and paying alimony to his ex–old lady, that might take a while. In the meantime, it pleased him to scrutinize. Course, who was he? Just the hippie on the night shift in most folks' eyes. Still, he had his theories, on which he was more than willing to expound, at least until somebody told him to shut up.

Scotia and the whole PL scene up here were just like the hobbits, Kelly Bettiga liked to say. Just like the goddamn hobbits, those little

THE TAKEOVER   13

people in the Tolkien books—a tiny world, separate from the rest of
reality, tucked back away from anywhere and anything, working by
its very own set of rules. It was a dead goddamn ringer. Real life
hadn't made a dent up here, not a dent.

Which was not to say that the necks up and down Main Street
weren't just as red as any other mill town—that's sure as shit—it's
just that none of the rest was quite the same. Most people who
worked timber couldn't count on much more than the sun comin'
up the next morning. One week you're working, the next week you
ain't; one week your town is booming, the next week it's dead. Here,
you could count on everything. Here, there were pensions, health
insurance, employee stock plans, the whole nine yards. None of the
other mills had anything like that. The Murphys had busted the
only union that ever tried to organize here but they always paid a
higher wage than any of the union shops and better benefits. Once,
when Stan Murphy was running things, he'd hired one of those effi-
ciency experts to look this place over and he came back with a long
list of jobs that could be eliminated. Old Stan read that damn list
and threw it in the shit can. He said, "I can't lay those people off.
They're all my friends." That's the kind of place PL was. When you
got on here, you were taken care of. Shit, some families, like the Bet-
tigas, had been workin here three generations, some for four. Most
lumber companies don't even last one generation, but this place
was organized to last forever. This was lumberjack paradise. It ran in
a closed loop, feeding on itself, you know, like something worshiped
by a bunch of Borneo niggers with bones through their noses. People here treated PL like it was part of the landscape, Kelly liked to
say, like the fucking Eel River or the Coast Range, a force of nature
that would just go on and on, doing what it did.

What PL did began at first light, out on the alluvial flats and precipitous slopes where the coast redwoods, *sequoia sempervirens*, grow.
These, of course, were no ordinary trees. The ones growing in the
company's virgin stands were often more than a thousand years old
and two hundred and fifty feet tall with a diameter of some fifteen
feet. During logging season—from April, when the rains tailed off,
to November, when they picked up again—the migrating "logging
shows" in which these colossi were harvested were scattered here
and there from the far side of the Van Duzen to the western reaches

of the Mattole. The doomed trees were transformed into logs by two men on the ground, a "feller" and his "bucker," and another man mounted on a Caterpillar tractor, usually of the high-powered D-8 variety. The Cat driver carved the hillside into a cushion of raised earth called a "layout" to catch the falling tree and save it from splintering upon impact. Then the feller, the show's lead artist, went after the trunk with his chain saw, severing the tree from its roots at just the right angle to ensure it would drop on the designated spot, cleaving through the air with such force that it sucked the breath right out of the feller's lungs on the way down. The final step belonged to the bucker, who mounted the fallen redwood, stripped it of its limbs, and divided its length into twenty- and forty-foot sections.

These logs were then "skidded"—winched from where they fell, secured to a D-8 Cat, and dragged to a "landing" where logs from all over the show were collected and marked with a "setting" that allowed the mill to track when and where they had been cut. Some were stored temporarily at the landing and others were loaded on trucks by Cats rigged with giant pincers that seized and lifted five-ton logs as though they were pick-up-sticks. Then, with a belch of diesel smoke and a hiss of air brakes, these eighteen-wheelers, hauling anywhere from three to seven logs cinched onto their trailers, made their way out the dirt track gouged into the hillside by the company tractors, onto the paved road, and on down the hill to Scotia. Most logs were stacked there at the "cold deck," a massive wall of cut trees more than a hundred feet tall and as much as a mile long, looming over the riffles where the Eel began its elbow. Others, destined for immediate use, were dumped in the company's thirty-one-acre millpond, abutting the cavernous Mill B.

Mill B was the Pacific Lumber Company's flagship, big enough to park a dirigible in, constructed out of steel girders, corrugated tin, and fiberglass siding, situated along the railroad tracks, downslope from the last two blocks of cottages at the south end of town. In Mill B, giant logs became boards. That process began at the "debarker," where high-pressure blasts of water stripped off the redwoods' skin, often as much as a foot thick. The clumps of stripped bark were hauled off on a conveyor belt to be dried, ground, sorted, bagged, and sold for an assortment of uses ranging from filter papers to soil conditioner. The naked log was moved on to the "head-rig," a ten-foot bandsaw run by a "sawyer" seated in an overhead control room. The sawyer examined the log with a laser scanner, looking for the pattern of cuts that would yield the most lumber, then maneuvered the log, using hydraulic jacks, and ran it through his rig, slicing it lengthwise. The resulting slabs, called "cants," were flopped onto their sides and conveyed to an "edger," where the "edgerman," again mounted in an overhead control room, divided the cants into marketable widths with a medley of circular saws. Finally, the "trimmerman" used eight remote-controlled power blades to reduce the edgerman's work to appropriate lengths and slice out defects.

These freshly cut boards were carried by conveyor belt to the "green chain," where a crew sorted them by grade and size. A few were shipped fresh from the saws but most were carried by overhead monorail to the massive outdoor drying yards and stacked in thirty-foot-high squares. There, they sat for anywhere from three months to two years. The higher-grade boards were eventually moved on to a "kiln," for a final seasoning inside a warm, moisture-controlled building. Next to the kilns was a factory, where planing machinery manufactured building siding, moldings, flooring, end-glued boards, and paneling. Next to that was a huge warehouse in which the shipping department assembled orders for the thousands of lumber yards, wholesalers, and manufacturers who were the company's customers. At the other end of town, next to Mill A, there was another manufacturing plant. All of the buildings were connected by a web of monorails, steam pipes, overhead cranes, and conveyor belts, feeding one function or another.

And noise pervaded everything, often so loud that men standing shoulder to shoulder could not be understood except by shouting at the top of their lungs: the deep reverberating clunk of logs rolling against one another; the screams and screeches of hard metal blades tearing at high speed through soft wood; the clatter of conveyor rollers; the liquid sighs of hydraulics; the thud of ponderous loads lifted and dropped; the hiss of compressed air; the splash of logs hitting the water; the guttural farts of tractors, front-end loaders, and heavy-duty trucks; the groans of metal on metal as cranes bent under their tasks; the soft rustle of fresh sawdust under foot; the constant crack of boards stacked on boards stacked on more boards. When the mills shut for the day, the silence was startling.

That silence, of course, was the setting in which Kelly Bettiga pulled his shift, after the afternoon whistle brought the entire cacophony to a halt. On the way to work from the coffee shop, he passed hundreds of men going home, smelling of sweat, fresh tree sap, and diesel fuel. Once such parades were a sight all over Humboldt County. Lumber companies and sawmills used to be as thick as fleas on a dog, but not anymore. What was there, five or six of them left in Humboldt now? There'd been more than a thousand once. There were still several dozen left between here and Canada, but none of them had lasted the way PL had. Because PL was never just any lumber company, at least not since the Murphys had owned it. It was, Kelly always pointed out, *the* lumber company. The rest, they'd just cut the shit out of the forest until they didn't have no more trees and then they'd move on someplace else. Not PL. As he liked to say, fuckin' PL was made to last forever. They cut slow and easy, so there'd always be trees left. By the time all the first growth was gone, the second growth would be just as big, and on and on like that forever and ever. The way the Murphys set this place up, there'd always be work. That alone made it one of a kind. There was no company like it, not another one. None of them treated their people like PL and none of them treated the forest like PL, either. Fucking one of a kind, was what it was, Kelly liked to say, and he guessed they all had old Mr. A. S. Murphy to thank for that.

Albert Stanwood Murphy was addressed by everyone at the Pacific Lumber Company as just plain "Mr. Murphy" when he became president in 1931 at the age of thirty-nine. By then he was an invariably formal man, a regular in San Francisco high society who was never seen at work, either in the city or on visits to Scotia, without his high stiff collar. When he first arrived in Humboldt to cast his lot in the timber business, however, barely twenty years old, standing on the deck of a four-masted schooner riding the tide over the bar at the mouth of Humboldt Bay, he looked more determined than imposing. His grandfather, a Detroit millionaire, had bought the company almost a decade earlier and his father was an officer in the family partnership that had overseen the Murphy properties since his grandfather's death shortly after the deal for Pacific Lumber had been made—but A.S., like all the Murphys who followed him, started at the bottom and worked his way up, learning all the small tasks done by hardhanded men in hobnailed boots before moving on to San Francisco to master the desk and ledger side of the business.

During his first decade as chief executive officer, Mr. Murphy earned the reverence that still surrounded the portrait of him hanging on PL's boardroom wall. Ignoring the pressures of the Depression—when PL was feeding all comers out of its Scotia cookhouse and running its mills at only a small fraction of capacity—he instituted two of the policies that were principally responsible for the identity assumed by Pacific Lumber for the next half-century. Both sacrificed short-term profits in favor of what A.S. expected would be long-term health.

The first of those policies redefined how the company would cut its trees. At the time, clear-cutting—felling every one of the trees in any stand during harvesting, leaving behind a bald patch of mountainside—was the industry's standard technique. The result when the rains came to Humboldt—as much as a hundred inches a year in some spots—was a tide of topsoil, stripped of its natural moorings and running off the slopes in rivulets, clogging the streams and tributaries, and transforming the mighty Eel from a narrow watercourse running deep and blue all year round into a broad, silted riverbed that ran clear and shallow in summer and overwhelmed its banks when winters were especially wet and the flow turned thick and dun-colored. By the time A.S. took the reins of PL, the devastation wrought by logging had been plaguing Humboldt for a good fifty years and the salmon, native to all of the county's rivers, had begun to diminish and disappear. A few areas were so badly damaged that the redwoods, which normally regenerate from their own stumps, had died out, deprived of the soil they needed to sustain themselves, and been replaced by alder and other "junk" trees worthless to lumbermen.

Mr. Murphy decided to take PL out of that destructive cycle and, shortly after his promotion to chief executive, shifted the company to a policy of "selective cut." Henceforth, when harvesting, PL cut a maximum of 70 percent of the mature trees in a stand, leaving the younger, most vigorous redwoods to hold the hillside and seed a new generation of forest. Those "residuals" would eventually be logged off after another half-century or so of growth. In the meantime, it was often difficult for the untrained observer to realize, once the Cat tracks had grown over, that the company's selectively cut acreage had even been touched. Part of A.S.'s motivation for the change in policy was California's mid-century timber tax system that made financial advantages available to loggers willing to leave a portion of their harvested timberlands intact; part was his belief that if lumber companies were typecast as the purveyors of ugliness and destruction, their political survival was doubtful; and yet another part was his personal distaste, as an avid outdoorsman and hunter, for the havoc loggers were working on the Coast Range. With those admonitions in mind, under Mr. Murphy's guidance the Pacific Lumber Company parted ways from the industry and pursued its own course.

Mr. Murphy's other major departure from the industry norm was over the pace at which PL's forests would be cut. The underlying issue was the same one that had driven the Murphys and the rest of the industry west. Simon Jones Murphy, A.S.'s grandfather, had started his first sawmill on the Penobscot River in Maine and then, as the ancient eastern forests played out, moved on to the St. Clair River in Michigan. There, his interests had widened into mining and real estate, but Simon's final investment, the purchase of PL, was a recognition that the Great Lakes forests were playing out as well. His grandson, A.S., had recognized, after barely twenty years in the business, that overcutting was the bane of timbermen, though most refused to recognize this. Lumber was an unstable industry because its production was market driven, leading sawyers to cut the maximum as quickly as possible and ignore the limitations nature placed on its resource. Even in the 1930s it was apparent that the same dynamic was holding sway among the redwoods along the Pacific. For 20 million years, California's entire northern coastal cusp, from Monterey Bay to the Oregon border, from water's edge to as deep as forty miles inland, had been dominated by *sequoia sempervirens*, a forest of some 2 million acres. After little more than seventy years of logging, that giant ancient forest had disappeared from all but the least accessible locales along the North Coast. Humboldt County would obviously be its last stand.

Mr. Murphy's response was another policy, dubbed "sustained yield." Others might cut themselves out of existence, but his company would never lack timber ready to fell. Its annual cut would always be limited and never exceed its timberlands' new growth. So each year since Mr. Murphy's policy commenced, PL's foresters had calculated how many board feet would be added to the company's holdings by the force of nature that season, and, each year, the cut never exceeded that figure, whatever the demand of the market-place might be. Instead of maximizing production and immediate profits, Mr. Murphy's strategy was to expand PL's timberlands when-ever possible and always to treat its forests the way he treated capital, maintaining the principal while living off the interest. Once again, PL's approach was at odds with every other company's on the North Coast, but, once again, that didn't deter Albert Stanwood Murphy. By July 1985, sustained yield, like selective cut, had been the com-pany's iron rule for almost half a century.

The fruits of Mr. Murphy's contrarian vision were now fully incorporated in Scotia's self-image. Shopping downtown at the gro-cery store up the block from the coffee shop or playing softball down at the ballpark where a sign at the top of the bleachers marked the high water mark of the 1964 flood, people here took great pride in their company's differentness. They smugly joked about Simpson Timber, which had cut through its 300,000 acres of ancient forest in thirty years and was now stuck with chopping rela-tively spindly second growth, or about Louisiana Pacific, which was on its third cut over the same ground, dropping trees barely bigger than eighteen inches across, the legal minimum. PL, on the other hand, was timber rich, still sawing giant logs and holding a virtual corner on the market in "uppers," the flawless, tight-grained, almost maroon-colored boards which could only be sawn from the heart-wood of ancient trees, seeded before Columbus sailed for America. PL, having limited its cuts, now owned almost 70 percent of the re-maining ancient redwood forest that was still in private hands and, by its own reckoning, had enough remaining to feed Mill B well into the twenty-first century. By then, the leading edge of its second growth would be close to a hundred and fifty years old and at the apex of the redwood's growth curve. Folks here bragged that PL was a company their kids and grandkids could count on working for, just as their fathers and grandfathers had. They figured they were part of the most stable institution in Humboldt County. And they were right. As Kelly Bettiga liked to say, there was nothing like it. He might just be the hippie on the night shift, but he could tell shit from Shinola, and Pacific Lumber was the best company that ever came down the pike, bar none.

That the future of the Pacific Lumber Company and the cosmos of the hobbits who served it might be up for grabs wasn't even thought possible in Scotia in July 1985. Since the company wasn't for sale, it never occurred to anyone here that it might be bought anyway.

3

Charles Hurwitz recognized no such cosmic implications in buying companies and Pacific Lumber was no exception. Buying and selling them was just a business and, while it had its philosophic elements, those were a matter of little more than mathematics: whatever companies he bought had to be priced cheap enough that the costs of borrowing the necessary money fit into the gap between the purchase price and the property's true worth, with enough room left over to drive a good-sized cash flow through. It wasn't as easy as it sounded, of course, but it was that simple. At least for Charles Hurwitz. Searching out such deals was the grist of his life, from early in the morning to late at night, Saturdays and Sundays included if the situation called for it. The economy always had its laggards and they could always be had for less than their actual value. They were Charles's calling. He prided himself in his ability to cull money from the cast of capitalism's lesser lights and, now, he was ready to make his break toward the big time.

Forty-five years old, always dressed in his trademark dark suit with every hair on his head slicked in place, Charles Hurwitz already controlled some $4 billion worth of businesses, mostly in real estate and oil, all heavily leveraged, and he still spent most days with the phone glued to his ear, checking out bargains, sampling interest rates, and picking up stock market scuttlebutt. When necessary, he caught a plane from his Houston headquarters to New York or Los Angeles, flying coach, working the in-flight telephone, and taking notes in a dyslexic scribble that looked like the handiwork of a second-grader.

In July 1985, Charles Hurwitz's quest took him to a five-story office building in Beverly Hills, on Wilshire Boulevard just off Rodeo Drive. The passing Los Angeles traffic identified the building by its ground-floor tenant, a showroom of Gump's, the luxury retailer, but the real action was on the inconspicuous third and fourth floors. They were occupied by the investment bankers Drexel Burnham Lambert's high-yield bond division—the fiefdom of Michael Milken, the pope of junk bonds, and mecca for the legion of corporate raiders who were driving the American economy through the eighties at breakneck speed. Limousines bearing such "acquirers" as Charles Hurwitz began lining up outside the Gump's building at 5:30 A.M., an hour after Milken arrived for work, and the last limo didn't leave until 8:00 P.M., when Milken finally went home. This was no run-of-the-mill bond shop. At the moment, it was the center of the financial universe.

Here, the likes of Charles Hurwitz and the man he'd come to see were transforming the rules of high finance. In the age of Milken, Big no longer ruled. Milken's high-yield shop provided such large quantities of capital on the basis of so little security that a $50 million company could now acquire a $500 million one—all it took was the right price to the shareholders and Milken's backing. Banks now loaned hundreds of millions of dollars on the basis of Mike's pledge that he was "highly confident" of selling a borrower's bond issue. It was now the outsiders' turn, Milken preached, and he recruited a cast of several dozen of them to make runs around or over sluggish managements steering valuable but stagnant enterprises. Charles Hurwitz was one of those outsiders. He and Mike had known each other since the early seventies when they were both making a killing bottom-feeding in the Real Estate Investment Trust market. Hurwitz had come to meet with Milken and the Drexel bankers today about making a run at the Pacific Lumber Company, headquartered up in San Francisco, and Milken's bond shop was his only option. No one else could raise the money he would need on the short notice his surprise attack would demand.

Hurwitz was greeted at the elevator on this day by one of

Milken's chief acolytes. Although they would be meeting in a plush private conference room, the banker first steered Hurwitz through the trading room that dominated the third floor. Drexel liked to show off the throb of activity on the third floor and, though Hurwitz had seen a lot of trading rooms, this was acknowledged around the money business as a one-of-a-kind place. Drexel recruited the best, the brightest, and the most greedy and here they were, in a large common room, watched over by Mike Milken from his roost behind an X-shaped desk in the middle of everything. He waved at Hurwitz from afar and, his man told Charles, would join them shortly in the conference room. Standing, his cheap toupee cutting across his forehead like a window sill, Milken was carrying on four conversations at once—on the telephone, to the man standing next to him, to someone another yard beyond that, and also to a guy walking by. This was Milken's knack and even while doing all that, Mike had an uncanny ability to overhear a conversation across the room concerning a trade about to be finalized. If he didn't like what he heard, Milken would stop everything and yell across the room at the banker to void the deal and make a better one.

Around Drexel's trading room, Hurwitz was thought of as much brighter and more capable than most of the men Mike was backing. Charles was no mere stalking horse. One of Drexel's board members had even predicted in *Business Week* that the Texan would become the richest man in America some day. He had the knack, though he was not always a particularly easy client either to deal with or to understand. Hurwitz kept his own counsel and, no matter with whom he dealt, he was prepared to argue over every nickel. He was friendly, but never chummy, and nobody here, except maybe Milken, had ever seen him in anything but his perfectly tailored dark suit. His assets were held in a maze of interlocking corporate shells that was virtually invisible from the outside looking in—an ideal arrangement for a takeover artist who needed to stalk his prey and pounce with the benefit of surprise, but also the kind of setup that made bankers a little jumpy, even with their better clients. He and Milken had first done business in 1982, when Mike helped him gain control of the United Savings Association of Texas, the largest savings and loan in the state—which was now, of course, a loyal purchaser of other Drexel issues. Mike had moved a second raft of bonds earlier this year to give Hurwitz cash to flash in his search for another target and Drexel's New York-based Mergers and Acquisitions division had been scouting prospects for him throughout the last year. Now, after exploring several other possibilities, he had focused on Pacific Lumber.

And had come back to see the only man who could make that possible. In the summer of 1985, thirty-nine-year-old Mike Milken was the most important banker in America, perhaps even the most important single figure in the entire economy. He had spent the last decade waging a remarkable sales campaign for the high-yield or "junk" bond, bearing both high interest rates and ratings in the C- range to reflect the hazards facing their corporate issuers and anyone who bought their debt. Previously, this was a financial species relegated to inconspicuous sales on behalf of the near-bankrupt, made out the back door of the premier investment houses in a plain brown wrapper. Milken ignored the common Wall Street wisdom and embraced the shunned instrument, relentlessly citing studies showing that, while these bonds were indeed riskier, the cushion provided by the higher rates meant that a spread of them included enough survivors over the long run to yield far better returns than the same investment in blue chip issues. The result of Milken's missionary work was a growing network of converts, first among private investors and insurance companies and then, once they were deregulated in 1982, among the Savings and Loan Associations. Those early converts had made money hand over fist and, by 1985, were crying for more high-yield issues. To meet that demand, Milken had recently steered his bond shop into the takeover business—where his capacity to raise hundreds of millions of dollars in half a day on the phone had given Milken an almost instant corner on the market in financing corporate stock raids. And it was a profitable corner. Where most houses made three quarters of a percent on an issue, Milken charged 3 or 4 percent just for selling the bonds, and did a land-office business anyway. The high-yield division had transformed Drexel into the most profitable house in the business and the range of annual bonuses in the Beverly Hills office ran from $1 million on the low end, up past $300 million and beyond. Charles Hurwitz could smell the money every time he walked in the door.

Milken only stayed long enough at the July meeting with Hurwitz to pass on a warm greeting and then excuse himself. He counted on his chief assistant and the other high-yield whiz kids to hold up

Drexel's end and was already gone when the discussion started. Mike was much too valuable back at his X-shaped desk to be tied up in a numbers conference like today's, even when it involved an important client such as Hurwitz.

Though he traveled without a number of the flashier accoutrements of wealth and power, Charles Hurwitz brought along a significant reputation in business circles. *Business Week* described him as an "inscrutable" and "enigmatic financier" whose "quiet Texas charm and baby face conceal a steel-nerved dealmaker who has stripped down companies and squeezed out their shareholders. . . . [His] smooth sidewinder style sets him apart from other raiders. . . . Day and night, Hurwitz studies takeover targets, poring through files or talking to former executives and investment bankers. . . . Patience is one of his biggest attributes. So is tenacity. . . . Hurwitz is tight-lipped about his next target. But he will not let himself become overconfident. . . . Most of the risks, it seems, are borne by the companies unlucky enough to catch his eye. . . . Charles Hurwitz doesn't bark, he just bites." In an economy in which predators were playing all the lead roles, Charles was recognized as a predator of the first order by all concerned.

Except, of course, Hurwitz himself. He bristled at allusions to himself as a corporate raider. Raider? It made him sound like some kind of damned armed robber. It was an insult, as though he were a parasite, preying on the helpless. He was no raider. He was a builder. The companies he bought were better for the change in ownership. They produced more under him. They made money. They were worth more. Where was the piracy in that? He paid more for their stock than anyone could have reasonably expected. He was a boon to ignored shareholders. Raider? He found no small element of anti-semitism in the term, applied, as it often was, by Ivy League goyem insiders to Jews who made money even without the Ivy Leaguers' old-boy connections. What was he? Some kind of gunslinger? Buying and selling was what this country was all about and, as far as he was concerned, he was just being run down because he was better at it than most.

Certainly his skills as a salesman were legendary—in his first job selling mutual funds in San Antonio, other salesmen used to crowd around his desk just to hear him work the phones, his drawl softening all the rough edges, his will managing to transmit itself down the line and snare his mark in its inexorable grip. Few could resist his hard sell when he chose to apply it.

Today, he let one of the bankers get the meeting rolling. Everybody had a sheaf of papers, many of them simply columns of numbers eight and nine digits wide, compiled by Drexel's Mergers and Acquisitions division in New York.

Pacific Lumber was only a "midsize" enterprise, but still far bigger than anything Charles had previously pursued. Under the logo PALCO, it owned 183,000 acres of timberland, almost all of it in Humboldt County, California. Pacific Lumber also owned the entire town of Scotia, two sawmills there, and one more in nearby Fortuna, as well as several thousand acres of agricultural land in the Sacramento Valley and a virtually brand-new headquarters building in San Francisco's financial district. In the early seventies, the company had diversified and added a cutting and welding business with the purchase of the Victor Equipment Company, which it now ran as one of two company divisions, called PALCO Industries. Last year the parent corporation made some $44 million after-tax profits on net sales of $280 million, most of it generated by the forest products arm.

Those were not the kind of numbers that made anyone's eyes bulge, but everyone in the conference room knew that if they were any better, the stock wouldn't be so damn cheap.

Shares in Pacific Lumber had been hovering between $24 and $25 for most of the summer. And that was after the company had staged a buyback late last year at $30 a share in hopes of driving up the price, then stuck at $22. The company tendered 10 percent of its outstanding stock and the buyback was oversubscribed by a ratio of five to one. From the look of things, this stock was just lying on its back waiting to be bought. An offer framed with a $10 premium over the current rate would be snapped up by the market, assuming advance word didn't leak out. Since June, Drexel had been fronting for Hurwitz's secret purchase of a 500,000-share foothold in the company, most of which was already bought. The price had risen in response, but not enough to catch the market's attention.

It was the company's assets that had Hurwitz and the bankers salivating. Most of Pacific Lumber's timberland was redwood and a good portion of that was old-growth redwood—monster trees that yielded the best softwood in existence. Nobody else in the forest products business owned anything like it. Those holdings gave Pacific Lumber a virtual corner on the market in high-quality redwood boards, a commodity already rare enough to almost guarantee it would escalate in price. Plus, the company hadn't even come close to exploiting those assets for their maximum value. They weren't harvesting their trees at anything remotely resembling the rates that were standard in the rest of the industry. Pacific Lumber was a Ferrari that had been managed like a Model T. Cranked up to a competitive pace, it could easily generate two or three times its current cash flow. Drexel's M&A boys in New York estimated it was actually worth $95 a share. Plus it was an ideal candidate for a leveraged buyout. It had virtually no outstanding debt—so it could be hocked to the hilt—and no one owned more than 5 percent of Pacific Lumber's outstanding stock—so control would be easier to buy.

In the ensuing discussion, Hurwitz's faith in his judgment of the company and in himself were obvious. The son of a successful haberdasher in Kilgore, Texas, pop. 9,000, he had become the architect of the largest mutual fund offering in Texas history at the age of twenty-seven. He'd then risen through a decade and a half of buying fading companies, stripping their assets, and turning what remained into prosperous enterprises. Along the way, he acquired a reputation for seeing what situations demanded and, without hesitation, responding in kind. When he was taking over MCO Resources, talk was called for and he'd been at his smoothest, convincing a hostile board and management, committed to fighting him tooth and nail, to sign on to his plans. When he tried to take over Castle & Cooke, talk was useless, so he'd been at his most intransigent. Sitting through a meeting with Castle & Cooke's president, at which the man sought an angry confrontation, Charles refused to even open his mouth, freezing him out until the furious and befuddled president finally stormed out of the room. Charles Hurwitz was sure he could handle whatever came up this time around.

The major worry discussed at the July meeting was that management would wage a fight over the company. Charles thought they would turn friendly when they were suddenly faced with a healthy tender offer, supported by a substantial block of stock accumulated without management's knowledge. In those circumstances, surprised and panicky, most boards lost their will to resist. He expected Pacific Lumber's would as well. They had some defenses in place,

but everyone thought those could be dealt with. Everyone also recognized that Mike's ability to raise a lot of capital quickly when the
time came would be critical. Assuming Hurwitz offered $36 each for
the company's more than 22 million shares, he was looking at a
transaction of more than $700 million and that figure might very
well escalate. Two of his companies, the Maxxam Group, his Houston flagship corporation, and MCO Holdings, his Los Angeles incarnation, had a total of some $150 million with which to construct an
initial equity position. The rest of the money would have to be borrowed. Part of the sum could be raised from more traditional bank
financing, once Drexel's assurances of backing were in place, probably in the form of a bridge loan which Pacific's welding business
could be quickly sold to repay. There were other disposable pieces
that could be translated into quick cash as well. The office building
could be disposed of and so could the farm land. Apparently, there
was also an overfunded employee pension plan whose at least $50
million surplus would be available once the takover was completed.
Even so, he would need some $400 million that Drexel would have
to generate from sales of its trademark high-yield bonds.

Everyone in the meeting also understood that Drexel had little
or nothing to lose by backing Hurwitz. When completed, the transaction and the bond sales would earn the firm tens of millions of
dollars in commissions. It would also keep someone in play who was
an ongoing boon for Drexel's business. Hurwitz's Savings and Loan
bought Drexel's junk bonds, and Hurwitz's use of them to finance
his own rise would only spread Milken's financial revolution. Men
like Charles Hurwitz were all part of Mike's plan, as, of course, he
was of theirs. That symbiosis elevated both parties to the apex of the
financial food chain. In addition, it was obvious that Hurwitz had a
real winner in his sights this time. Its assets made the Pacific Lumber Company an unmitigated steal.

Several in the room betrayed excitement at the prospect but,
typically, Charles kept his feelings in check. He was simply not the
type to do otherwise. About the only emotion most people had ever
seen him display was when talking about his dead parents. They'd
both been stricken simultaneously with cancer several years ago and
when he described them being wheeled down the hallway in Houston's M. D. Anderson Hospital on side-by-side gurneys, holding
hands, tears welled up in his eyes. Otherwise, he tried to keep his

presence a closed book. Business had no room for sentiment or self-revelation. All that emotional hemorrhaging got in the way of the numbers, and numbers were the whole point. They were the language of money, and money was how Charles, Mike, and Drexel Burnham Lambert kept score in life.

The final word in their July discussion was supplied by Milken, speaking through his assistant. Mike had checked everything out, the man announced, and he was satisfied. The values were there. The numbers worked, any way you ran them. Mike believed in this deal.

Hurwitz and Drexel had yet to reach a formal agreement on the exact terms of their collaboration, but when Charles left that afternoon, heading up Wilshire Boulevard in a hired car, he knew he could count on having all the capital he would need. Mike and his Drexel money machine were in his corner. "They thought that this was a financeable transaction," Charles would explain to a subsequent congressional investigation. "They thought that they could [make] a financing commitment."

Though oblivious to the threat, the Pacific Lumber Company was now at serious risk.

Among all the research Charles Hurwitz and his Drexel bankers collected on PL, there was little information about its chief executive officer, Gene Elam—even though Elam, forty-six, would be the field general for any resistance the company might offer. They knew that he had been an accountant most of his career, that this was his first posting as a c.e.o., that he was still relatively new to the job, that he made $220,000 a year, and that he owned less than one tenth of 1 percent of his company's stock. None of this was particularly impressive and Hurwitz and his cohorts didn't figure they needed to know a whole lot more.

Theirs was not an uncommon response to Gene Elam. He worked under a long shadow at PL and, in his less guarded moments, resentment leaked around the edges of his restraint. It was this damned Murphy mystique. Everything was A. S. Murphy this and Stan Murphy that, as though the whole company were no more than a conglomorate for selling artifacts of its dead saints, monopolizing the company's identity to such an extent that even most of the California financial press believed PL was still a family company, just like back in 1932. Elam was Pacific Lumber's third c.e.o. since Stan's death, but the first one who hadn't been one of Stan's henchmen, and it was no secret he was resented. He knew what was said about him behind his back: that he was a pencil pusher who wasn't fit to wash Stan's jockstrap, an alien who had no roots in the mill, a numbers guy with an adding machine for a heart and no feel for the company's soul. Well, to hell with them. Their beloved Stanwood Murphy was no world beater as an executive and old A. S. Murphy hadn't had a private line to God, either. The truth was that damn legend was suffocating a fine company. Ed Carpenter and Bob Hoover had been too close to the Murphys' myth to scrape the barnacles off PL when they had Elam's job, but he wasn't. He meant to give the company a little rule by the numbers for once—enough with just doing everything the way A. S. Murphy set it up. Elam meant to prove there were other ways to run a lumber company than walking along in the Murphy footsteps. And that there was also a damn sight more to Gene Elam than all those Murphy groupies let on.

Elam, of course, still had no idea that he would soon be called on to defend Pacific Lumber from the designs of a Texas invader. He'd only been chief executive officer for three years and had spent much of that time nursing the company through a recession, with California construction starts deflated, lumber sales anemic, and, for a short while, the mills in Scotia scaled back to a four-day week. Gene's concerns were provincial at best. He focused on running the company and on whatever crossed his desk and on little else. Wall Street strategy and national corporate warfare were well outside his accustomed field of vision.

Still, Gene Elam knew something was going on. The numbers told him so, their message like a faint hum muffled behind a closed door. In June, the price of PL stock had begun to float slowly upwards, beginning the month at 25 and ending it at 26½, pushed by a corresponding escalation in trading volume. During May, an average of 60,000 PL shares a week had changed hands. The average for a week in June was 85,000. July was the same story, only more so. By the end of the month, stock price jumped to a high of $29 and average weekly volume reached 184,000 shares with no obvious explanation. Gene wanted to believe that the market had finally responded to PL's virtues and the stimulus of last year's buyback. The company had, after all, clawed its way out of the residues of the recession and was on its way to a banner year. But, since there was no way to tell for sure, he opted simply to track developments and carefully recorded the daily permutations of trading in PL's stock and plotted the numbers on a tidy-looking graph he stored in his desk drawer.

Elam also put the mysterious inflation on the agenda for discussion at the regular July meeting of the board of directors in Pacific Lumber's San Francisco headquarters. While not necessarily anything to worry about, he told the board, it was certainly out of the ordinary.

By then, this unanticipated demand for PL stock was old news to the Pacific Lumber Company's board. The increase in market price had enlarged some of the longtime directors' paper wealth by hundreds of thousands of dollars and captured the attention of the newer members with much smaller stakes in the company, as well. Because they were accustomed to a steady but inconsequential traffic in the company's shares, the developments of June and July were already an established topic among them, but none saw this as a warning of imminent danger. Like Elam, they all wanted to believe that the anonymous forces of the market were finally bringing their company's value into clearer focus and, until proven otherwise, they were in no hurry to look this gift horse in the mouth. That July, the issue was discussed as almost a *pro forma* obligation.

The director with the least to say at the meeting was also the board member who had gained the most from the price escalation. Suzanne Beaver, Stan Murphy's remarried widow, was Pacific Lumber's largest shareholder. She was also, along with Ed Carpenter (her late husband's right-hand man and best friend), John Bates (Stan's old socialite, San Francisco lawyer, buddy), Bob Hoover (the current chairman who had headed PL's sales department under Stan), and Charlie Moran (Stan's cousin, whom family wags ridiculed as never having recovered from falling off the burning Green Goose's roof and landing on his head), the board's last personal links to Pacific Lumber's good old Murphy days. Upon Stan's death in 1972, Suzanne had inherited more than 600,000 shares, some 3 percent of the company. She had always been a housewife, with no more knowledge about business than she could pick up over the dinner table after Stan got off work, and was still self-conscious about her presence on the board after thirteen years as a director. She knew she was only there as a tribute to her late husband and often felt intimidated by her own shortage of qualifications. She spent a lot of time trying not to get in the way and customarily followed Ed Carpenter's lead on issues of substance.

Suzanne Beaver was not, however, without her own opinions. She had voted to promote Gene Elam three years ago, mostly on Carpenter's recommendation, but she didn't trust him. She didn't trust anyone who combed his hair up in a dippy little wave the way he did. Everyone she'd ever met who looked like that had been a dud. She was also annoyed by his insecurity. For months, the board had been urging him to train an understudy so the company would not be stripped of leadership should he be incapacitated. All his predecessors had done as much, but Elam dragged his feet, as though he were worried about being anything but irreplaceable, and he still hadn't complied with the board's wishes. She was equally annoyed by his self-righteousness. She was a Catholic, like all the Murphys, and so was Elam, but he was always making a point of how devout he was, wearing his religion on his sleeve. And she also thought he was plain silly. Every president of PL since Mr. Murphy had maintained a membership in San Francisco's exclusive Pacific Union Club, but he'd turned down the opportunity in favor of spending his lunch hours playing checkers back in the office. Increasingly, she thought of him as someone less than the job deserved.

Suzanne's son, Warren Murphy, told her that Elam's rise was due in large part to a flaw in PL's traditional system. The company had always drawn its executives from the inside, grooming a lot of self-made men, short on formal education, who started without prospects on the mill floor or in the woods and rose by dint of native talent and devotion to the company. The one skill consistently lacking in that group, however, was the ability to manipulate numbers and make decisions with the aid of little more than a ledger book and a sharp pencil. They were all rough-and-ready seat-of-the-pants guys, like Stan himself. In most companies, skills similar to Elam's were a dime a dozen, but at PL, they looked like something special. Warren said the guy should never have risen past preparing the company's tax returns, the post where he'd started, and Suzanne found herself agreeing with him more every day.

At the July meeting, Suzanne Beaver kept quiet, accepting Elam's sanguine approach to the stock activity conundrum mostly because Ed Carpenter and Bob Hoover apparently shared it. And even if this was a sign that some corporate shark was stalking PL, hidden among the shadows of the market, she, like the rest of the board, had no idea what more the company could do to defend itself.

Pacific Lumber was not one of those companies that had failed to anticipate the threat of a stock raid. Far from it. In 1981, during Bob Hoover's last year as c.e.o., when Elam was still learning the ropes as chief operating officer and the economy's binge of corporate assaults was still in its early stages, PL's stockholders had approved a package of antitakeover bylaw changes recommended by the board. Those revised bylaws were now the basis of PL's defense fortifications. At the time they were installed, PL's consulting bankers had pointed out that a company like theirs, which operated on a pay-as-you-go basis and husbanded its resources, was almost guaranteed to be undervalued in the prevailing bull market and become a ripe target for corporate raiders simply because of the kind of company it was. They could either change the way they did business, loading up on debt and maximizing their short-term profits—all of which was anathema to the board—or make themselves difficult to swallow. The directors had unanimously chosen the latter approach.

This was necessary, the board's 1981 proxy letter to shareholders explained, because "your Board . . . believes that corporations have an obligation to society as a whole. In particular, companies charged with the stewardship of scarce resources such as timber have a duty to use such resources wisely. . . . Continuity and stability of management are necessary for the intelligent development and harvesting of the company's timber resources. . . . The Company was a pioneer . . . in developing and applying the continuous yield forestry principle . . . complemented by . . . selective harvesting [managing] its timberlands to insure the continued productivity of these lands in perpetuity. . . . Uninvited attempts . . . to take control of the Company [and institute] a management philosophy which would seek a dramatic increase in the short-term yield of the Company's redwood-producing properties would have a destructive long-term impact on the Company [as well as] the company's stockholders, employees, customers, suppliers, [and] the communities where the Company operates."

To block any such uninvited attempts, the 1981 bylaw revisions laid out a series of obstacles, all of which were supposed to make a hostile takeover inordinately expensive or cumbersome. The most daunting of those was the provision requiring that anyone who purchased 5 percent or more of Pacific Lumber's outstanding shares without the unanimous approval of the board of directors and then, in the standard corporate raider strategy, sought to merge PL into another corporation, would have to receive at least 80 percent approval of the company's stockholders, affording the die-hard minority enormous leverage with which to defend the company's independence. To further bolster the status quo, the bylaws also revised the standard definitions of directors' fiduciary duty when faced with an uninvited tender offer. Traditionally, a board's legal obligation was simply to negotiate the best price possible for the shareholders, using the existing market as a yardstick—a standard often invoked in court by raiders trying to force boards to accept their unwelcome overtures. PL's board, however, was now instructed to take into account not only such short-term calculations, but also "the future value of the company as an independent concern, including the unrealized value of its properties and assets" and "the social, legal, environmental and economic effects of the acquisition on employees, customers, suppliers and other constituencies of the Company [and] the communities and geographical areas in which the Company and its subsidiaries operate." The board was legally empowered to reject any proposal that failed to meet the company's standards in those additional areas of concern.

In truth, when its board of directors met that July, the Pacific Lumber Company was better equipped to fight off a stock market raid than virtually all of its peers.

Whether it was prepared to actually wage such a battle, however, was another question. The board's discussion of the summer's stock activity had all the substance of wet spaghetti. Suzanne Beaver would later remember only that everyone almost automatically followed Gene Elam's less than aggressive lead.

What they needed, the c.e.o. suggested, was more expertise. PL ought to hire an investment banking firm to answer questions like these. He had some other issues about which he needed expert consultation and perhaps the bankers could also come up with some suggestions about further bolstering PL's defenses.

The board unanimously approved the idea and instructed Elam
to select and retain investment bankers to suggest how to deal with
this mystery. Then, the directors proceeded to the next item on
their July agenda.

Hiring "experts" to evaluate the situation was typical of Gene
Elam's approach to management. Experts provided him with something solid on which to base a judgment, something with the aura of
fact that could at least approximate the absolute truth of numbers.
He resisted the notion that expertise was relative and there were
subjects immune to the presumption of certainty. The ledger book
was Gene's paradigm and, for him, "expertise" transformed the vagaries of business into integers.

In this instance, however, he was in no great hurry to put it to
use. Armed with the board's instruction to hire bankers, he dawdled, figuring that the task could wait while he concentrated on
more pressing concerns. The new power plant for Scotia had to be
planned and he was caught up in negotiations with the Irving Trust
Company over its financing, so, for the rest of July and all of August,
he did little besides collect information on possible firms with which
he might eventually consult.

And, of course, he continued to maintained the graph in his
desk drawer. During August, PL's share price stabilized, floating
between $28 and $29, with an average volume of 95,000 a week—
about half of the traffic of July, but still well above the stock's customary turnover.

The one concrete step Gene Elam took to flesh out the invisible
force pushing PL's stock through the market at such an exceptional
pace amounted to little more than a half-assed stab in the dark. Pacific Lumber hired an industrial relations firm, D. F. King & Co., to
perform several small tasks during August and, in the course of
their conversations, Elam asked the firm, whose principal business
was preparing stockholder mailings and staging corporate proxy
votes, if they would also conduct "some investigative work" on just
who or what was so interested in Pacific Lumber stock.

Not surprisingly, given that King & Co. was not particularly well
suited to the task, it came up empty. The firm reported that no one
in the securities business had any idea if someone was out there accumulating PL stock and, if there was, who. Nor did anyone seem to
take the prospect very seriously.

5

It was well after Labor Day before Elam gave priority to hiring some experts to apply themselves to the mysteries accumulating on the graph in his desk. During the first three weeks of September, trading volume in the company's stock had jumped, averaging 127,000 shares a week, and the month was almost over when Elam concluded his search for consulting investment bankers. First, he narrowed the broad field of available firms to three finalists; then, after a second round of interviews, he selected Salomon Brothers. Nicknamed "Solly" on Wall Street, Salomon was one of the nation's premier bond merchants but not yet much of a player on either side of the takeover game. Despite Elam's pitch to the board for expertise, Solly's relative lack of experience in the subject at the heart of their commission did not seem to bother him. In fact, he had selected them primarily because they were familiar. Solly was already PL's primary agent in purchasing short-term commercial debt and money market investments, and its West Coast bankers were on a first-name basis with the headquarters crew at PL, so there would be no adjusting to new personalities or worries about educating strangers in the idiosyncracies of company practices.

During the last week of September, Elam announced his decision at a meeting with the managing director of Solly's West Coast operations. This was not a working meeting, just a brief drop-in to shake hands and offer congratulations, but Gene nonetheless ran through a brief synopsis of the situation Solly was being hired to address.

He was having trouble getting the company's bottom line up where he wanted it, he complained, and there were several long-term development questions that needed to be plumbed and strategized. Getting things rolling the way he wanted them was no simple proposition.

In addition, Gene Elam noted with the air of someone including an afterthought, there had been "some unusual trading" in Pacific Lumber Company stock.

6

While Gene Elam was slowly selecting a banker to defend the company, Pacific Lumber pursued business as usual throughout August and into September. Scores of gargantuan *sequoia sempervirens* floated in one end of Mill B and tens of thousands of prime redwood planks clattered out the other, day after day, week after week—workdays framed in steam whistles, weekends strung between softball games down by the river, shopping trips up the coast to Eureka, and drunken midnight encounters in the parking lot of the bowling alley in nearby Fortuna. The only break in the pattern came on September 4, when PL's board of directors arrived at the company offices on Main Street and convened a meeting in the redwood-lined conference room.

Scotia was accustomed to visits from the board, usually once a year. The largest house in town, the Directors' Cottage, a fancy two-story wood frame structure catty-corner from the hospital, was at their perpetual disposal should they desire to spend the night. To the townsfolk, those visits usually amounted to a brief appearance by a gaggle of city dwellers, done up casually by their own lights but still dressed several notches above the common Humboldt fashion, who trooped through with brand-new orange safety helmets perched on their heads and lingered briefly in the distance to observe the dog and pony shows arranged by management to evoke the artistry of lumberjacking. Earlier this year the board had assembled in the company forest south of town to witness one of the company's best fellers address a two-hundred-foot "sucker"—a secondary growth protruding at an angle out of the side of a three-hundred-foot trunk—and drop it into a tiny lane cleared from the surrounding forest. The feller's only glimpse of the directors was an irregular line of orange dots, safely out of the way up a nearby ridge, too far for him to hear their clapping when he laid the sucker down without putting a scratch on any of the surrounding trees. The only surprise in the board's next visit, on September 4, was that they were back again so soon.

September 4 was not, however, an official meeting of the board. Those only occurred quarterly and the next wasn't scheduled until October. Rather, this was an informal "working session," at which no minutes would be kept and no official actions taken. Gene Elam had scheduled it in response to a request during the winter from Mike Hollern, an Oregon lumberman who had been added to the board in 1984. Hollern thought at least the board's newer members ought to have an opportunity to familiarize themselves with PL's timber inventory, the record system the company used to track that inventory, and the PL forestry department that actually did the tracking. Elam decided to hold the session in Scotia and ordered Forestry to prepare a presentation for whoever among the twelve directors decided to attend. In addition to Hollern and Tim Skinner, a northern California utility executive who'd come onto the board that April, longtime members Elam, Bob Hoover, Ed Carpenter, Charlie Moran, and Suzanne Beaver were all present on September 4. Elam was accompanied by several other executives from San Francisco headquarters. The host for the gathering was the company's aggressive new executive vice president for forest products and boss of Scotia, John Campbell.

The board's newer members were only acquainted with Campbell from his maiden appearance before the directors in April, during his first few months as executive vice president. John could charm the warts off a toad when he had a mind to and his April performance, blending hard-edged energy with banker's competence and bluff Aussie sociability, had been impressive. He obviously meant to get somewhere and carry the company with him. The older members of the board were hardly surprised. Campbell had been a member of Pacific Lumber's extended family for quite a while, first appearing in PL circles when he married Ed Carpenter's daughter, Cindy, back in 1967. As a gesture to Ed, who was Stan Murphy's best friend, the Campbells' wedding reception had been hosted by Stan and Suzanne in the picturesque lodge old Mr. Murphy had built on the family's ranch along Larabee Creek, abutting the Eel about halfway between Pepperwood and Holmes. The newlyweds first settled in John's native Australia, on the coast north of Sydney, but, within two years, Cindy's homesickness brought them back to Humboldt and John, at his father-in-law's recommendation, was put on Pacific Lumber's executive trainee fast track, just like the Murphy boys would be several years later.

Scotia had known John Campbell as a comer for a long time and no one disputed his talent or, of course, his pull. This was, after all, a guy whom Stan Murphy had invited deer hunting while he was still just learning the company ropes, a sure sign of induction into PL's inner circle. Most accepted John's rapid rise as a matter of fact. Only the last step of it, the one that landed him on Scotia's top rung, had bred any noticeable resentment.

Warren Flinchpaugh, the man Campbell replaced as executive vice president, had been something of a venerated figure on the mill floor. Flinchpaugh, fifty-eight, had instant recall of everyone in the county who ever worked for PL and never forgot even the slightest fuck-up, but he rewarded genuine effort and had nursed dozens of PL men of all stripes up through the pay grades. Most notably, he had godfathered the training of both John Campbell and Warren Murphy, personally guiding their careers up the chain of command until John reached the station immediately under his own. Flinchpaugh himself had started with PL when Mr. Murphy was still running things, eventually manned Scotia's front office under Stan, and now saw himself as the gatekeeper of the Murphy way of doing things. In that scheme, dictated by Mr. Murphy himself, Scotia controlled lumber production according to its own calculations, and the San Francisco office, even though it was the apex of the company chain of command, had to accept Scotia's decision as a *fait accompli*. Mr. Murphy had always said he didn't want the salesmen in San Francisco telling the mill how, what, or when to cut—an admonition Warren Flinchpaugh continued to enforce. Gene Elam thought that was a typical case of the tail wagging the dog but, whenever he sought information from Flinchpaugh that would allow him to increase his control over the company's production, he received only vague responses to the effect that the numbers weren't available.

Not surprisingly, Elam considered Flinchpaugh an obstruction. John Campbell, his rise now halted by Flinchpaugh's presence above him, felt the same way and, eventually, Campbell stumbled upon a situation that would solve both their problems.

John, son of a former operative in the Australian intelligence service, was a fanatic about gathering information and, to that end, had built a network of informants to keep him secretly abreast of the side talk and scuttlebutt on the mill floor. In the fall of 1984, one of his informants brought him a story then being tossed around among the teamsters down at the log deck. PL had hired an independent logging outfit, known in the business as a "gypo," to harvest some of its lesser stands and the talk among the truck drivers was that this gypo was defrauding the company on a massive scale. Gypos were paid by the log, according to two rates, one for standard tractor or "Cat" logging, and another for "yarder" logging. Yarder logging involved using cables and hoists to extract trees from slopes too steep to be safely worked with tractors and, since it was by far the more difficult of the two techniques, received the higher rate. The gypo's accounts were tracked at the mill by the markings or "settings" on the logs trucked down from his show, which indicated whether each was to be counted at a Cat or yarder rate. PL's gypo was forging his settings and, according to the talk among the men hauling his logs, had been getting away with it for years.

Campbell's detractors claim John bypassed the chain of command and carried the news of the scandal straight to Gene Elam. This ripoff was too big and had been going on too bloody long to just leave it to Scotia to clean up, John allegedly pointed out. That gypo bloke's hand had most likely been in the till for years. At the very least, his transgression marked a major breakdown in company operations and, for that, the finger had to point all the way up the ladder to Flinchpaugh. God knows why old Warren had been looking the other way, but if he hadn't, this would never have happened. Campbell was quick to point out that he didn't mean to say that Flinchpaugh was in on the crookedness, not at all, only that he should have been on top of the situation and, for some reason only he knew, he wasn't. That alone was enough to convince Campbell that someone of Elam's stature ought to plumb this issue. Elam could see where Campbell was heading and fell in step without further prodding. Yes, he agreed, this was a case where the San Francisco office's insight was essential.

The gypo controversy apparently took Warren Flinchpaugh from his blind side. Flinchpaugh had long since delegated responsibility for overseeing the gypos to the woods boss and from him to the forestry department, which, lax and lazy, had dropped most of the procedural safeguards and opened the till to pillaging. It was a typical case of the sloppiness that tended to infect PL's "one big family" approach to management, but Flinchpaugh, a confirmed straight arrow and company loyalist, was flabbergasted that anyone could imagine it as anything more. The innuendo grew, however, until Flinchpaugh, a proud man who recoiled at having his reputation dragged back and forth through the mud, finally, late in 1984, applied for early retirement.

The changes that had accompanied Campbell's promotion to executive vice president were obvious by the time the company officers assembled in Scotia's conference room. For starters, San Francisco no longer had a problem getting numbers from the mill. Every week, Campbell had Warren Murphy assemble all the information Gene Elam wanted, dress it up in the best possible light, and ship it south. Elam, now feeling welcome, also started visiting Scotia regularly and, whenever he did, was impressed at what a good choice Campbell had been for Flinchpaugh's old job. The big Australian meant to whip the place into shape and let everybody know it. Years of kindly paternalism had left PL's operations hidebound, encrusted with wasteful habits and deficient personnel, but those days, he announced, were over. Changes were on their way. Some people would be buying ties, others, work gloves, but nobody's place was safe. Company policy kept him from firing anyone for anything short of outright dereliction, but transfers and reassignments abounded. The company's personnel director for the last seventeen years was sent out to the shipping department to restart his career in overalls, assembling orders of boards, while one of Campbell's allies from the mill was promoted to the front office and then sent back to the cutting floor dressed in a tie, carrying a stop watch with which to measure who among his old compatriots were dragging their feet. John Campbell was a hard charger and, now that he had Scotia by the short hairs, he meant to turn his fief into a hard-charging kind of place as well.

Though it hadn't been part of the gathering's advance billing, Campbell envisioned the loose agenda for the board's "working session" on September 4 as another opportunity to extend his vision for a reborn Pacific Lumber Company. This time, he was taking aim at the most sacred of the company's sacred cows. He was convinced that if PL was ever going to become the kind of aggressive company he had in mind, it would have to alter its cutting policies. By the prevailing standards of the logging business, Pacific Lumber's Murphy approach was positively backward. Old Mr. Murphy's ironclad restrictions to selective cut and sustained yield resulted in a return on investment so low that Campbell, trained in Australia as a banker, considered it an embarrassment. Other companies with only a fraction of PL's assets consistently outperformed it on the bottom line. Why in the hell should they keep living in the past? It was awful bloody-like managing with one hand tied behind his back, and it had to stop. He had first raised the subject to the board at its April meeting, when he made vague references in his address to them about the need to eventually adjust Pacific Lumber's traditional harvesting philosophies. Since then, he had developed a plan for immediately increasing the annual cut from 130 million board feet to 170 million and now, in the course of Forestry's briefing on its timber-tracking techniques, he hoped to push the issue even further.

Campbell was counting on Bob Stephens, PL's "forest manager" and head of the forestry department, to provide the impetus. Scoutmaster to a generation of Scotia boys, Warren and Woody Murphy included, Stephens had managed to survive the purges that followed the fall of Flinchpaugh even though his department was the most culpable for the gypo's malfeasance—an outcome some speculated was a direct function of the alacrity with which he signed on to Campbell's new approach. Others thought he was still around because his intimate knowledge of every corner of the company's forestlands made him irreplaceable. In either case, Stephens, fifty-eight years old and cheery, was the featured act of the September "working session" clustered in the company's redwood-lined conference room. His presentation to the assembled board members was accompanied by the distribution of a seven-page document titled "Forest Management Proposal."

Stephens began by addressing the company's timber inventory. As the board no doubt knew, the most complete assessment of timber inventories was through an elaborate process called a "cruise," where trained timber estimators analyzed maps, aerial photographs, and ground-level observations and derived an estimated yield measured in board feet of merchantable lumber. PL's 183,000 acres of timberlands hadn't undergone a full-scale cruise since 1956, when the independent forestry firm of Hammond Jensen & Walling had produced one under commission from Mr. Murphy. That thirty-year-old analysis was still PL's basic yardstick, living on in a collection of maps, delineating the various timber stands, and tables, in which the stands were broken down by type and volume. To obtain current estimates, the Hammond cruise was resifted through a complex regimen of updates centered on Forestry's cutting maps, recording which stands had been depleted on what date. The cruise numbers were further modified by a numerical factor derived from a dozen or more sources in hopes of calculating the amount of volume added to a stand during the years since it was cut or last calculated. The company inventories were divided into three basic types—Old Growth, the virgin forest that had never been logged; Residual Old Growth, the mature trees left behind after a selective cut; and Young or Second Growth, the even-aged forest that grew up in the aftermath of previous cutting—and each type brought a different growth rate to the equation. The final step was to further modify the numbers with an adjustment factor, to account for the inevitable discrepancy between paper estimates and mill floor realities.

The result, Stephens announced, was the Pacific Lumber timber inventory as of September 1985—5,197,000,000 board feet.

Stephens next moved on to the material covered in his "Forest Management Proposal" which, while somewhat tangential to the original purpose of the meeting, was nonetheless of compelling importance. Simply put, he explained, the selective cut system just wasn't working out as well as it should and the time had come for the company to modify its traditional approach if it wanted to maximize the productivity of its resource base. PL needed to start clearcutting, like everybody else in the business.

Warren Murphy was one of several Scotia executives who were in the conference room along with the board when Stephens put forward his proposal and, at first, Warren wondered if he was hallucinating the whole thing. He'd known Bob Stephens all his life and Bob had always been an almost religious devotee of the old Murphy system, proselytizing for it at every opportunity. When Stephens proposed abandoning selective cut, Warren would have been less surprised if the scoutmaster had shown up at church wearing a nose ring and a chartreuse Mohawk hairdo. Warren looked over at Campbell to see if he was equally taken aback but Campbell showed no expression at all.

Stephens's arguments in favor of a change amounted to little more than a compendium of all the arguments that had been used against him over the years when he'd defended PL's system: selective cut no longer carried tax advantages, the regrowth generated after a selective cut was less vigorous than that following a clear cut, the residuals left behind were less cost-effective to harvest because of the reduced density of the stand, residual harvests harmed the second growth. "Variety" was the answer, Stephens concluded. Pacific Lumber needed to be free to use "a range of forest management techniques" and apply whatever harvesting approach best suited any situation. Clear cuts were the missing part of the equation and they were, despite their reputation, often the best option for a healthy forest and a healthy lumber company.

When he'd completed his arguments, Stephens welcomed the board's questions, but *welcome* was, in retrospect, a poor choice of words. According to Warren Murphy, the question and answer session did not go at all well for PL's forest manager or for the interests of his boss, the executive vice president for forest products.

First, Stephens's credibility was shredded by Mike Hollern's cross-examination on inventory procedures. The new director picked out several plots on the forestry department maps and asked for more details about how the numbers attributed to the forest there had been reached. Stephens, however, had no such details at his fingertips and could only invoke the computer process that had yielded the conclusion. Hollern kept pressing, plot after plot, and Stephens kept confessing he couldn't answer the questions. Warren Murphy cringed at the spectacle. It would have been downright comical if it hadn't been so damn embarassing. With every fresh twist, it looked more and more as though the forestry department had no real idea what was out there on those 183,000 acres. There could have been twice as much, or half, and the ill-prepared forestry department looked like a bunch of jerks who were guessing their asses off.

Stephens fared no better when the questions switched over to his new forest management proposals.

Exactly which parcels did he think the company ought to clear-cut? Well, he wasn't sure. He'd have to look into it. His remarks had all been preliminary.

Did he have more examples of places where selective cutting was working against the company's interests?

Well, again, he'd been speaking in generalities and he'd have to get back to the board on that. Like he'd said, his proposal was preliminary.

Gene Elam, his jaw clenched against his own rising anger, soon joined the front ranks of those hounding Stephens.

What do you mean preliminary? Elam snapped. You've had half a year to prepare for this meeting.

Well, there hadn't been personnel available to sort out this kind of detail.

What in the hell had those personnel been doing if not getting ready for this?

Stephens was reduced to shuffling his feet in silence.

For his part, John Campbell had abandoned his initial attempts to fend off some of the pressure on Stephens and, almost as angry as Elam, just shut up and let the forester take his beating.

The "working session" ended with an informal consultation among the seven board members in order to provide the forestry department with some sort of response to its proposal. Harvesting by selective cut and abstaining from mass clear cuts was, they emphasized, an essential part of PL's identity, which they were unwilling to forsake. To do so would mean abandoning an image that was among the company's most valued assets. Still, they didn't want to give Stephens an absolute "no." They were willing to permit an occasional, small clear cut, if there were special circumstances that required it. During the previous decade, for example, they had allowed a reasonably extensive clear cut when a windstorm had wreaked havoc in one of the virgin old-growth groves. But that was it, no major changes in policy, only an occasional exception to prove the rule.

Next on the board's September 4 agenda was a reception over in the Directors' Cottage, and between the two gatherings Elam and Campbell managed to find enough privacy to share their thoughts. Elam was furious. He'd been made to look like an ass, he fumed, inviting all these directors up here only to have Forestry botch the whole thing. Campbell was doubly pissed, both on his own account and because of how much it had upset Elam, but all he could do was wail. He had warned Forestry to have all its ducks in a row, he assured Elam, but they'd just fucked it up. Elam told Campbell that he wanted the information Stephens had spent the day failing to deliver and if he didn't get it double quick, someone in that goddamn forestry department was going to be headed down the road looking for a new job. John told him not to worry.

To the surprise of no one who knew what had gone on with the board, John Campbell spent a good portion of September 5, when the board was gone, yelling at Stephens loud enough to raise blisters on the side of Stephens's head. Campbell's fury was genuine. He didn't like looking bad in front of the boss and, thanks to Forestry's laziness, he'd been tainted with their bungling. The incident hadn't damaged John's relationship with Gene Elam but, just to make sure, Campbell gave Elam a call later in the day to let him know the forestry department had been pilloried and was now hustling its ass off to fill in the blank spots.

By then, Elam had returned to San Francisco and resumed his search for bankers who might unravel the fluctuations on the stock graph in his desk drawer.

7

John Campbell's organizational purview did not, of course, extend to the public trading of the company's shares, but, through his father-in-law, he knew of the summer's ongoing mystery and the board's deliberations on the subject. The extreme sensitivity of the issue, always couched in secrecy, prodded his interest and, as September progressed, work whistle to work whistle, Campbell tracked PL's stock as it escalated back toward the inflated levels of July. Most of John's attention, however, was simply consumed with the daily September responsibilities of being Pacific Lumber's big fish in the small Humboldt County pond.

One of the county's largest September events was the annual Ducks Unlimited auction and banquet at the Eureka Inn, Humboldt's finest hotel. The evening was staged to raise funds for maintaining duck habitat along the western wildfowl migration routes and ensuring an ample supply of birds to hunt. PL's front office was well represented at this benefit, as it was at most Humboldt charity enterprises. Such attendance was a part of his job John enjoyed. He was a hearty mingler, up for a chance to down a few drinks, slap some familiar backs, flirt with a few women, and rub elbows with people he didn't yet know all that well.

At one point in the cocktail hour, Campbell ended up chatting with Bill Bertain, a local attorney, grandson of the man who'd moved the family laundry-processing business into Scotia's old Green Goose whorehouse, and son of the man who'd run the laundry since A. S. Murphy had first assumed PL's presidency. Bill and Campbell had crossed paths before, but had only talked enough on that occasion to ensure that neither had to be introduced to the other when they hooked up again. Naturally enough, Pacific Lumber soon occupied the center of their conversation.

Campbell broached the subject with an unsolicited defense of the changes he'd instituted at the company. It was simple, he explained. Pacific Lumber had just become bogged down in the years since Stan had died, God rest his soul. That kind of thing happened all the time with businesses. People just became set in their ways and lost their flexibility and initiative. Now it was his task to free the company of all that calcification. It needed to be shaken up and that was what he'd been doing since he got the job. And you could bet your bloody rent check that he wasn't through yet.

Bertain, one of the few people in Humboldt who read *The Wall Street Journal* every day, responded at something of a tangent. Quite frankly, he pointed out, he wasn't so sure that PL's sluggishness was the central issue. From where he sat, its absurdly low stock price looked like the real threat to Pacific Lumber's future. The market was full of sharks these days, Bertain argued, hunting for companies to steal on the cheap, and PL looked like the most undervalued company in the country.

As soon as the words came out of Bertain's mouth, Campbell gagged on his drink, went white as a sheet, and then flushed deep pink. Finally, having caught his breath, he stammered that PL might be *one* of the most undervalued.

With that, John Campbell turned abruptly on his heel and walked away, terminating the conversation without so much as a by-your-leave.

Bill Bertain watched him disappear into the crowd of duck hunters and wondered what in the hell PL's executive vice president was so damned uptight about.

8

While Gene Elam dawdled through his search for bankers, Charles Hurwitz made considerable progress. The Texan hustled from Houston to New York to Los Angeles, concealing his intentions, plying the telephone at every opportunity, and staying several steps ahead of the Pacific Lumber Company's status quo.

In August, when Elam asked D. F. King & Co. to take their fruitless look at the escalation in PL stock trading, Hurwitz acquired a surreptitious survey of PL's timberlands that indicated the company's holdings might well contain 8 billion board feet of lumber, 3 billion more than Elam assumed. While Elam and the board began September by meeting with the forestry department in Scotia, Hurwitz was in New York, meeting secretly with the Irving Trust Company and arranging the bridge loan that was a key element of the financial substructure supporting his planned assault. During the last week of September, when Elam was just making up his mind to hire Salomon Brothers, preparations for Hurwitz's assault were almost complete and he set up a Manhattan command post, midtown on Third Avenue, inside the law offices of Kramer Levin Nessen Kamin and Frankel. From there, he planned to manage his endgame. The command post was manned by a few operatives from Hurwitz's New York office and some young lawyers from Kramer Levin who would process all the last-minute details of the approaching corporate ambush. Hurwitz planned to leap from hiding and announce his tender offer at the end of the first week of October.

He chose to operate out of Kramer Levin Nessen Kamin and Frankel because of Ezra Levin, one of the firm's senior partners. Ezra, several years older than Hurwitz, was his *consigliere,* a quiet, professorial man whom he had first retained in the early seventies, after encountering him as an adversary in a negotiation. Next time, Hurwitz had remarked after their initial encounter, he wanted that fellow Levin on his side of the table, and Levin had been there ever since. Hurwitz counted on Ezra's steady intelligence and insight to bolster his own judgment and looked to Levin as a kind of emotional older brother on whom he could depend, whatever the circumstance. Levin was also a very able attorney, a skill for which Hurwitz had a relatively constant need. Over the last decade and a half of empire building, Hurwitz had been enjoined by the Securities and Exchange Commission, settled civil fraud charges, shed subsidiaries via the bankruptcy statutes, jousted with state and Federal regulators, and woven his way through assorted lawsuits—all without a substantial legal blemish on his record since Ezra Levin came on board.

Like most of those who worked with Hurwitz, Levin did not credit his friend's fearsome raider's reputation. Levin, after all, was a securities lawyer who saw a lot of these big-time stock players up close. By comparison, Charles behaved like a rabbi. The guy was without any particular ostentation, scorning the corporate jets and stretch limos to which so many of his peers were addicted. And while he might work the fast lane, he didn't live in it. For years, even though he was worth tens of millions, perhaps hundreds, he occupied the same relatively modest house in one of Houston's better neighborhoods, but not its best. He was still married to his college sweetheart, Barbara, with whom he dabbled occasionally in Houston high society, and he always found time to spend with his two teenage sons. He kept big French poodles at home and a tank of tropical fish in his office. He didn't take his underlings to task in front of others and, despite maintaining the demeanor of a funeral director when under public scrutiny, his sense of humor was evident in private, where he exercised an attractive deadpan wit. Charles wasn't an observant Jew like Levin, but he honored his heritage and was a serious supporter of Israel. You could do a lot worse around

Wall Street than Charles Hurwitz, that was for sure. And, of course, he was terribly talented at what he did. People thought there was something easy about being an acquirer like Charles but they were off their rockers. It took tremendous skills. It required analysis and independent thinking and the kind of quick intelligence that was a rarity anywhere in life and especially in business. You also had to have the humility to know your limitations and cover them. Then, Levin noted, when all the thinking was done, it required a truckload of moxie to pull off. There was nothing simple about it. You had to be at the top of your game to play at Charles's level.

The first significant legal obstacle along Hurwitz's path to the Pacific Lumber Company was the recently enacted Hart-Scott-Rodino Act, which began looming over the transaction within days after his meeting with the Drexel people in Beverly Hills. This Federal statute reflected the Congress's feelings that the Securities and Exchange Commission's requirement of public filing by anyone puchasing 5 percent of a company's stock was insufficient to cope with the new wave of stock raids. Accordingly, Congress had added a requirement that anyone purchasing $15 million worth of a company's stock must file with the Federal Trade Commission and halt all further purchases for fifteen days while the FTC investigated possible antitrust issues. The object was to strip would-be takeover artists of their protective cover even earlier in the financial process, increasing the difficulty of their maneuver and decreasing its likelihood of success.

In the case of Pacific Lumber, the $15 million Hart-Scott-Rodino limit amounted to some 2.5 percent of the company's stock, a level Hurwitz began approaching through his hidden Drexel-engineered purchases at the end of July, so he halted short of the legal trigger point and waited for Ezra Levin to figure a way off the horns of his dilemma. It was still far too early in his stalking to come out into the open, but he needed a lot more than 2.5 percent of Pacific Lumber's stock in hand if his sneak attack was going to carry sufficient weight to overcome his expected opposition. He had to accumulate a stock position significant enough to panic Elam and his board and make them feel he was already inside their defenses, rendering further resistance pointless. Surfacing too early with too little would only give them time and space in which to muster themselves.

As August began, Levin recommended that Hurwitz employ a

maneuver known as the put-call agreement. Under this arrangement, Hurwitz would agree to buy a specified amount of Pacific
Lumber stock from a seller at a prearranged price on a future date.
Earlier that year, the Federal Trade Commission had ruled that a
stock holding, subject to such an agreement, was not countable under the Hart-Scott-Rodino limits until the transaction was actually
consummated. Levin consequently figured the put-call would let
Charles stay legal while accomplishing exactly what the law had
been written to thwart. All he needed was someone willing to accumulate a position in PL shares and sell it to him at some point down
the line.

Hurwitz, as it turned out, knew just the man for the task.

Boyd Jeffries, founding partner of the Jeffries & Co. brokerage
house, was a dominant figure in the rambunctuous "third market"
of stock trading that had come into its own in the frantic pace of
eighties transactions. Unlike the "first market" of tightly scrutinized
stock exchanges and the "second market" of publicly registered
over-the-counter trading, Jeffries bought and sold stocks twenty-four
hours a day, under any circumstance. His acuity at arranging very
large, secret transactions on short notice had made him the darling
of the takeover crowd and he was known around The Street as one
of Michael Milken's favorites—someone who, by his own admission,
was unable to say no to a client, whatever the request. Among the illegal activities Boyd Jeffries would later confess to having engaged in
on behalf of clients were "parking" stock to conceal its true ownership, keeping false records, violating Federal "margin" requirements, and manipulation of stock prices. When Charles Hurwitz was
confronted with the Hart-Scott-Rodino ceiling on his PL purchases,
Jeffries was already involved in trading large blocks of other stocks
on Hurwitz's account.

Charles informed Jeffries in early August that he was interested
in some 500,000 shares of Pacific Lumber Company under a put-
call due at the end of September. That figure would keep Jeffries's
purchase below the Hart-Scott-Rodino limit, keep the total shares
Hurwitz was amassing under the 5 percent level triggering the SEC's
reporting requirements, and still make Charles Hurwitz the largest
single Pacific Lumber shareholder, unbeknownst to everyone else in
the market. As expected, Boyd Jeffries accepted the assignment and,
by August 6, was buying PL shares on the accounts of several union

pension funds under his management. Lawyers for Hurwitz and Jeffries began drafting their actual put-call agreement immediately but stopped when the two principals decided simply to draw up all the paperwork at the time of sale instead.

Now, almost seven weeks later, that time was rapidly approaching. In Hurwitz's Kramer Levin Nessen Kamin and Frankel command post, spread between Ezra Levin's corner office and the small law library next door, sorting out the details of the Jeffries transaction was just one of the tasks caught up in the momentum of the endgame, when everything seemed to compress as the assault accelerated relentlessly toward its target and, with only a dozen or so days to go, the throw weight of months of stealthy anticipation increased geometrically. The quarry Hurwitz's team had tracked for almost a year was locked in their crosshairs and, after all those accumulated months of patience, they were haunted by an anxiety that now, just when it seemed as good as grabbed, Pacific Lumber would somehow manage to elude them, that some stray gust of karmic wind would strip away their cover and alert their prey, or, even worse, that some other predator, also in hiding, would pounce on it before they could strike.

The underlings' principal focus was writing the formal tender offer, a composition framed in intense legalese and straightjacketed by all the requirements of full disclosure under penalty of law. This document would be presented to the shareholders when Hurwitz revealed himself and proposed to purchase all their shares in one fell swoop, thereby placing Pacific Lumber completely under his own control. The drafts of the tender offer being circulated in the Kramer Levin offices still had the name of the company to be acquired blocked out in the interests of secrecy. The final prospectus would eventually run to some forty-one letter-sized pages in small print, detailing the procedures of the buyout, the financial status of the acquirer, the conditions attached to its financing, and similar constructs.

The document's only direct mention of just what Charles Hurwitz had in mind for Pacific Lumber once it was his came in a paragraph on page eighteen, under the heading "Debt Service": "The Purchaser expects to require funds substantially in excess of the amounts currently generated by the operations of the company in order to pay the principal of the bank loans and Notes [so] the Purchaser has considered . . . increasing the Company's annual lumber production . . . to a level which . . . would equal two times or more the Company's 1984 production [and] may consider selling some or all of the Company's cutting and welding operations [and] taking . . . action . . . to cause surplus assets held by the Company's defined benefit [pension] plan to revert to the Company." If old Mr. Murphy was capable of turning in his grave, he did so when that ink hit the page.

As the drafting proceeded, Hurwitz came in and out of the command post and when he was in, he was usually closeted with Levin in the corner office, where the fortieth-floor window behind the desk looked north without obstruction, over Central Park, across the Bronx, and up the Hudson toward the Tappan Zee Bridge. The two of them, however, paid little attention to the view. They had a couple of major problems to resolve.

The first was in assuming ownership of the stock that Boyd Jeffries had accumulated. Their put-call strategy was coming apart. On Monday, September 23, Charles and Jeffries spoke on the phone and completed their negotiations over price, settling on $29.10 a share, two and a half cents less than the market had closed the previous Friday. Charles told the broker to have his lawyers send their draft of a put-call agreement to Levin, who would work out the final details. That draft arrived on Tuesday but proved absolutely unacceptable. Jeffries's lawyers were worried over possible future liabilities and had inserted language into the agreement requiring Hurwitz and Maxxam to "confirm and represent" that they had taken no "substantial step or steps to commence . . . a tender offer," a representation that couldn't have been further from the truth, and Jeffries's lawyers steadfastly refused to delete the requirement. Ezra advised Charles that he couldn't sign off on that kind of language and their August plans for sidestepping Hart-Scott-Rodino would have to be revised. But, he reassured him, it wasn't that big a thing. He could structure other legal means with which to accomplish the transfer. The impasse wouldn't squelch the deal. It just required some figuring,

Levin had no such quick fix for their other problem. Relations with Drexel were also at loggerheads—not with Milken's Beverly Hills end of the firm, but with the New York Mergers and Acquisitions division, which spoke for the firm as a whole. By now, Drexel's

M&A bankers had been through a year of Hurwitz's stalking: they had identified PL in the first place; they had calculated its worth; they had arranged for surreptitious aerial surveys of its timberlands; they had secured Hurwitz's fiancial base, including a letter signed by Michael Milken attesting to Drexel Burnham Lambert's intent to float the necessary bonds; and, with less than two weeks to go, they continued to consult on strategy, disputing Hurwitz's inclination to offer $36 a share in his tender offer, arguing that was just low enough to allow someone else to top his offer and leave him in the lurch. Now, the monetary value of those services was at issue between them and the negotiations over Drexel's fee were increasing in acrimony with each passing day. The bankers had submitted a draft of a fee agreement to Hurwitz more than two months earlier, but he had ignored it and, in what the bankers interpreted as a bargaining ploy, waited until the last minute to begin discussions and, true to form, was contesting every nickel. For its part, Drexel, calculating its payment in points of the buyout's total value, was not only insisting on more points than Hurwitz wanted but also on warrants to buy stock in the Maxxam Group Ltd., Hurwitz's principal corporate front. Hurwitz thought that his bankers, having him over something of a barrel, were now trying to get into his pants as well. He was, he continued to repeat to them, quite prepared to walk away from the whole deal and flush all the preparations of the last year right down the tubes.

By Thursday, September 26—the same day Gene Elam informed Salomon Brothers they'd been hired—the fee discussions between Charles and his bankers had still gone nowhere, but everyone in the command post was confident the difficulties with Drexel would be ironed out in the ten days left until their planned announcement. Work on the tender offer continued to progress with a single-minded grind. The only significant diversion was side talk about Hurricane Gloria, working her way up the Eastern Seaboard in New York's direction. Otherwise, Hurwitz's team of lawyers and M.B.A.'s just cast an occasional glance outside at the shroud of overcast darkening Third Avenue and concentrated on polishing the latest draft of the tender offer. Thursday, September 26 seemed like just one more run-of-the-mill day at the fortieth-floor language factory.

Then all hell broke loose.

Two hours before the New York Stock Exchange closed, Kramer

Levin's stock ticker started spewing out quotes on PL that bounced around the room like live grenades. With each printout, the numbers grew, by eighths, by quarters, by halves, even by a point at a time. The volume being traded was light but the bidding on those shares that did move was obviously ferocious. Someone out there was exceedingly anxious to get their hands on a piece of PL. It had closed Wednesday at $29; this unexplained surge of last-minute trading pushed PL up to $33 by the time Thursday's final bell rang. By then, of course, work in the command post had long since ceased while everyone monitored the ticker, dumbstruck. Hurwitz himself soon rushed in to consult Levin. What in the hell was going on? This stock had barely gone up four points throughout the entire summer when it was under all the pressure of his own buying. Now it was duplicating that in two hours? Somebody must be wise to them. What in the hell was going on?

Hurwitz was soon on the phone to Drexel. Had they seen what PL was doing? What in the hell was going on?

Of course they'd seen it. No one could miss a jump like that. Drexel was calling all over The Street trying to find out what was going on and had learned nothing. Nobody had the faintest idea. Someone said they'd heard that a little weekly newspaper in Pennsylvania had run a story predicting a Pacific Lumber buyout, but Drexel had checked that out and it proved to be false. It was a giant mystery. Fewer PL shares traded than any day this week and the stock still ran right up the elevator shaft.

The inexplicable character of the escalation did little to dispel the gloom that was settling in at Hurwitz's command post. Everyone there knew the news could hardly have been worse. Explained or not, an episode like this would bring half the market players on Wall Street swarming over PL when trading opened Friday morning. They would reason that something must be happening and they would want in on it, even if they had no clear idea what it was. The ensuing stampede would drive the price up another $5, maybe even more, and all the calculations upon which Hurwitz's strategy had been based would collapse. Suddenly, with the market running out of control, Charles Hurwitz's takeover of the Pacific Lumber Company looked as though it was about to end before it had even begun. It seemed for a moment that only a miracle could save them.

And then the phone rang.

Drexel was on the line again. This time the bankers had a miracle to report. The National Weather Service had issued a hurricane warning for the entire New York metropolitan area on Friday and the regional civil defense planners were preparing for a state of emergency when Gloria finally made her landfall. Throughout the city, shops had already begun boarding up their windows. To cooperate with the officials' request that travel in the area be kept to a minimum, the Stock Exchange had just announced that it would stay closed on Friday and trading would not resume until Monday, September 30.

Had the track of Hurricane Gloria been a hundred miles east or west, Charles Hurwitz might never have gone any further in his stalking of Pacific Lumber and Pacific Lumber might never have heard of him. Instead, the arrival of a random weather front provided him with a reprieve, and he moved immediately to take advantage of it.

They had three days in which to button up their offer, he announced to the command post. If they hustled, they could still get their takeover out in the open before trading commenced on Monday and the price of Pacific Lumber went through the roof.

9

On Friday morning, while the eye of Gloria was cutting a swath through Long Island to the east and her wide skirts were tearing limbs off the trees in Central Park, the fortieth-floor lights were on at 919 Third Avenue. The command post team labored on the tender offer in the library and Hurwitz and Levin sat in the corner office and managed to corral enough working phone connections to convene a telephonic meeting of the Maxxam Group's board of directors, a body composed of Hurwitz employees and old friends. Without discussion, the board formally granted him the power to issue a tender offer for the Pacific Lumber Company on Monday if he saw fit.

Hurwitz and Levin also ironed out the problems with Jeffries. Levin was now of the opinion that since the broker was in the legal position of being simply a party in possession of a large block of shares unencumbered by any formal obligations, they should just buy them from him outright. To stay legal, the purchase should be made by Hurwitz's MCO Holdings, rather than Maxxam, though Maxxam would have to agree to idemnify MCO against any potential losses. That arrangement would satisfy all of the companies' "arm's length" fiduciary obligations and also, because of the technicalities of Hart-Scott-Rodino's treatment of stock purchases by subsidiaries, still dance around the statute's requirements for public notice. Charles got back on the phone with Boyd Jeffries and explained the new tack their arrangement was taking now that the put-call was dead. For his part, the cooperative Jeffries, even though he had no legal obligation to the terms of the put-call, agreed to sell his position in PL at the price they'd negotiated on Monday, despite the stock having now risen almost $4 a share. Jeffries's cooperation cost the pension funds who actually held the stock at least $2 million in unrealized profits. Nonetheless, Jeffries & Co., transferred some 530,000 shares of Pacific Lumber Company stock to MCO Holdings on Friday at $29.10 a share and, by the time Hurricane Gloria had spent herself thrashing about in Connecticut, Charles Hurwitz held 4.6 percent of the company and nobody outside his Third Avenue command post knew it.

Negotiations with Drexel, however, made little progress. They went from intractable on Thursday to intractable on Friday to intractable on Saturday. On Sunday, September 29, Hurwitz called Michael Milken in California. Hurwitz thought the M&A boys were trying to screw him, and he wasn't going to put up with it. He'd rather have no deal than that deal and, if it came to it, he'd just let this whole thing get trampled by the market on Monday, sell his Pacific Lumber stock for a tidy profit, and forget about it.

Milken agreed to give his New York associates a call and see if something couldn't be worked out before it was too late.

10

Each ring of the phone poked a fresh hole in Gene Elam's sleep, but he resisted opening his eyes, hoping the ringing would somehow cease and allow him to reclaim insensibility. His hope, however, lasted only seconds. Then his wife bolted up in bed. It was 5:30 A.M. Pacific Daylight Time, Monday, September 30, and Mrs. Elam, convinced that a phone call at such an hour could only be an emergency, exclaimed that something must have happened to Michael, their son, away for a college semester in Rome. That thought jump-started Elam and he snatched the receiver out of its cradle.

The man's voice on the line was unfamiliar and rounded on its edges by a melodious drawl. Elam might have expected him to open with an excuse for the hour of his call, but there was none forthcoming. His tone was comfortable, direct, and all business—the voice of someone convinced he had nothing to apologize for, least of all calling when it was still dark outside, California time. He said his name was Charles Hurwitz and he was in the oil and gas business in Texas. He'd phoned as a courtesy to let Elam know that this morning in New York he was announcing a tender offer for the purchase of the Pacific Lumber Company—all of its outstanding shares at $36 apiece.

Elam's heart raced and strained to bring his brain up to speed, but he still groped for a response. This was all so sudden, Elam stammered. Before Hurwitz launched a tender offer, wouldn't it make sense to get together and talk about it?

Hurwitz said it was too late to postpone his offer. The announcement was being circulated as they spoke and he expected a report of it would be transmitted over the Dow Jones ticker any minute. Elam would have no choice but to come to terms with a new reality, and do so in a hurry. But that didn't mean Hurwitz was opposed to talking. On the contrary. Charles Hurwitz believed in talking. And he hoped they could sit down together as soon as possible and negotiate his purchase of Pacific Lumber on a friendly basis.

Elam growled that a phone call out of nowhere at 5:30 A.M. with this kind of news was hardly his idea of how to start a friendly discussion.

Hurwitz was undeterred by Elam's irritation. He could understand that the man was shocked and said he'd feel the same way in the same circumstance. He left unsaid his assumption that, in truth, the two of them had little if anything in common. Charles Hurwitz would never have let anyone sneak up on his business like this, not in a million years. He was nobody's easy pickings. But that was beside the point. His goal now was to belly up to the table and cut a deal as soon as possible. He told Elam he was prepared to fly out to San Francisco immediately. All Elam had to do was say the word.

Elam hedged. He didn't want to commit himself to anything until he'd had a chance to get his wits about him and structure some kind of strategy, but, having raised the issue of talk, he had a hard time refusing. After a brief resistance, Elam gave in and made an appointment to sit down with the Texan late that afternoon.

Hurwitz closed the conversation by poking some fun at his adversary's predicament. His accompanying chuckle had a swagger to it. Elam probably wouldn't need a shower to wake up this morning, he said, would he?

Hurwitz chuckled again and, when Elam didn't respond in kind, he rang off. The phone call had lasted less than five minutes and Charles Hurwitz was off to as good a start as he could have hoped for.

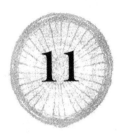

11

Elam, however, jolted awake and then ambushed, had to fight off panic. This was not a turn of events he'd anticipated. The freakish last-minute updraft in Thursday's stock transactions hadn't set off any alarm bells around the PL offices or among the consulting bankers he'd hired at Salomon Brothers, so, after an unperturbed Friday, Elam had spent a typical weekend out at his home in the East Bay suburbs, taking in his usual Sunday morning Mass. It had never occurred to him that his company would be going to the mattresses before the sun rose on the new work week. Once he'd collected himself, he called Bob Hoover, the chairman of the board.

Hoover, sixty-nine, lived in San Clemente in southern California. For the first two years after handing the company presidency over to Elam, he'd commuted between there and San Francisco, working three or four days a week, looking over the younger man's shoulder at the request of the board, but since Elam's elevation to chief executive officer, Hoover's commuting had ceased and he had retired completely, save for a half-dozen board meetings every year. He was always proud to point out that there'd been Hoovers connected with PL almost as long as there'd been Murphys. His dad, Gus, a lumber wholesaler, had become the company's southern California sales agent in 1909. Bob himself had worked directly for the company for a brief stint in 1939, right after finishing at

Stanford Business School, and then, after two decades in his father's firm, had returned as PL's vice president for sales under Stan Murphy. Hoover was still a salesman by personality. He was a go-along-and-get-along guy, even less equipped than Elam for the kind of merciless corporate combat into which PL had just been thrust.

Bob Hoover was stunned when awakened by Elam's phone call and informed of the latter's 5:30 A.M. conversation. Like Elam, he'd never heard of this fellow Hurwitz, but he assumed the Texan was deadly serious. Unfortunately, that's the way business was these days. History counted little and Wall Street was God. Hoover knew right away that they would have to deal with Hurwitz but wished they didn't. He wished Pacific Lumber could have just gone on the way it always had, but he expected that would be impossible. People like Hurwitz held all the cards and it was either their game or none at all. He advised Elam to get into the office and start working the phones. In the meantime, he'd catch the next plane north and be there before lunch.

Gene Elam's first phone call after he reached the office was to the company attorneys in the San Francisco firm of Pillsbury, Madison and Sutro. They weren't securities specialists, but they knew enough to say in no uncertain terms that negotiation with Hurwitz at this point would be an error of considerable magnitude, so he immediately canceled the appointment into which Hurwitz had pressured him.

Elam figured his next call ought to be to Salomon Brothers, the consulting bankers he'd hired on Thursday. He clearly needed guidance from some "experts." Before he could call, however, the director of Solly's San Francisco office called him. Solly's man in the city had learned of PL's most recent development from the firm's New York Mergers and Acquisitions division, who had picked it up off the Dow Jones wire. M&A had been quick to note that what had been a minor consulting contract had just been transformed into a major piece of work with significant implications. Solly was a late-comer to the takeover game and this was a chance to build their M&A reputation against some major players. The New York bankers knew full well who Charles Hurwitz was and, though his official tender offer document had yet to be released, they expected it would reveal that his principal backer was Drexel Burnham Lambert, the biggest player of all. The action in the Pacific Lumber account had definitely moved to the deep end of the pool, and M&A wanted in on it. That they might very well be in over their heads was never discussed with the client. Instead, Solly's San Francisco director assured Elam that the firm had a special division based in New York that dealt with nothing except these kinds of situations. He also pointed out that last week's understanding would hardly cover what PL now needed. Rather than wait until their contract would be rewritten, however, the two agreed on a stopgap two-month retainer at $100,000 a month. The remainder of Solly's fee would be negotiated as they went along.

The first service Pacific Lumber received for its money was an immediate conference call for Elam with Salomon's Mergers and Acquisitions bankers in New York. The bankers assured him they would have a team of their best people out to California by tomorrow afternoon to begin collecting the information they would need to brief the board and lay out Pacific Lumber's strategy. In the meantime, Solly's M&A men thought the company ought to retain a top-of-the-line New York securities law firm to participate in that process. They recommended Wachtell Lipton Rosen & Katz and Elam accepted the recommendation. The bankers promised to bring the lawyers along tomorrow as well. Since Hurwitz hadn't released his actual tender offer document, their immediate analyses would all be tentative but, once those documents were out, Solly could crunch the numbers and get a more definite take on just where PL stood. There was no cause to panic, they assured Elam. They dealt with this kind of stuff day in and day out. His company was in good hands and they would be out to see him in person tomorrow.

In the meantime, Bob Hoover arrived at PL's headquarters, just as he'd promised. By then, of course, word of Elam's 5:30 A.M. phone call had spread throughout the building and monopolized the workforce's extracurricular attention. Everyone knew why Hoover was there. Many of those who greeted him evinced a spirited defiance, rallying to their embattled company, but the chairman of the board had to work at not being glum. He remembered the days when old Mr. Murphy patrolled the front office in his stiff collar and when Stan ran the woods crew, tin hat on his head and logging boots laced up to his knees. Now, with the company "in play," change was inevitable, whatever the outcome of Hurwitz's offer—

change into a company that made more money more quickly and
with less heart—and, in that process, lumberjack heaven was sure to
be replaced by an arrangement more in line with the stockbrokers'
lowest common denominator. Over the next three weeks, Bob
Hoover would consult with Gene Elam at least once a day, often
three or four times, trying to make sense out of developments, and,
from Day One, Hoover was convinced they were just acting out bit
parts in a genuine tragedy.

The behavior of the stock market only darkened his mood further. During Monday's trading, PL, goosed by Thursday's run-up
and news of Hurwitz on the morning's Dow Jones, opened at $36.50
and closed at $39. Some 656,000 shares were traded, only 200,000
shares less than had been traded during the mysterious escalation
that consumed the entire month of July. By the end of the trading
week on October 4, 2,793,000 Pacific Lumber shares would have
moved through the New York Stock Exchange—more than 10 percent of the company in a matter of five days. The stock reached
its all-time speculative high of $41.12 a share on Thursday, Octo-
ber 3—almost twice what PL had sold for only a year ago. By then, it
was obvious to Bob Hoover and everyone else with an eye on the
ticker that "the arbs" were now in the act.

The presence of these arbs—arbitrageurs, who speculated in
takeover stocks—was often the kiss of death to companies faced with
unwelcome tender offers. Once the arbs controlled a critical mass of
shares, intending to hold them only long enough to turn a quick
profit on their resale, the struggle over a company was reduced to
an auction in which the only loyalty was to the highest bidder. Leading the charge at PL was "the King of the Arbs," Ivan Boesky, perhaps the most notorious player on The Street and, thanks to
countless newspaper features, the reigning American symbol of
bull-market capitalism. The mere presence of Boesky was sufficient
to confirm the most dire of Hoover's premonitions, but the still secret truth behind his interest in PL was even worse.

After Tuesday, when Boesky took his profits at $39 on the Pacific
Lumber shares he'd collected in Friday's third market at $33, he re-
mained in the PL hunt solely on behalf of Drexel Burnham Lambert. Securities law forbade Hurwitz's bankers from accumulating
PL shares themselves, so Michael Milken and Boesky, who'd worked
closely on some of the arb's more spectacular ventures, cut a deal.

Milken, wanting a hedge against the possibility of his client Hurwitz being preempted by another bidder, knew that the combination of Boesky's reputation and the block of stock he would accumulate would likely be sufficient to keep the market's other predators at bay. And Boesky, anxious to please the man whose junk bonds had made his anointment as King of the Arbs possible, owed Milken more than one favor. After each day's trading, Boesky called one of Milken's principal associates to report and settle up the day's accounts. Boesky would eventually purchase more than 5 percent of PL's outstanding shares for his covert partner, all very much outside the law and to the benefit of Drexel Burnham Lambert. But that was still a secret. At the time, all Bob Hoover and Gene Elam could discern was that the Pacific Lumber Company seemed to be surrounded by vultures on all fronts.

Solly's M&A bankers offered no immediate escape when they arrived on Tuesday, October 1. Four of them and a lawyer from Wachtell Lipton spent the heart of the afternoon closeted with Elam, Hoover, and several other PL executives. Their role, they explained, was to assist management and the board in meeting their obligation to the stockholders. Their independent certification of whether a tender offer was a "fair price" or not would be critical in avoiding later stockholder suits. They would also help develop a strategy for maximizing the stockholder benefits in the situation, analyzing Hurwitz's offer, and soliciting others, should that be called for. Their first product would be a written and oral report to the board at its regular meeting, scheduled for October 9. To begin, they needed to work up a complete financial picture of the company and would start analyzing PL's books and other proprietary information immediately. Once Hurwitz's documentation was available, they would start breaking it down as well.

That process began the next day, Wednesday, October 2, when Hurwitz's formal tender offer was finally released. According to its terms, Pacific Lumber Company shares would be officially purchased by the MXM Corporation, a subsidiary of Maxxam created solely for the purposes of this transaction, to be merged into its parent once the process was complete. As expected, the document also identified Drexel Burnham Lambert as Hurwitz's chief backer. Drexel would collect a series of percentages of the transaction's aggregate value in payment for its various advising and financing functions which, combined, stood to earn it at least $24 million, plus warrants to purchase some 500,000 shares of Maxxam common stock at pre-merger prices. The biggest surprise to Solly's analysts was the document's indicated price. Over the two days since his call to Elam, Hurwitz had dropped his plans to open at $36 and brought the offer in at $38.50 instead. Hurwitz was known to be a tight spender, so the most popular analysis was that his hand had been forced by the market or Drexel or both. In either case, it was an obvious move to preempt any other bidders.

The tender offer also made it clear that Hurwitz intended to fight any attempt by Pacific Lumber to exercise the defenses built into its bylaws, either by legal challenge or by purchasing enough shares to amend them out of existence. This, however, was not an aspect of the document to which Solly devoted a lot of attention. The head of the visiting M&A delegation had already made it clear that he considered bylaw defenses such as those PL had adopted of little value. In discussing strategy, there was no mention made of all the other constituencies besides shareholders or issues besides price that the bylaws obligated the board to consider. Nor was there any ruminating over the possibilities of mobilizing the company's shareholders to fight back or of declaring the offer "hostile" and utilizing the 80 percent rule to sabotage any planned merger. These, the experts from Solly told Elam and Hoover, were useless gestures fraught with legal dilemmas and strategic pitfalls. Elam and Hoover, in over their heads, accepted Solly's expertise. On Thursday, Pacific Lumber's management issued a press release announcing that it had received Hurwitz's "unsolicited" offer and that the board would meet shortly to consider it. In the meantime, the company was "studying" the proposal.

Behind that noncommittal veneer, a strategy was taking shape, however, and it was most visible in the agreement Elam and the bankers were busy laying out to cover Salomon Brothers' fees. According to the terms of this new contract, should Solly fend off any takeover and maintain the company's independence or should Hurwitz succeed at $38.50 a share, Solly would be paid a flat fee of $2.5 million. Should, however, the bankers succeed in negotiating a price in excess of $38.50, either from Hurwitz or some other buyer, the payment schedule would switch to a piece of the action and Solly would be due one half of 1 percent of the transaction's value. At a sale price of $38.51. a share, an increase of only one penny, that piece of the action represented a far more lucrative fee of some $4.2 million. The implications for strategy were obvious. Whatever the company's public position, the incentives behind the scenes all pointed in one direction.

12

None of that drift was obvious in Scotia. When word first got around about Hurwitz's announcement, no one there thought this Texas motherfucker stood a chance in hell of taking over PL and everyone assumed the people down at headquarters were preparing to fight tooth and nail. Pictures of Hurwitz clipped from the *San Francisco Chronicle* were posted here and there around town with Hurwitz's image defaced and doggerel scribbled on them. A few of the boys down on the mill floor even talked about strapping on their ammo belts, taking up their deer guns, and waylaying the son of a bitch at the freeway exit ramp if he ever ventured into Humboldt County.

That sense of resistance was just as apparent in the front office, and the front office always set the tone for the town. At one point during that first week, one local executive was walking along Main Street, headed in the direction of the Scotia Inn, when he passed an immigrant millworker who was identified by everyone in town as the resident German. In what passed as Scotia humor, it was common practice to kid him about being a Nazi, a ritual the executive had engaged in like everyone else. Now, taking off on the town's combative mood toward the current stock market assault, the executive added another to the ongoing string of Nazi jokes.

"Better stoke up those ovens again, Heinie," he shouted at the German. "We got us another Jew to burn."

13

By the second week of October, Charles Hurwitz's tender offer had become the tune to which everyone in Scotia danced. Mill hands now clustered together with every break whistle, feverishly hashing and rehashing the situation, usually referring to the Texan as "that son of a bitch" and speculating what he'd look like strung up on the bridge to Rio Dell. Scotia housewives now discussed junk bonds over back fences and in the grocery checkout line. Diners at the Scotia Coffee Shop, once content to debate the 49ers' chances of returning to the Super Bowl, now scoured the *San Francisco Chronicle* financial pages hoping to enlarge the town's pitifully meager supply of real information about its fate. When not deriding Hurwitz, most took to speaking wistfully of Stan Murphy. Had "that son of a bitch" tried this shit when old Stan was alive, the outcome, everyone agreed, would never have been in doubt. Stan would have kicked his ass all the way back to Texas, end of story.

Stan, however, now dead more than thirteen years, would not be coming to Scotia's rescue. The only Murphys available to act as Pacific Lumber's protectors were Stan's widow, Suzanne Beaver, and his two sons, Warren and Woody.

Of them, Suzanne, sitting on the PL board, was in the best position to help save the company. She was also the least equipped by either experience or character for doing so. Suzanne arrived at

Pacific Lumber's San Francisco headquarters for the October 9 board meeting in a state of high confusion. She made no pretense of understanding how on earth things could have reached this state of affairs. That a stranger might come in from nowhere and buy PL seemed nonsensical. The prospect violated all the rudimentary economics she'd managed to accumulate when Stan talked business at the dinner table. Even as a girl, growing up not far from Stan in San Francisco's well-heeled Pacific Heights, before she'd even imagined becoming a Murphy herself, her father ritually admonished everyone in the family never to sell the Pacific Lumber stock. It would, he claimed, pay dividends forever. Then, at a summer party down in the sunny horse country along the Peninsula south of the city, to which all the scions of San Francisco society had been invited, Suzanne, now past debutante age, met the dashing young Stan, his arm bandaged from a logging accident. He could talk of nothing but Humboldt and felling the big trees that grew there. The company was already Stan's life and, once he asked her to marry him, it became hers. From that point, selling the company was absolutely unthinkable. Having such a possibility discussed, even four decades after Stan first cornered her at the edge of that innocent crowd of white frocks and linen jackets, filling her ears with exotic tales of peaveys and bucksaws, was extraordinarily disorienting.

The board meeting on October 9 did little to resolve her confusion. It was so full of bankers and lawyers that, to Suzanne Beaver, the room seemed to tilt toward the end of the table where all the new hired guns from New York swarmed into chairs on either side of Gene Elam. Among them, only Elam's haircut looked like it came from somewhere other than Brooks Brothers.

The bankers from Solly opened the discussion by distributing the report upon which their M&A group had been laboring for the last ten days. It ran some sixty pages, including graphs, charts, and tables, all under the code name "Operation Weldwood." Suzanne quickly gave up any notions of reading the document on the spot—it would take her a good week to digest anything that complicated. Instead, she waited while the bankers took turns at the podium, walking the board through "Operation Weldwood," page by page. Using the company's own timber estimates, Salomon Brothers calculated that Pacific Lumber was worth somewhere between $60.28 and $77.96 a share. In light of those numbers, Hurwitz's $38.50 tender offer was clearly "inadequate." They also considered his financing suspect. Even Drexel might not be able to deliver the cash this kind of deal would require and, if they did, they were still loading some $460 million of long-term high-interest debt on a company whose available cash flow was currently only about $12 million a year. On its face it was a recipe for financial collapse, Solly argued.

Unsure what to think of all this banker talk, Suzanne took some comfort when she noticed that both Ed Carpenter and Bob Hoover were bobbing their heads in agreement.

The company's New York lawyers from Wachtell Lipton eventually took their turn at the podium as well. Like the bankers, they made almost no reference to the defenses already in the company bylaws. Instead, the attorneys led off with a boilerplate lecture about the board's responsibilities to look out for the interests of the shareholders and then proposed some immediate legal tactics. They had two lawsuits ready. The first, to be filed in the Federal District Court for Northern California, described Hurwitz as "a notorious takeover artist [whose] background demonstrates a conspicuous absence of [the] integrity, competence and fitness necessary to control or manage a substantial business enterprise" and asked the court to block him from any further pursuit of his tender offer. The second, a petition to the Federal Reserve Board, claimed that the tender offer, which would be accomplished almost entirely with money in effect borrowed against the stock to be purchased, was a violation of the Board's regulations and sought Federal Reserve intervention. The Wachtell Lipton attorneys seemed pessimistic about the ultimate success of these moves but noticed they might at least slow Hurwitz down and give him something to think about.

Suzanne Beaver glanced over at Carpenter and Hoover for confirmation and both men were still nodding.

When the reports finally ended after several hours, the focus of the meeting moved off the company's hired guns and onto the board itself. Once they'd formally voted to reject the tender offer, most of the directors scoured the laundry list of standard anti-takeover practices provided by the bankers from Solly, looking for more roadblocks to throw into the path of Hurwitz's advance. The two they selected were familiar tactics among all the players of the takeover game. First, they expanded the company's "golden parachute" provisions, providing its executives with severance benefits.

The October 9 resolution passed by the board enlarged the benefits already provided for Elam and his top five underlings and set up additional benefit packages for another thirty-four managers in both the welding and timber operations. If Hurwitz thought he was going to walk in and clean out PL's upper echelons, it would cost him several million to do so. Suzanne voted for the arrangment because the men in question had "given their lives" to PL.

The second resolution passed by the board was a much more significant threat to Hurwitz. The directors meant to deny him access to Pacific Lumber's overfunded pension plan as well. By unanimous vote, the board passed provisions ensuring that, should the company be taken over against its wishes, the $55 million pension surplus would be automatically vested in the employees, reserving it for the exclusive use of the company's retirees. Suzanne cast her vote without second thought. Though Bob Hoover pushed this move as an excellent way to exert additional leverage on Hurwitz, she never really thought of it as a negotiating ploy. It was simple justice. What had been put away for the employees ought to remain true to its original purpose.

Six hours had now passed but the men from Solly were not yet ready to allow the board to adjourn. All of these tactical moves were fine as far as they went, the bankers pointed out, but none of them would take Pacific Lumber off the hook. The simple fact was that it would be impossible to wrestle with this tender offer without the company undergoing a significant "restructuring" of some sort. Like it or not, PL was "in play" and it would have to transform itself in one way or another to escape that status. The last pages of "Operation Weldwood" contained a list of seven options to solve PL's larger dilemma. They ranged from another self-tender, similar to the 1984 buyback, to a leveraged buyout, in which the company would borrow enough money to outbid Hurwitz and take itself out of public circulation. The bankers worked their way through the list, advancing arguments why one option after another wasn't feasible. According to the bankers, only the last two on the list were genuine possibilities. The first of those was identified as "Pursue White Knights." This involved management's use of the legal waiting period, during which Hurwitz was prevented from purchasing further stock, to solicit another buyer. The second option endorsed by Solly was "Negotiate with Maxxam." They could get a better price, they assured the board. Hurwitz had more money to spend than he'd yet offered. At Elam's urging, the board unanimously agreed to give management permission to pursue these two possibilities.

Numbed by the marathon discussion and aching for adjournment, Suzanne Beaver voted for this final resolution largely because both Hoover and Carpenter thought it was the best thing to do. Afterward, she was not at all clear about what she'd voted for. She thought she was just giving Elam more room to maneuver and bringing to a close the longest board meeting in which she'd ever participated. It was only weeks later, when the whole tragedy had played itself out, that Suzanne Beaver realized that she and the other directors had just pushed the company one step closer to being sold.

The second of Stan's heirs who might have seized the savior's gauntlet, Suzanne's elder son, Woody, had none of his mother's confusion around the issue, but none of her power either. Woody—Stanwood Albert Murphy, Jr.—was the first and only Murphy ever to be fired by the Pacific Lumber Company. Unlike his little brother, Warren, he'd never had any ambivalence about working for PL. In truth, Woody had never wanted anything else as long as he could remember. The day after Stan had died, Woody was found down in his father's Scotia office, sitting behind the desk, ready to do business. As elder son, he assumed the job of running PL was now his. Ed Carpenter gently disabused him of his fantasy and sent him back to his job on the logging show by Bear Creek, but shortly thereafter Woody was placed on the executive fast track, just like John Campbell before him and Warren yet to come.

Woody did not, however, demonstrate much in the way of executive potential. Stanwood Albert Murphy, Jr., was just a good ol' boy, a little short on intellect and built like a fireplug, who loved mucking around in the woods on heavy equipment and always felt as though someone was about to hang him every time he knotted a tie around his neck. He'd jumped off the fast track almost as soon as it took him out of Humboldt and down to the San Francisco headquarters. Then he'd landed back in the forest, running a crew that spread gravel on PL's logging roads. Woody stayed at that posting for the better part of a decade. His relative lack of status had only begun to chafe a couple of years earlier when he got in a heated dispute with his supervisor. Then Stanwood, Jr., made an abortive effort to reclaim at least some of his standing as a Murphy. He was tired of being treated as the "nigger in the woodpile," he complained to John Campbell. Campbell, a family friend and old hunting buddy, told Woody he'd see what he could work out. Two months later, John called the elder Murphy son into his office and told him there was no place for him inside PL anymore. Despite owning a little less than 1 percent of its stock, his career with the Pacific Lumber Company was over. Devastated, Woody had nonetheless managed to suppress the quiver in his voice and the tremble along his jaw as he turned on his heel and walked out of the office where his dad had once run the show. Woody now ran his own independent timbering and log export business, based in Fields Landing on the mudflats of lower Humboldt Bay.

When Woody heard what Charles Hurwitz was up to, he called his attorney, Bill Bertain. Bill, the last of the Scotia laundryman's ten children, had once taught Woody and Warren their altar boy chores at St. Patrick's church and had grown up into Woody's kind of lawyer—a homeboy who'd never forgot where he was from. Bill had tried the big-city-lawyer routine after graduating from the University of San Francisco Law School, but had barely lasted six months up on the ninth floor of some high rise, trapped in an office where the windows didn't open, before he'd fled back to Humboldt and set up practice in the county seat. Shorter even than Woody, Bertain had built a local reputation as a crusader when he led a long but successful legal campaign to restrict a sewage plant planned for the north end of the bay. Woody had hired him earlier in the year to put his new timber business on proper legal footing. Now, Woody, who still loved PL despite being fired, wanted to know what in the hell he could do to stop this son of a bitch Hurwitz.

The two consulted in Bertain's office on J Street in Eureka, on the second floor of a two-story building across from the County Jail. Bertain's desk was covered with mounds of papers, arranged according to a system only he could interpret, and the aluminum frame window to its left overlooked a waterbed salesroom. The other walls were covered with cheap machine-pressed wood veneer that made a hollow sound when knocked upon. The lawyer's twenty-year-old Oldsmobile was parked in the lot out back and he wore cowboy boots and no tie, his usual workaday uniform. Relentlessly good-humored, Bill resembled a cross between an elf and a pit bull. When he made his usual lunchtime journey for a burger at the A and A Lounge across the three one-way lanes of Fourth Street that carried southbound U.S. 101 through town, half the people he passed along the way greeted him.

One of the first things he told Woody was that he was not well-versed in securities law and would have to do some reading before he could give much in the way of an opinion.

That didn't matter much to Woody. What mattered was he trusted Bill. He knew what Bill was made of, which is more than he could say about any other lawyer.

And if they did end up taking any action, Bertain continued, he would have to hire on one or two big San Francisco firms to carry the brunt of the legal work, lawyers who were used to these kinds of cases. But there was time to plan all of that. In the immediate moment, nothing could be done until it was clear what Elam and the board were going to do. The ball was in their court.

Woody understood that. He was about to leave for Wyoming and his annual fall hunting trip—blood sports were a Murphy tradition that Stanwood Albert, Jr., indulged at every opportunity—and he wasn't going to let this son of a bitch from Texas disrupt that. But he wanted Bill to track the situation for him while he was gone.

Bill agreed. And what about Warren? he asked. Would Woody's little brother be involved?

Woody told his lawyer that he was sure Warren would be right there with him if the shit hit the fan, but, in the meantime, his brother was somewhat between a rock and a hard place.

Warren, the third Murphy who might figure in a rescue effort, was indeed hamstrung. His instinct was to leap into the fray but, as manager of lumber operations, he had to act as a loyal soldier and line up with the rest of management behind the pencil-pushing Gene Elam. Warren doubted Elam had the stomach for a real fight, but he figured he had no choice but to wait and see.

Warren Murphy's doubts only intensified during the week after the October 9 board meeting. He'd picked up the scuttlebutt from the boardroom, both through his mother and scraps passed on by John Campbell, but the drift of events was brought home by a succession of corporate delegations who suddenly began flowing through Scotia's head office. These were the "White Knights" Solly recommended the company pursue. The ones with the most interest flew private planes into the Hydesville airport, on the bluff between Fortuna and Rio Dell—the same airport where thirteen years earlier, PL's company plane had skidded to a halt while, inside the passenger compartment, desperate efforts were being made to restart Stan Murphy's heart. It had stopped beating during their approach run at the end of a flight up from San Francisco. The irony of the parallel arrivals was hardly lost on Warren. His father had died in one and the company might well die through the other, but Warren soldiered on, producing the numbers the visitors requested from John Campbell as they pored over the Scotia production records, then watching them drive off for Hydesville and the return trip to their own companies when they had all they wanted. Sometimes he and Campbell discussed them afterward, sometimes Warren just gritted his teeth and went back to his daily tasks.

By the end of the week, however, Warren's patience gave out. The company was already set up to fight off someone like Hurwitz but, as far as Warren could tell, no one was gearing up to do so. Certainly finding someone else to buy the company wasn't any way to make that fight. Someone had to invoke PL's bylaws and mobilize the shareholders. A lot of them remembered Stan and his vision for PL and if the company's loyalists would seize the opportunity, they had leverage enough to control the situation. Warren was convinced that sufficient numbers to block the tender offer would hold out if someone would just recruit them to resist.

He took his frustration to John Campbell, both because Campbell was his boss and because the two men were friends. Warren told John the time had come to start pushing the issue. The company had to mobilize its friends and do it now.

John listened, flashing an occasional sympathetic grimace and snatching glances out the window toward Main Street. It was drizzling outside and rainy season was clearly on its way. When Warren paused, John leaned forward in his chair and tried to slow him down. Before he did anything, Campbell advised, they'd better clear all this with Elam.

Five minutes later, he had Elam and Bob Hoover on the other end of a conference call, listening to Warren implore them to start mobilizing the stockholders.

The call was barely under way when Elam announced that he'd heard enough. "No" was the mildest part of his response. He ordered Warren Murphy not to approach anyone with this scheme. He wasn't to call anyone; he wasn't to mention it. He should just sit tight in Scotia and do his job and keep his nose out of business where it didn't belong.

After Elam hung up, Murphy and Campbell sat in silence for a moment.

John finally broke their paralysis with a resigned chuckle. Well, he offered, that's the end of that bloody idea.

Warren just nodded and headed back down the hall to his own desk.

14

Gene Elam and Warren Murphy, headed in opposite directions at a rapid pace, were even further apart than it seemed at the time of their phone conversation. By then, unbeknownst to either Murphy or Campbell, Pacific Lumber's c.e.o. had already concluded that the White Knight strategy would likely prove fruitless. None of the candidates for rescue had yet offered more than $37.50, a dollar less than the tender offer already on the table, and, while not every possibility had weighed in, the promise of a genuinely competitive offer was slim at best. Without such an offer, the only remaining option endorsed by Solly as workable was negotiation with Hurwitz, and Elam meant to take it, though, of course, he never considered telling the Murphy kid of his plans. That would have only been inviting trouble. Like it or not, Elam felt he had no choice but to deal with the Texan and he didn't need some sentimental junior executive yapping at his heels when he did so. For Gene Elam, barely three years in the job, this was an opportunity to prove he could shepherd his company through a difficult situation, playing in the big leagues, head to head with Wall Street's sharpest. Charles Hurwitz, of course, cast as the spider to Elam's fly, had expected they would end up in this kind of face-off all along.

It was actually initiated by the respective bankers involved. While John Campbell and Warren Murphy were seeing to the needs of the

White Knights trooping through Scotia, the M&A boys from Solly invited a couple of their counterparts from Drexel to stop by Solly's Manhattan headquarters for a chat. There, the two sides circled each other warily.

Solly pointed out that Elam and PL's board were just looking out for their shareholders. And everyone in the room knew $38.50 was not the best Hurwitz could do. The stock had begun the week selling on the exchange at $40, for Christ's sake.

Come on, Drexel responded. Those numbers were all market fluff that would last only as long as the next puff of wind that came wandering up The Street. The fact was that without Charles, Pacific Lumber would still be bumping along at $25 and lucky to be there. PL was fortunate that Charles wasn't just some arb fooling around but was instead a serious businessman, who wanted to own and run the company. He was also a reasonable man and, despite the slander of PL's lawsuits, still open to sitting down at the table and talking all this over.

Solly said they were glad to hear it.

Charles wanted a friendly deal, the Drexel delegation continued. Making a fight over this would be bad for everyone concerned. In that context, the cooperation of PL's board with his tender offer "might be worth something" when it came to nailing down a final sales price.

Solly said they were glad to hear that as well.

The bankers' meeting lasted twenty minutes and ended with an agreement that Hurwitz would come to San Francisco the next Saturday, October 19, and begin negotiations.

Both Gene Elam and Charles Hurwitz got what they wanted from this preparatory conversation between Solly and Drexel, but both of them arrived at their initial sit-down at least somewhat aggravated.

For his part, Hurwitz was angered by Drexel's promise to Solly that "something" would be added onto the final price in exchange for the possibility of a friendly deal. The Texan went through the roof when first informed of it. He hadn't commissioned Drexel to talk price, he complained. What the hell were they doing making offers like that? He didn't need to give on the price. Couldn't they see that? These guys had no place else to go. If nobody panics, the deal is a winner at $38.50. His irritation had subsided somewhat by Saturday, but it still lingered, submerged behind the veneer of pomaded serenity he customarily presented to the world. On the other hand, Elam's irritation was running at full throttle. He was furious at Hurwitz. On Friday, less than twenty-four hours before negotiations were to commence, Maxxam had filed suit against Pacific Lumber in the state of Maine, where PL was incorporated, attacking most of the measures adopted by the board on October 9, dismissing these defensive maneuvers as absolutely unwarranted windfalls for management and employees. As far as Elam was concerned, the gall of this fellow Hurwitz knew no apparent bounds. Suing on the eve of a "friendly" discussion—which he had initiated—that was beyond the pale, Elam raged. By Saturday morning, steam was leaking out of the PL c.e.o.'s collar as he waited with flushed cheeks for Hurwitz's arrival at the company's otherwise empty headquarters.

The Texan was accompanied by one of his Maxxam executives and two men from Drexel. Elam and he were introduced by their respective bankers and then they all sat down together in one of the headquarters' conference rooms. Hurwitz began by reaffirming that he was there to make this into a "friendly" transaction.

Elam almost choked. Friendly? He hadn't done a damn thing since this all started that even remotely fit any definition of friendly with which Elam was familiar—starting with his 5:30 A.M. phone call and running through yesterday's lawsuit. Suing on the eve of negotiations was hardly the stuff upon which friendly relations are built, Elam pointed out.

Hurwitz's response was unruffled. He hadn't known that suit would be filed, he claimed. His attorneys must have proceeded as a matter of course without checking with him first. Had he known he would have stopped it.

Elam was incredulous. He didn't believe for one minute that Charles Hurwitz's lawyers went around filing suits without his knowledge, and he said so. He was nonetheless careful not to let the negotiations get stuck in recriminations. He did not approve of the way Maxxam had proceeded, he added, but this was beside the point. Hurwitz had asked for a meeting and now he wanted to hear what Hurwitz had to say.

Hurwitz answered that he wanted to make this deal. It was as simple as that.

If that was the case, Elam pointed out, then he'd better be ready to raise his price above $38.50. Otherwise, there was nothing to talk about. With that, Elam and his Solly bankers ran down a long list of reasons why Hurwitz's pending tender offer was "inadequate."

Hurwitz listened and then launched into his own list of reasons $38.50 was more than fair. He was a generous man, he insisted, and Pacific Lumber's executives would learn this firsthand if they stayed on to run the company for him. He then began listing the incentives he was willing to offer PL's management.

Elam interrupted. He was here to look out for the shareholders, not management, he admonished. All those incentives didn't mean a damn unless Hurwitz got up off of $38.50.

Well then, Hurwitz challenged, what price did Elam want for the company?

The company wasn't for sale, Elam snapped, but if Hurwitz had an offer to make, he'd listen to it.

Before the discussion could deteriorate any further, one of the men from Drexel intervened and suggested the two principals separate and let the bankers talk. After discussing it among themselves, PL's delegation agreed and relocated to one office down the hall while Hurwitz and his executive moved off to another, leaving Solly and Drexel to retrieve the negotiations from the corner into which they'd been driven by the intractability of the two principals.

Once it was just banker to banker, one of the two men from Drexel seized the initiative. He suggested they pass on the foreplay and get right to the bottom line. There would be another $1.50 on the table for a friendly transaction, he assured his counterparts, so why didn't Solly just go back to their clients and put this thing to bed?

After lingering just long enough not to seem anxious, Solly headed back down the hall. They were sure $40 was an offer that would carry a lot of weight, and to have gotten it so quickly made it even more impressive. But before they could do more than begin briefing Elam and the other PL executives on what Drexel had proposed, they were interrupted by a knock on the office door. It was the man from Drexel who'd just moments earlier sanguinely urged putting this whole thing to bed. From his expression, it was clear that Charles Hurwitz's irritation was now doing a lot more than lingering. The Drexel man's presence almost reeked of singed flesh.

He was sorry, he stammered, but he'd made a mistake. After checking with his client, he'd discovered they were only willing to go up to $39, not $40.

When the door closed again, the PL delegation had no trouble making up its mind. This was preposterous, no way to behave, and, they agreed, it was time to gather everyone together again and just tell Hurwitz good day.

That, however, was not easy. The Texan, always certain of his ability to convince anyone else of anything, struggled to keep the negotiation alive, advancing a spate of arguments for the suitability of his $39 offer.

Elam didn't buy it.

In that case, Hurwitz threatened, Maxxam would just proceed with its tender offer, without the board's cooperation, and buy the company at $38.50, whether Elam liked it or not.

Elam told him to go ahead and do whatever he had to and that Elam would do the same.

Fair enough, Hurwitz snapped. He certainly wasn't going to hang around here and bid against himself.

With that, the meeting, a little more than two hours old, ended. Hurwitz and his entourage drove off for the airport and Elam watched them disappear into the sparse Saturday morning traffic in San Francisco's financial district. Round One was over, and Gene Elam thought he'd won.

At this stage of the game, such assessments were, of course, meaningless. Both sides knew there would be a Round Two, though nothing had been done to arrange it. Indeed, that possibility was the principal subject of a Hurwitz war conference over lunch back at his New York hotel on Sunday. The two Drexel bankers were there and the Maxxam executive, but, this time, Ezra Levin was there as well. Normally, Levin would have been part of the delegation that had gone to San Francisco, but he did not travel on the sabbath, so Charles had done without him. That would not be the case for Round Two.

It was clear, Charles began over brunch, that, whatever their pretensions, the Pacific Lumber people were in a weak position. They would never have agreed to talk otherwise. Come October 24, when the waiting period was over, the company's stockholders would start cashing in their shares as though they were going out of style. Then it was just a matter of time before they could dismantle all the booby traps in its bylaws and swallow it whole. The deal was a winner at $38.50, without giving up a nickel more.

That might be so, the men from Drexel responded. The emphasis, however, was on *might*. On the other hand, Elam might well be putting together another deal with which to blindside them as they spoke. Everyone on The Street knew he was out there fishing and, judging from the market, most were betting he would find one. Charles should also remember that even if they were able to force the issue and win, PL still might be able to deny them the pension fund surplus. That alone would cost him $2.50 a share, making him look penny-wise and pound-foolish, to say the least.

To Drexel's surprise, Hurwitz agreed without having to be bludgeoned. He admitted that he was prepared to go up past $39. How much past, he didn't say, but the bankers didn't push the issue further.

Now the question was how to get PL back to the table without looking weak or tipping their hand. The strategy the Maxxam Group settled on was a third-party intervention, using Pacific Lumber director Michael Coyne as the third party. Coyne was notoriously jumpy. He'd been calling Elam several times a day since Hurwitz first surfaced and was anxious for a deal to be made. He'd become a major Pacific Lumber shareholder when Stan Murphy had bought his cutting and welding company and turned it into a PL division. This was Coyne's chance to cash out at prices he'd never imagined would be available to him. Hurwitz's people already knew he'd been intensely disappointed at yesterday's collapse of negotiations. They approached Coyne on Sunday through a banker from a house other than Drexel. The banker knew Coyne personally and Coyne leapt at the opportunity to put the banker in touch with Elam. The banker then offered Elam his assistance in coaxing a "reluctant" Hurwitz back to the table. By that afternoon, California time, Elam and Hurwitz were talking on the phone.

It was a shame to let all this become an outright fight, Hurwitz offered. They ought to talk again. He was prepared to pack his people up and be in San Francisco tomorrow morning.

Elam told him that if he wasn't ready to sweeten the price and offer some "significant protections" to PL's existing program of employee benefits, the trip would be wasted.

So just what price was Elam looking for? Hurwitz pressed.

Elam squirmed, trying to avoid giving a number, but unable to pull it off. Finally he allowed that $42 would be a figure that the company would have to seriously discuss.

Hurwitz said the numbers don't work for $42.

Elam had nothing to say about Hurwitz's numbers but he was confident the board would find $42 acceptable.

Hurwitz, rather than haggle on the phone, suggested they get into the details of possible offers tomorrow morning, at PL's headquarters.

Elam agreed.

Just why he'd done so was not immediately apparent on Monday morning. The first hour and a half of Round Two were little more than a reprise of Round One, with Hurwitz devoting enormous energy to making the case for $38.50 as a great price. Before the situation could blow up, however, the bankers took matters in hand, separating the principals and shuttling back and forth between them. That process slowly pushed the price up, usually a quarter at a time, until Hurwitz sent the bankers back to PL with an offer of $39.50.

After giving it brief consideration, Elam rejected $39.50 as well.

That pissed Hurwitz off, and one of the Drexel bankers was sent back down the hall. The $39.50 was it, he said. There would be no more offers forthcoming. If that wasn't good enough, then Hurwitz would just proceed with his original tender offer on Thursday, when the waiting period ended.

Shortly thereafter, a banker from Solly was sent shuttling down the hall to Maxxam's room with a response. Hurwitz could save his ultimatums. PL's final answer to $39.50 was no, period. If Hurwitz couldn't go higher, then he should go back to New York or Texas or wherever.

The messenger from Solly was followed shortly by Elam himself. When he got there, the Maxxam delegation were packing up their briefcases. He repeated that $39.50 was insufficient and, playing the good host, walked them to the front door. There, they paused to shake hands.

Hurwitz spoke first. He read Elam's good host routine as a way to hang around hoping the deal might still get done. He suggested they talk a moment.

The two men, escorted by one banker apiece, stepped aside into a nearby office and closed the door.

Hurwitz was to the point. What price did Elam need to support his offer to the board?

Elam would later liken the moment to running a bluff in a high-stakes poker game. He knew his hand was weak. That morning, the last of the candidates for White Knight had bowed out without so much as making an offer. The time had come to fold and take what he could get. Forty dollars a share, he told Hurwitz.

The Texan gave the number thirty seconds worth of deliberation. O.K., he said, they had a deal.

The enormity of the moment was captured only by some sucking of breath out in the hall when the two men emerged and announced their accomplishment.

15

Whatever celebration might have surfaced was quickly suppressed. This was still far from a done deal. All the details still had to be collected and sold to the board. Ezra Levin was already on the phone, summoning a team of his firm's attorneys west to work through the night drafting the legal documents with Drexel and Solly, in company with PL's lawyers from Wachtell Lipton. Gene Elam and Bob Hoover were soon working the phone as well, summoning the members of the board of directors to meet at 9:00 A.M. the following morning, October 22. The directors were told that the situation with Hurwitz had come to a head.

Suzanne Beaver remembered the October 22 meeting as even more top-heavy with hired guns than the one on October 9, though most of the lawyers and bankers were outside the actual meeting room, in adjoining offices, still hammering away on language in their ongoing all-night attempt to put together a document. Elam seemed "smug" and Suzanne felt a sense of panic about what was about to transpire.

He and Mr. Hurwitz had reached an understanding, Elam announced. He'd agreed to increase his offer to $40 a share and to guarantee existing employee benefits for the next three years. In return, Elam was asking the board to accept the offer and recommend it to the shareholders, transforming the Maxxam Group's tender offer into a "friendly" transaction and defusing all of Pacific Lumber's defenses. Current management would be left in place for at least six months and PL would grant Hurwitz an option on 6 million shares of stock and withdraw all the legal actions that had been filed against him. Because the details of the actual language was still being worked on, this morning's session would be informational. They would then recess and meet again in the afternoon when all the paperwork was ready.

Elam allowed that this was a sad turn for a proud company but pointed out that there was no choice. Even if the company opted to obstruct Hurwitz, using all of its defenses, Hurwitz would still collect enough stock at $38.50 to overturn all their efforts and take control of PL anyway. If a miracle happened and they succeeded in driving off Hurwitz, the company's stock, which had closed yesterday at an eighth of a point under $39, would collapse. They'd be back to $25 overnight, and that drop would set off a host of shareholder suits against the board, and the members would be held collectively and *personally* liable for the losses. This, he pointed out, would amount to a disaster for everyone concerned.

Elam then called on Solly's lead banker for a report. With no small amount of revulsion, Suzanne Beaver listened to him recite the failures of their White Knight search and tout the acceptability of $40 a share. She thought all these damn bankers were just a sham. They were supposed to defend PL and, as far as she could tell, all they'd done was turn the company into duck soup for Charles Hurwitz. Some defense. Suzanne tuned out a lot of what he had to say, as she did with the Wachtell Lipton lawyer who got up and reiterated that the board members were likely to be held personally responsible if they should obstruct this windfall.

Finally, the floor was thrown open for discussion among the board. Mrs. Beaver had been hoping that Ed Carpenter or Bob Hoover would come up with something that could turn back the tide, but they only echoed Elam's conclusions. Michael Coyne spoke up, calling it a "damned shame" that they had to sell and endorsing the deal wholeheartedly. Everyone else found ways of asking essentially the same question. Wasn't there something they could do? And Elam's answer was the same every time. No, there wasn't. Even Suzanne herself got into the act.

If Hurwitz was going to leverage the company to the hilt to take it over, she asked, couldn't the company do the same thing and buy itself?

No, he answered, it couldn't. Management and Salomon Brothers had looked into the possibility and it wasn't feasible. Suzanne felt like she'd been given short shrift but kept her peace. It was hard enough for her to ask a question, much less dispute Elam's answer. She was uncomfortable with what was happening, but the momentum behind this deal with Hurwitz was more than she could imagine trying to confront. When the morning session finally came to a close and Elam recessed the board until 4:00 P.M., the recess felt like a reprieve.

But the reprieve was, of course, momentary. At 4:00, the board returned, only to sit and stew in its own juices. The document was not yet done, so the members waited in the boardroom while the language was delivered to them page by page and paragraph by paragraph. It was not until 7:00 that the pages stopped coming and the board had a chance for one last lap through the arrangement. Elam again led the charge and, if anything, made his predictions of liability even more dire for the board should they choose to resist. No one on the board spoke up against him.

Suzanne wished it would all slow down, as though somehow prolonging the issue might ensure that it would never come to fruition. She wished someone else—Ed Carpenter, maybe, or Bob Hoover—would have objected and given her permission to step back from the abyss, but no one did. She felt miserable about what was about to happen, but there was no way out. Sometimes in life, she told herself, you don't have any choices. As much comfort as she took in that thought, the room still sucked in on her, constricting her throat, and, when she looked their way, the eyes in Stan's photograph, staring blankly from their frame on the wall, seemed tortured.

At last a vote was taken, and Suzanne Beaver, the final representative of the long line of Pacific Lumber Murphys, heir to Stan and A.S. and Simon J., voted yes like all the other directors. On October 22, at 7:30 P.M., by unanimous vote of the board, Charles Hurwitz's raid on the Pacific Lumber Company became a "friendly" transaction, virtually guaranteeing its success. The lawyers assembled down the hall were already at work on a letter to the shareholders explaining their action. "We are pleased to report . . .," it began.

While the lawyers drafted, Gene Elam brought the victorious Charles Hurwitz in and ushered him around the boardroom, introducing him to each of the members. Hurwitz was smiling and shaking hands, exuding his legendary Texas charm.

Suzanne Beaver was dazed. Later, she could remember almost nothing about Hurwitz other than he was well groomed, pleasant, and polite. Everything else went by her in a blur.

16

Warren Murphy would never forgive his mother for her role in the board's October 22 submission. Although there was no personal confrontation between them and they still shared summers up at Larabee, her moment of weakness was tattooed across the face of their relationship forever after. It didn't matter that he still loved her, he would explain. She'd done the wrong thing and, whether she meant to or not, her transgression had severed the lifeline tying the Murphys to the forest and to each other. There was no excuse good enough to wipe the slate clean.

Warren learned of what had transpired down in San Francisco about the time Charles Hurwitz was making his way among the directors, shaking hands in the wake of his victory. Warren was working late in Scotia's front office. Outside, Main Street was bathed in the half-light cast by a sun already over the horizon but not yet set. Sprinkled among the undulations of the Coast Range beyond town, the aspens that invaded the old clear cuts too played out to support redwoods anymore glittered like fool's gold. John Campbell burst into Warren's office without knocking.

The bloody board's done it, he blurted. They're selling to Hurwitz.

Warren sat there paralyzed. Only his anger prevented him from dropping his head on the desk and crying like a baby.

The next day, Murphy collected himself and paid a visit on

Campbell, seated in the office that had once been Warren's father's and his grandfather's before that. Since Hurwitz's tender offer had surfaced, he and John had talked often about the situation and always seemed on the same page. John, like Warren, had vowed they would never allow the company to go to the likes of Hurwitz, not in a million years. John, like Warren, had also vowed to man the barricades in that cause. He seemed the logical person with whom Warren should commence whatever was going to come next. Campbell was seated, moving paper from "in" tray to "out" at his usual rapid pace.

John, Warren began, we've got to get together and fight this thing.

Warren was taken aback almost as soon as the words left his mouth. His call to arms just splattered against Campbell's indifference like a six-mile-an-hour bug hitting a sixty-mile-an-hour windshield. There was nothing of the friend in Campbell's reaction, only the senior company executive.

The board has decided, John answered, and we'll abide by that decision.

Murphy stuttered. He had trouble believing he'd actually heard what he had. Abide? Abide? The hell we will. John, John, he pleaded, we can still turn this around. All we've got to do is fight.

Campbell repeated what he'd said.

Warren drew himself up and began to stand. He was going to fight it, whether John signed on or not.

You're doing the wrong thing, Campbell said.

No, John, Warren answered, I'm right and you should be in this with me.

The two men, once friends, stared at each other for a moment and then Warren Murphy walked out, returning to his own office down the hall. It would never be the same between him and John Campbell again.

The next stop on Warren Murphy's quest for resistance was the law offices of Bill Bertain. He was accompanied by his brother Woody, who'd cut short his hunting trip and driven straight through from Wyoming to be there.

Like the brothers, Bertain had been stunned by the October 22 action. He saw it as a betrayal by Elam and the board—a betrayal that included not just Pacific Lumber but all of Humboldt County.

Something good and true and special here was about to be devastated. He knew about guys like Hurwitz. They were the takers of the world, those who wanted it all now and wanted it all for themselves. Hurwitz would devour the future of the county's grandchildren just to make himself and his buddies over at Drexel Burnham Lambert richer than anyone in Humboldt would ever be. When Hurwitz was done, there'd be nothing left to carry on with.

And what was about to be lost was precisely what had nourished Bill Bertain through childhood. Bill had toddled to Scotia's old Labor Day picnics down by the river and risen to Eagle Scout in Scotia's Boy Scout troop. He'd learned to swim in the old swimming hole behind the sand bar in the Eel and been there when they fished out the body of the drowned boy that finally convinced the company to build a more traditional pool. He remembered walking on the last of the town's wooden sidewalks, he saw his first movie down at the Winema Theatre, and, along with the family laundry, he had weathered the floods of '55 and '64. His roots were sunk into PL all the way back to his grandfather, who'd jumped ship in Humboldt Bay before the Murphys even owned the company. Now was the time to pay back what Humboldt County had given his family. This was his fight too, he told the Murphys, every bit as much as theirs.

He also told the brothers that he was prepared to go after Hurwitz, but he wanted them to know ahead of time that it would probably cost a lot of money. They would have to retain a couple of San Francisco law firms with a background in securities law and they would be fighting some big boys. That meant lots of billable hours on the Murphy tab.

Woody said he didn't give a shit if they were up against the goddamn Shah of Iran. He wanted a piece of this son of a bitch.

Warren added that their sister, Suzanne, wanted to be a party to their lawsuit as well.

Their biggest problem, Bill went on, was that their legal complaint would have to focus on the mechanics of Hurwitz's takeover, a subject about which they knew virtually nothing. Everything except the actual tender offer and the announcement of the board's final decision had been concealed and, if Hurwitz and Elam had their druthers, would stay that way. Somewhere in the planning and execution of that hidden maneuver were the grounds upon which they could base their case and then, once they'd found a crack in the wall surrounding it, they could bust Hurwitz's act wide open. But finding the crack was not going to be easy. Even Bill, already known as Humboldt's patron saint of almost lost causes, had to admit the odds against them were steep.

The brothers told him to proceed anyway.

Barely a week after the board endorsed Hurwitz's tender offer, *Stanwood Murphy, et al. v. The Pacific Lumber Co., et al.* was filed in the Federal District Court for Northern California in San Francisco. Three days after that, it received its first and only hearing in front of a judge. Neither the Murphys nor Bertain were present for the hearing, having been assured by their high-priced San Francisco attorneys that it would be a *pro forma* appearance. They had patched together a twenty-one-page complaint against PL and Hurwitz, alleging, among other things, that the Texan and his Drexel bankers had violated the 5 percent provisions in Pacific Lumber's bylaws and that the tender offer had to be submitted to the shareholders for a vote requiring 80 percent approval. The allegations were long on speculation and short on proof, amounting to little more than several well-calculated shots in the dark, but were sufficient, the San Francisco attorneys were convinced, to win a restraining order and, at the very least, the right to exercise the discovery privileges that would allow them to amass the proof they needed.

The arguments were heard by one William Schwarzer, a Ford administration judicial appointee with a reputation as a scholarly conservative. In addition to the briefs submitted by the Murphy, PL, and Hurwitz attorneys, the only "evidence" considered by Schwarzer was a short affidavit from a vice president in Drexel Burnham Lambert's New York office. The Drexel vice president swore under oath that, "as of the close of business on October 22, 1985, Drexel owned, beneficially, directly or indirectly, no shares in its firm accounts, including arbitrage accounts, of Pacific Lumber Company stock." His affadavit, of course, made no mention of Ivan Boesky's secret purchases on Drexel's behalf, now some million PL shares, almost 5 percent of the company, available for Hurwitz's purposes along with Hurwitz's own similarly sized stake, held by Maxxam and MCO. Citing the Drexel affadavit, Schwarzer not only denied the Murphys' requests for an injunction and discovery privileges, he also peremptorily dismissed the entire case.

The Murphys' San Francisco attorneys were shell-shocked by the ruling and Bertain was stunned. He notified Warren and Woody and they couldn't believe it. It never occurred to them they would be drop-kicked out of the game before they even had a chance to make their point. But they weren't yet prepared to give up, so they set Bertain and the San Francisco lawyers to the task of finding another legal strategy that still might cut Hurwitz off before it was too late.

The immediate effect of their efforts was not on Hurwitz, however, but on Warren's working conditions down at the Scotia offices. As far as John Campbell was concerned, once the lawsuit had been filed, Warren had crossed over the line and become a "fifth columnist" inside the company. He stormed into Warren's office shortly after their abortive conversation about fighting the board's decision and demanded that Murphy immediately return all the company financial reports in his possession. Warren handed them over. He would get no more of these, Campbell announced. Nor would he be allowed to participate in any of his usual meetings. He was still manager of lumber operations but he no longer had any responsibilities. Manager of lumber operations was, at least while Warren was in his "fifth column mode," a blank spot in the chain of command.

Warren asked if John was going to fire him.

No, he wasn't, John answered. He liked Warren; he didn't want to fire him. He was prepared to wait for him to come around. Perhaps all he needed was a little time to think it over and get his head together.

In truth, Campbell hoped that this would prompt Murphy to resign—freeing the company of the onus of firing him. That, he thought, would be the "proper thing" to do. Murphy, however, had no such sense of propriety. He was not about to give Campbell and Hurwitz the satisfaction of leaving on his own volition. Better to just hunker down and endure.

On most days, as October melted into November, Warren Murphy rose as usual and took his customary morning walk down the block to the office, arriving ahead of the steam whistle that commenced the cacophony of lumber production, only to sit at his desk with absolutely nothing to do. Occasionally, he walked around the mill, but those excursions only accentuated the weirdness of the situation. Word that the young Murphy was *persona non grata* had spread quickly among the workforce, so having him around was like a visit from the plague. It was assumed that the name of anyone fraternizing with him would get straight back to Campbell. When Warren walked up, conversations ceased and the idle immediately found pressing tasks at the other end of the mill. The same men, if they crossed paths with Warren down at the grocery after working hours, often made a point of letting him know that they were behind him all the way and hoped that he and his family would keep up the fight until that son of a bitch was back in Texas where he belonged. At first, the dichotomy threw Warren, but he learned to live with it, as he did the inactivity.

Laughter helped. When at his desk first thing in the morning with nothing to do, instead of calling his secretary and ordering a cup of coffee, as had been his habit, he simply turned the light out and sat in the dark. When his secretary asked why, he explained that he was just a mushroom here, so he was going to sit in the dark until he was ready to pick.

It was no surprise to Warren that the first response of the men on the mill floor was to keep their distance. For all their private grumbling, the people of Scotia were not the kind who challenged their bosses. This was, after all, a company town. They were used to being taken care of and most had long since accepted the notion that the company was always right. Standing up to the front office was, as a rule, much more of a risk than they were prepared to bear. The last occurrence remotely resembling rebellion had been the strike of '46, when every mill in Humboldt had been shut down. Old Mr. Murphy had broken the back of PL's role in that effort within six months and no union had been seen around Scotia since. It took the resistance of old A.S.'s grandchildren almost forty years later to provoke Scotia to stick its head out of the trenches again. When that happened, everyone, including Warren himself, said they'd never seen anything like it.

The outburst began in the company's shipping department. Shipping was already notorious as the outpost of PL's "liberals" and had been loud in its collective derision of Hurwitz. During the second week of November, one of the department clerks phoned Warren Murphy after he'd returned home from work. The guys in shipping wanted to help stop the takeover, the clerk said. What could they do?

Warren was circumspect in his response. His San Francisco lawyers had warned him that if he and Woody ever went so far as to frame a competing tender offer to Hurwitz's, they couldn't be part of any effort to publicly discredit their competition. Specifically that meant they could not under any circumstances participate in organized protest efforts. All Warren could suggest was that the clerk give Bill Bertain a call.

Bertain was under none of the strictures placed on the Murphys and quickly fell into strategizing. The upshot was plans for a protest letter to be signed by PL employees and run in the Sunday *Times-Standard*, the county's leading newspaper. This was not, however, a simple proposition to pull off. The letter would have to be circulated at work and that meant there would be only a limited window of opportunity before the front office got wind of it and shut the effort down. There would nonetheless have to be a significant number of signatures collected because most employees would condition the actual printing of their names in the paper on there being enough signatures to assure them the protection of being only one in a crowd too large to act against. The attitudes of the front office also ensured that they would have to collect all those signatures without any advance notice.

The petition hit the mill floor on Friday morning. It was considered an especially fortuitous moment because John Campbell was away in San Francisco, consulting with Elam and headquarters. Word of what was going on spread like wildfire from work station to work station and copies of the petition followed close behind. Distribution was begun by a core group from shipping and coverage was sporadic, depending on who knew who in what part of the mill, but almost everyone approached for a signature gave it. As expected, word soon reached people in the front office, but, due to Campbell's absence, they were slow to respond. Finally, Campbell was telephoned down at the San Francisco headquarters. He was furious and demanded an immediate written directive to all the foremen in the bloody company, ordering them to put a stop to any further unauthorized use of company time. In the meantime, he would catch a plane back.

When the directive reached the mill floor, some supervisors enforced it immediately, others chose to be slow, letting whoever was circulating the letter collect all the names he could before stopping.

During the last hour of the letter's circulation, the core group of supporters fell back to operating on a hit-and-run basis—grabbing whatever names they could before the foreman noticed and then retreating to another location to try for more. By 11:00 A.M., all signing had ceased. In the few hours it had circulated, the shipping department's open letter received some 340 signatures, 40 percent of all the company's employees and an overwhelming majority of the workers in Scotia, the only location where signatures had been collected.

When one of the men from shipping drove the letter up to the *Times-Standard*'s offices in Eureka during lunch hour, he passed John Campbell, headed south from the Arcata airport. Campbell was driving like "a bat out of hell," with his hands strangling the steering wheel. He was so pissed, the man reported, he looked like the top of his head was going to lift off.

The following Sunday morning, *Times-Standard* readers stumbled across a full-page ad titled "Heritage in the Balance":

"Some people," the open letter pointed out, "are comfortable with the efforts of Charles Hurwitz and his MAXXAM group to establish ownership of the Pacific Lumber Company. Most of us certainly are not! We . . . do not feel that this impending takeover would be in the best interest of ourselves, the shareholders, and the communities in which our company serves. Most of us are hardworking individuals who feel that PALCO was an honorable, well-serving company, with a heritage that we could be proud of—not only a secure place to work, but one which dealt conscientiously with the preservation and proper management of our vital resources: our people and the redwoods.

"In all earnestness, we do not feel that a company of real estate investors from the east coast can manage resources such as ours with the consideration that has been shown all these years by the Murphy family . . .

"The fight is not yet over. [Due to a series of minor shareholder suits in state court] MAXXAM has not yet been allowed to actually purchase any tendered shares. . . . It is our sincere belief that if the company's leadership were back in the hands of the Murphy family, the company's business, our environment, and the communities in which we all live will continue to prosper. There may be some changes in our company in the days to follow but we collectively support, with confidence, the Murphys' efforts to save the Pacific Lumber Company."

That printed page was the high point of Scotia's resistance.

The exclamation point of the uprising came not long afterward on a workday morning, when lines of men, Warren Murphy among them, again trooped to the mill. The rainy season was now under way and Scotia's streets were shiny and slick with mist. Close to seven inches of rain had fallen on Humboldt's coastal flat during the last few weeks and, up in the Coast Range, the slopes that fed the mighty Eel had received at least twice that much, beginning the river's annual transformation. The lazy August shallows that curved past town now roiled and raced and, where the water in the main channel once reached a man's knees, it was now over his ears. Few of the passing workers noticed the river, though. They were so used to it that only the occasional odd detail, out of place with the ordinary, caught their eye.

This morning, that oddity was hanging off the bridge linking Scotia to Rio Dell. A stuffed homemade dummy, the size of a man, was suspended by its neck from the span, dangling over the murky current at the end of a rope. There was little wind, but the vibration from traffic crossing the bridge was enough to set it swinging to and fro. A hand-lettered cardboard sign was attached to the effigy's chest.

The sign, flopping with the dummy's sway, read "HURWITZ."

17

December was different. Kelly Bettiga later remembered that he could smell the change. He might be no more than the hippie on the night shift but he was third-generation PL and he knew this goddamn town, sure as shit. And he could smell the fucking fear roll in like the fog while most everybody started looking for a way to cover their butts. Folks around here had no heart for fighting losing battles and, by December, nobody was kidding themselves. That son of a bitch Hurwitz was kicking ass, left, right, and sideways.

The state court restraining orders that had momentarily stalled the Texan's juggernaut had been shunted aside with relative ease and he had succeeded in purchasing some 60 percent of the company's stock before his tender offer expired at the end of November. That was enough to seize control of the board and amend the bylaws to clear the way for merging PL into Maxxam and assuming 100 percent ownership. He financed his initial moves with his bridge loan and an initial issue of short-term debentures. Among the largest subscribers to the debenture issue were the Bass brothers, in whose names the first feelers toward PL had been made. The only remaining obstacle was a last-ditch lawsuit filed by Bertain and the Murphys' San Francisco lawyers in Federal Court for the state of Maine, where Pacific Lumber was incorporated. Not many around town were prepared to bet their jobs on the Murphys' chances and no one suggested collecting more signatures for another newspaper ad.

Resentment lingered, however, and much of it focused on John Campbell. Hurwitz was still "that son of a bitch," but everyone knew he was just doing what he'd always done, however ugly that might be. Campbell, on the other hand, was considered a turncoat. He'd come to town fifteen years ago, knowing nothing and nobody, and had been accepted. He'd played softball at the park by the river and knocked down beers at Mingo's Tavern in Rio Dell. He'd hung out at the Fortuna Bowl and plunked deer in the pine forests above Larabee Creek. Then he'd gone over to Hurwitz and hung all that history out to dry. To punish his disloyalty, people stopped talking to him. If they had to work with John, they conversed as they needed to, but, otherwise, he was shunned. When he passed someone in the hall with a greeting, it was not returned. When he stopped at Mingo's or the Scotia Inn for a drink after work, he drank by himself. Scotians had no control over whether or not John Campbell was executive vice president but they still chose their own friends and, by December, he was an outcast.

Though painful, that ostracism did not affect Campbell's work, at least as seen by the men over his head. John traveled to San Francisco to meet with the boss with whom he'd thrown his lot, and Hurwitz, still in the midst of the stock tender, was impressed. Charles readily admitted his ignorance about logging shows and sawmills but now he had to figure out how to implement his plans for his latest acquisition, and he quickly recognized Campbell's potential value. John, of course, spoke both Charles's language and Scotia's and was an obvious candidate to tutor Hurwitz in the vagaries of the timber business. The Texan intended to listen and learn, saying little and committing himself to less, while others advanced positions for him to consume. Campbell fell into that strategy without missing a beat. Charles's immediate interest was in how the company could increase its cut and generate more cash.

Why couldn't PL just double the shift at its mills, he wondered, and in so doing, double its production in one fell swoop?

Cutting boards was not that simple, Campbell explained. The variables involved were multiple and easily thrown out of whack. Mill B, the old-growth mill, wasn't structured to consume that amount of timber. It would be better to simply increase its shifts to ten hours from eight and purchase another old-growth mill, like the one Louisiana Pacific was trying to sell up next to the Van Duzen in Carlotta, and rig it for double shifts. Similarly, there weren't enough old-growth fir logs to double the output of Mill A, which cut nothing but fir. The second-growth redwood mill in Fortuna could double its shifts easily enough but, like all the mills, was limited by the capacity of its drying yards. To maximize its value, lumber had to be dried and, at the moment, there was neither the outside yard space nor kiln capacity to handle a double load of boards. The shipping department, which would have to handle the doubled output, didn't have the necessary space either. All those problems could be solved with the investment of time and money. If they went ahead and doubled the cut out in the woods in the meantime, the company would have a lot of raw logs it couldn't saw itself and would have to sell to other sawyers. Marketing logs was an option the old company had treated as anathema, but it would generate additional cash flow immediately. In short, Campbell summarized, the transition would be tricky, but as long as the variables were well managed, the cut could be doubled, and doubled soon.

Eventually, Charles Hurwitz would follow all that advice.

18

John also thought it would be wise to stroke Scotia. The town wasn't used to changes and this one was an enormous shock. The company didn't need any labor troubles and the Woodworkers Union, sensing dissatisfaction, had opened up a storefront across the river in Rio Dell, the first time they'd shown their faces around PL in forty years. They'd probably get bloody nowhere even if Charles did nothing—these people weren't union fodder—but it might be wise for Charles to let the company's employees see him up close and hear from his own mouth that their jobs were safe.

Hurwitz agreed and, nine days before Christmas, paid his first visit to Humboldt County. The occasion was a companywide meeting convened in the Winema Theatre, which all employees were expected to attend.

It was the second such meeting in the course of Hurwitz's takeover. The first had been on the day before Halloween and featured Gene Elam, trying to explain the board's capitulation. For that one, Kelly Bettiga had found himself a seat right in the front. He wanted to scope out what was really coming down and figured the only way to do that for sure was to watch their eyeballs twitch. Campbell was there, sitting in one of the folding chairs facing the theatre loges, but Elam, the fucking numbers jockey from the city, did most of the talking. It was, Kelly observed, a real snow job. After spending the last month painting Hurwitz as the bogey man of the century, Elam turned completely goddamn around. Now that son of a bitch was really a good guy, just the kind of boss old PL needed. To Kelly, that line smelled. Sure Hurwitz was a good guy and, oh by the way, the goddamn Eel had decided to flow south, just for the hell of it. Bettiga didn't trust Elam's squirrelly mouth and didn't believe a thing he said, but he had to admit he pushed the words out like he believed them.

Elam was there to subdue any panic the workers might have and to convince them to, as he put it, adopt a new perspective. The employees had been taken care of in this deal, he assured them. Their benefit package was guaranteed for the next three years, no small concession. Nor did they have to worry about their jobs. If Maxxam really did what it said it planned to, there was going to be more work, not less. Even so, he and the rest of the current management planned to convince Hurwitz not to change the traditional PL approach and to stay on the familiar path. It would be foolish to make wholesale changes and he was counting on the fact that Hurwitz was smart and would listen to what Elam had to say. In the meantime, no one should fall into circulating unfounded rumors. They should have a little faith. Everything was going to work out. He, Gene Elam, was looking out for their interests.

More than a few men on their way out joined Bettiga in noting that if this pencil pusher was masquerading as the millworkers' fairy godmother they must have called fucking Halloween a day early.

Few were so feisty come December.

Except, of course, Charles Hurwitz. Charles felt no intimidation, descending on the town he was about to own. Nor did he possess any doubts about whether he could talk anyone here around to his side. After a night in the Scotia Inn, he, Gene Elam, and John Campbell strolled up Main Street, Gene with his hair combed back in his dippy wave, John with his tie knotted, Charles in his trademark black suit, impeccably shined shoes, and pressed shirt. He smiled at anyone they passed and everyone who saw them stared.

Campbell and Elam began by giving Hurwitz a guided tour, starting in the front office. Elam seemed nervous but Campbell was much more at home in the role, leading the new boss down the hallway, stopping to shake hands with everyone they came across. Eventually, they reached Warren Murphy. Though Hurwitz knew full well who Murphy was, he showed no signs of recognition when Campbell made the introduction.

This is Warren Murphy, manager of lumber operations.

Hurwitz extended his hand. Hello, he said.

Warren's stomach turned but he was determined to match the Texan's manners. Hello, he answered, taking the offered hand.

After a brief shake, Charles moved on down the hall and Murphy returned to his office to continue playing mushroom. He later remembered that shaking hands with Hurwitz was like reaching into a paper bag and grabbing a dead fish.

When Hurwitz arrived at the monorail shop, one of the mechanics there marveled at how pale the man was. Being a whiz at business and all, the mechanic guessed, the guy just never got out in the sunshine. As at most stops, Hurwitz did most of the handshaking and let Elam and Campbell do whatever talking was required. One of the monorail mechanics tried to put a question straight to him.

So how are you gonna pay for all this? he asked.

Campbell, visibly irritated that someone would raise such questions during their tour, intervened immediately. You let us worry about that, he snapped.

Hurwitz smiled, shook the man's hand, and moved on.

Campbell and Elam's nervousness only increased the closer their tour came to the shipping department. When they finally arrived there, Elam was the color of an oyster and looked like a candidate for open-heart surgery. Campbell was more together, but he looked terrible as well. The shipping department was still a hotbed of antitakeover sentiment. The workers here had chalked slogans like "Axe Maxx," "Where's Uncle Charlie?" and "We've Been Maxxed" up on the walls and on the side of the department's crane.

Hurwitz, however, acted as though none of the messages were there. Again, he introduced himself around, shaking hands and making small talk in his soft drawl. Eventually he approached one of the newspaper ad's principal organizers, who was sitting on a stack of redwood boards.

Boy, Charles opened with a wave of his hand at the boards, that sure is good-looking stock.

The shipping clerk responded with grim pride. These were the best boards cut anywhere, he bragged.

Later, the clerk would wish he'd said more and given that son of a bitch a real piece of his mind, but he didn't; and after a couple more handshakes, Hurwitz was out the door and on to the next stop.

When the tour was finished, Charles and one of the aides who had accompanied him from Houston stopped at the Scotia Coffee Shop to kill time before the meeting. The cafe was virtually empty except for a tall, thin, scruffy-looking millworker reading the newspaper at the counter. That was Kelly Bettiga and, while he held the newspaper up, he was only pretending to read. His eyes were really locked on to Hurwitz.

Bettiga noted that this guy was obviously Wall Street to the max, a number-one arrogant bastard. His shoes probably cost more than the motorcycle Kelly had parked outside and the price tag on his suit would probably cover six months' worth of Kelly's alimony payments. He was there to give them the word and Kelly could tell right away, just from how all the people who came in tiptoed around him, that the son of a bitch was going to pull it off. It was like he was some god, some foreign god, a Vishnu or a Shiva, just plopped right down in the middle of goddamn Scotia ordering a coffee with cream and sugar. Most of the people in this town thought the dudes that worked in the front office were big time. A guy like this just didn't compute.

Kelly Bettiga stopped his musings and gulped down his pie when Hurwitz checked his watch and got up to go. At that point, Kelly bolted out and hustled up to the Winema to make sure he got a good seat.

The air inside the theatre was laced with the smell of fresh sawdust and dried sweat. The raucousness of the day before Halloween had given way to a somber reflection. The dark redwood walls and shadowy ceiling beams only added to the mortuary feel of the occasion. There were none of October's jokes and joshing back and forth, just the sounds of heavy boots clattering across the floor and nervous coughing by those who'd already found seats. Many of the assembled men had grown up with the Winema, watching Saturday matinees or the annual American Legion talent shows and elementary school graduations. Still, no one seemed entirely comfortable there today and when they looked over the men up by the microphone, they eyed warily the guy with the rich suit and slicked-back hair. They'd expected a bigger man but, regardless, they could only hope if they gave him the boss's due, he'd treat them the way the bosses always had.

Once John Campbell formally introduced the dignitaries, Gene Elam opened the event with what would prove to be the longest speech of the day. He wanted to make it clear that the process begun by the tender offer was practically a done deal. All that remained was a formal stockholder vote on merging with Maxxam and since Hurwitz now owned 60 percent of the stock and the merger only required a majority approval, the outcome was a foregone conclusion. The actual vote would probably be held toward the end of February. In that process, he emphasized, the employee pensions would be 100 percent safe, even if Maxxam "reorganized" the pension fund. And no one should place a bunch of false hope in any of the lawsuits still floating around.

Warren Murphy was sitting in the lineup with all the other front-office types and a number of eyes in the audience automatically flitted in his direction. Warren's expression didn't change.

These lawsuits were absolutely without merit, Elam continued, utterly baseless. They wouldn't prove anything because there was nothing at all to prove. They hadn't the faintest chance of success and were a disservice to all the other shareholders.

Finally, PL's president tied off his remarks and gave way to Charles Hurwitz, the man everyone had come to hear. Hurwitz betrayed no hints of nervousness. He said he'd been looking forward to this day, when he could finally meet all of PL's loyal employees face to face and share some of his thoughts about their mutual future. He'd read a lot of newspaper stories about himself over the last couple months, claiming to explain who he was and what he was up to. Most were unrecognizable and several were bad enough that he hoped his mother never read them.

Hurwitz gave no indication his mother had been dead for several years and the audience tittered, breaking the crust of their reserve.

The truth was that he always tried to get involved with companies that had "great long-term prospects," he continued, and he planned to be involved in PL for the long term. He'd already decided to sink some $30 million in a new power plant—the same plant Elam had been planning for the last year—and was also commiting a half a million dollars more to commission a new timber cruise so the company could "better coordinate" its "planning goals." He was currently considering a whole batch of other extra expenditures and had also instructed his boys in Houston to keep their eyes open for other "forest products and related companies" he might acquire. His pocketbook would do his talking for him. All these claims repeated over and over in the press that he would strip the company and then take off were false. So was all the talk about jobs that might be lost in the process. On the contrary, almost everyone in the company would be working plenty of overtime when Maxxam got its show rolling.

A murmur of approval ran through the audience at the reference to fuller work weeks and larger paychecks.

This, Hurwitz emphasized in closing, was "a great company with a brilliant future" and he was excited about working with all of them.

After Hurwitz's presentation, the floor was thrown open to questions. Elam acted as moderator, answering some questions himself and directing others to Campbell and, of course, Hurwitz.

One of the first came from the same mechanic in the monorail shop who'd tried to question Hurwitz during his tour. The mechanic repeated that he'd tried to run the numbers himself and he couldn't see how Hurwitz planned to pay for this place.

The question was interrupted by a brief smattering of applause.

He'd studied up on this, the mechanic went on, and PL usually cleared about $25 million a year and, if he understood all the fine print, Hurwitz was taking on a debt that would eventually demand payments of some $100 million a year. He couldn't figure it out, he repeated. How the hell was Hurwitz going to pay it?

Hurwitz grinned. First, he said, they'd cut back on electricity.

The audience erupted in laughter and Hurwitz used the opportunity to slough the question off.

Seriously, Hurwitz continued, he thought they had a good plan for the company—a very long-term approach of the type he was used to. Next question?

Several more about benefits and the like were fielded by Elam. Then someone asked if the company was going to double its cut, like they'd heard.

Elam shuffled that question to John Campbell. John said he

wasn't aware of any plans for that size increase. It was important that everyone know that the company's operating margin had narrowed dramatically from the previous decade and that meant they would have to "operate the company a little harder [and] a little faster," no doubt about it, but the company was still studying just what the increase should be. They were currently looking at an escalation of around 20 percent.

Rumor was that if they did increase the cut, the next questioner pointed out, they were going to put on more gypos and curtail the company's own logging operations.

Campbell denied that rumor in no uncertain terms. If anything, he promised, they'd be increasing the company logging rather than signing on more contractors.

More questions followed about rents in Scotia and health insurance which, again, were answered by Elam. Hurwitz only spoke in response to several other inquiries that focused on his own reputation for stripping companies of their assets.

He had no idea where this came from, he claimed, and he was offended by it. He came from a little town, Kilgore in east Texas, and his history was one of building, not liquidation. The only evaluation that he was making relative to PL was just to try to understand the business a little bit better. If he got any message across today, it was that he didn't want any changes. He expected "Gene and the management" to do "whatever they did in the past."

Several minutes later, someone asked about the future of "Gene and the management." What about Elam and the rest? Was Maxxam going to send its own people in to run things?

Hurwitz grinned again and returned to his sense of humor. Only if the profits disappear, he quipped.

That drew more appreciative laughter. Most of the audience had no love for Elam and it was fun to see the new boss goad him a little.

Hurwitz, buoyed by the success of his jokes, figured he was on a roll and, pausing from the flow of questions, decided to pursue more humor.

You know, he said, there's an old story about the golden rule. He chuckled and paused, setting up the punch line. The story, he then continued, is "that those who have the gold rule."

Down front, Kelly Bettiga dug his fingers into his seat cushion. He wanted to jump up and strangle that son of a bitch on the spot.

He'd never heard such goddamn arrogance. This motherfucker ought to have his face rearranged.

Kelly expected the rest of the audience to growl along with him, but they didn't. Instead, they laughed the biggest laugh of the day. Guffaws ricocheted around the Winema, led by the front-office crowd clustered up near Hurwitz.

Bettiga noted that John Campbell was laughing the hardest of all. Only Warren Murphy abstained from the humor. His mouth was grim and taut, like a cable strung between a Cat and a redwood log, all bucked, choked, and ready to winch.

19

Warren Murphy's enounter with Charles Hurwitz in Scotia nine days before Christmas was not their final contact. That final encounter came shortly before New Year's, when Warren and Woody were meeting with Bertain in his J Street office. Outside, it was raining. Night had fallen like a cast-iron safe down an elevator shaft, suddenly reducing the nearby highway to a few short jabs of light suspended in unremitting darkness. Inside, the brothers and their lawyer began discussing their repeatedly unsuccessful efforts to initiate a bidding war against Hurwitz but, with 1986 bearing down on them, their conversation soon turned nostalgic. They all agreed that just a year earlier they could never have imagined themselves in this position. An avalanche of memories of the old days followed, when they were kids in Scotia and lined up with all the others for the company Christmas presents. The reminiscences were populated with ghosts of Stan and old Mr. Murphy and a host of others—dirty faces and strong backs, trooping through the forest in boots laced up over their calves. They agreed that "that son of a bitch" with all his talk of the golden rule could never hold a candle to those men.

It was Warren who then came up with the idea of phoning Hurwitz. Just call him straight out, Warren said, and ask him if he wanted to sell. Warren had Hurwitz's home number in Houston.

What'd they have to lose anyway? Maybe he was just waiting for an offer.

Why not? Bill and Woody agreed.

After three rings, Hurwitz himself answered.

Warren and Woody were each on one of Bertain's extensions and did all the talking. Warren identified himself and said he'd called with a business proposition. His family was prepared to make an offer above the $40 a share that Hurwitz had been paying. Warren did not attach a specific number to his offer, hoping that Hurwitz would express an interest or make some indication that he was indeed prepared to take a quick profit and get out.

Instead, the Texan laughed.

The Murphys were momentarily nonplussed.

He didn't mean to be impolite, Hurwitz explained, but he simply wasn't interested.

The Murphys were at a loss for what to say next. That they had only the sketchiest idea of what they were doing was obvious.

Charles Hurwitz, however, was not about to wait for them to learn. While it was apparently amateur night out in Humboldt County, it was after 8:00 P.M., Houston time, and he had other things to do. Good evening, he said, and Happy New Year.

With that, all contact between the Murphys and Hurwitz ended forever. Henceforth, only their lawyers spoke to each other.

20

And even that didn't last much longer. The lawsuit filed on behalf of the Murphys in the Federal Court for Maine had been bounced to California to be heard by Judge William Schwarzer in San Francisco, the same judge who had dealt with them so summarily in the fall. Bertain cringed at the thought. It was, he allowed, "lawyer's hell" to be sent back to Schwarzer's court again. The Murphys' San Francisco lawyers, who'd recommended against filing this second suit—favoring abandoning the struggle instead—agreed.

Still, Bertain was not about to give up. And, having sunk his teeth into the Pacific Lumber situation, his curiosity and outrage had both escalated geometrically. He still knew almost nothing about what had gone on in Hurwitz's maneuvering for the takeover, but he had stumbled across two key fragments of information. The first was the presence of Ivan Boesky. All fall, Bertain had been receiving regular calls from an underling in Boesky's office inquiring about the Murphys' legal plans, but he had no idea what Boesky's interest was until his niece, studying in Europe, mailed him a November clipping from the *International Herald Tribune* reporting that Boesky had amassed over 5 percent of Pacific Lumber. That set Bill to wondering if there was any connection between the King of Arbs and the "parasites," Hurwitz and Milken, who now had PL by the jugular.

The second piece of information Bertain stumbled upon turned his curiosity to fury. Late in January, as he was preparing for the Murphys' second bout with Judge Schwarzer, an anonymous envelope arrived at his J Street office. In it, without any cover letter or explanation, was a copy of Pacific Lumber's final formal agreement with Salomon Brothers. Bill suspected it had been sent by someone sympathetic in PL's front office, but he had no idea who. As he read the document, he muttered—at first in a muted way and then louder and louder. By the time he finished, he was pounding on his desk, sending papers scattering off the heaped mass there. Pacific Lumber had been doomed before it even got in the arena with Hurwitz. With Solly conducting its defense under the terms of that agreement, it was like offering the army a bonus for every battle it lost. And that, he suspected, was just the tip of the iceberg.

But those suspicions were a long way from proof of any behavior outside the law and, of course, of no use whatsoever in front of Schwarzer. Having been denied discovery in this case, as in the first, the Murphys' legal team was again long on argument and short on evidence. Their complaint ran on for some fifty pages, alleging that the Maxxam tender offer and the PL board's subsequent recommendation that its shareholders sell their shares were "materially false and misleading" in myriad ways; that Hurwitz had violated the Securities Exchange Act of 1934 through excessive use of credit for purchasing securities; that both the PL board and the company's officers had violated their fiduciary duties, taking care of themselves to the detriment of the shareholders; that the directors were never adequately informed of the value of the company before making their decision and, specifically, had no accurate notion of how much timber the company owned; and that Hurwitz and the board had "fradulently conspired to manipulate the corporate machinery . . . to enrich themselves."

On February 12, Bertain and four of the Murphys' San Francisco lawyers occupied the plaintiff's table in Judge William Schwarzer's courtroom. The Murphy siblings were seated in the front row of the spectator gallery. Schwarzer had already denied the plaintiffs' requests for a full evidentiary hearing at which witnesses could be heard under oath and was allowing only oral arguments. The defendants' was made by an attorney from Ezra Levin's office, the plaintiffs' by one of the Murphys' San Francisco hired guns. As soon as they finished, Schwarzer pulled out a twenty-two-page opinion he'd written days earlier and began to read out loud. By the time he'd finished, the judge had savaged every one of the Murphys' arguments. He denied everything for which they'd asked and invited the defendants to make a motion for dismissal that would "bring this matter to a reasonably early conclusion," and, with that, court was adjourned.

Having now spent some $400,000 in legal fees, the Murphys had lasted a total of less than an hour in court. Bertain felt as though he'd been hit in the solar plexus with a baseball bat. One of the defense attorneys was introduced to him as the lawyers were collecting their stuff and clearing out and Bertain, normally cheery, even with his opponents, was barely civil.

I hope you're happy, he snapped. This is going to kill Humboldt County.

21

As soon as he was back in Eureka, Bill Bertain began constructing yet another last-ditch strategy. Bertain was a serious practicing Catholic, making daily prayers and often attending Mass twice or three times a week, and he felt that of the three theological virtues—faith, hope, and charity—hope was the least understood. Because hope was the affirmation of possibility from which all good flowed, he considered it all the more important to practice hope when running against the drift of events. In the immediate moment, his hope was that he might muster some of the local community governments to join in a suit under the theory that Hurwitz's merger would violate the PL bylaws' requirements that the local area's welfare be considered on at least an equal footing with the financial rewards of the shareholders. Using the connections he'd made over the years in Humboldt County Republican party politics, Bill began calling mayors and city councilmen.

He found almost everyone increasingly distracted. By Thursday, the day after the Murphys' latest disaster in Schwarzer's court, Humboldt had been hit by the scattered northern edge of a major weather front driving hard off the Pacific. In Mendocino and Sonoma Counties to the south, which bore the brunt of the storm, some locations received as much as eighteen inches of rain in the space of twenty-four hours. And many of those were along the watershed of the mighty Eel. By Friday, the river was rising steadily as it reeled north, tumbling through the Coast Range, around the elbow at Scotia, and out onto the coastal flat. The current was the color of milk chocolate and carried logs floated off their moorings and uprooted trees swept away in the mad rush to the sea. By Saturday morning, at Fernbridge, north of Scotia in the Eel delta, the river was almost over its banks and all day Saturday, the coast was battered with the heaviest rains yet. Until Sunday, of course, when the rainfall was even heavier. By then, the dairies around Fernbridge were under several feet of water.

Scotia was still dry but Bertain was worried. At Mass Sunday morning, he prayed for the family laundry, situated at one of Scotia's lowest points, separated from the river bank by little more than the embankment supporting PL's railroad spur. The laundry had been covered by four feet of water in the great flood of 1964. Sunday night, Bill and his fiancée, Rebecca Holmes, headed up there to have a look. They parked his old Oldsmobile at the laundry and walked along the tracks to the ball park near which, after 1964, the company had erected a gauge to measure the Eel's depth. Though still below its natural bank, the river was over forty feet deep and had spread to cover the entirety of the bed, which, in August, had been acres of bone-dry gravel. As it careened through the elbow around Scotia, the Eel roared like several full-speed freight trains side by side and its surface, rife with flotsam, broke into riffles deep enough to swallow a house. Bill and Rebecca stared, awestruck.

Eventually they noticed another figure watching the river from a vantage point closer to the ballpark. Bill finally recognized the burly shape backlit by the night lights at the mill as John Campbell, all by himself, contemplating the possibility of flood. The two men did not exchange greetings.

Had the circumstances been different, the sight of Campbell alone, silhouetted against the mill and flanked by raging waters, might well have touched Bertain's charitable impulses. There was an aura of sadness around John these days. His isolation inside Scotia was, if not complete, nearly so. And that had been further compounded several weeks earlier when his wife, Cindy, had officially separated from him and begun preparations to file for divorce. There were a lot of stories flying around town about what precipitated the split but John himself gave a great deal of credit to the furor over Hurwitz's takeover and his own cooperation with it. In any case, he had sustained considerable personal damage over the last four months.

But if Bertain felt sorry for PL's executive vice president, the feeling was only fleeting. He figured Campbell deserved what he was getting and, while it might be sad, his ostracism was just. Bill also recognized that in his final desperate Humboldt County attempt to thwart the scheduled merger, John Campbell was his principal immediate opposition. Indeed, the two men were on the verge of locking horns in a battle over the loyalties of Rio Dell. There, across the mighty Eel from Pacific Lumber's Mill A, Bertain would make his last stand against Hurwitz's assault.

His strategy began on Monday when he and several veterans of the PL employees' petition drafted another petition for citizens or close neighbors of Rio Dell, to be submitted to the Rio Dell city council meeting Tuesday evening, asking the council to take "whatever action necessary to oppose and prevent the takeover/merger." The petitioners then proceeded to collect some one hundred and fifty signatures over the next twenty-four hours.

By the Tuesday night council meeting, however, Rio Dell had lots of other things to worry about. On Sunday, flotsam had begun collecting around the footings of the freeway bridge supporting the northbound lanes of U.S. 101 where the roadway arched over the snaking course of the river north of town. The understructure of that bridge supported the water main from the city's wells on the other side of the Eel, its telephone cable, gas main, and its connection to the county's electric power grid. City officials had immediately begun badgering Caltrans, the state transportation agency with jurisdiction over the threatened bridge, to remove the debris but Caltrans dallied and, by the time Bertain and his allies were out collecting signatures, a logjam had formed against the structure's legs. Caltrans then moved a crane out onto the bridge and began dismantling the tangle of debris below, piece by piece.

Disaster struck at 1:00 A.M. Tuesday. As Caltrans's crane yanked, part of the bridge's base shifted in the sloppy river bottom, gave way, and, with a shower of sparks, several of its footings sank into the mud and two sections of the northbound span dropped twenty feet, carrying Rio Dell's electrical cables, telephone lines, and water main with them. When they were finally able to fully assess the damage in the first light of morning, the prognosis was not good. Though the last of the storm seemed to be on its way and rainfall was lessening, the raging Eel sent shudders through the wobbly bridge, leaving significant doubts about whether it would remain standing through another night. The city's water main, though not severed, was so damaged that it could only be used to fill the city's water tanks once or twice a day, leaving Rio Dell with water pressure that was weak at best and often simply nonexistent. The electricity and telephone connections could be rewired along the adjacent southbound freeway bridge but the water problem would take much longer to solve. The best stopgap measure was to run a temporary pipe overground from Pacific Lumber's wells in Scotia and across the still undamaged Scotia–Rio Dell Bridge at the other end of town, upriver from the mangled freeway span. City officials quickly began working out the details of a such a temporary arrangement with John Campbell.

In the meantime, however, Rio Dell's position worsened even further. The weather began to clear toward the middle of Tuesday but, at the same time, fire broke out in the one of the businesses in the city's tiny downtown. The Rio Dell Volunteer Fire Department responded but, with no water pressure with which to battle the blaze, it soon appeared as though the flames, now uninhibited by rainfall, would spread unchecked and consume the entire business district. Black smoke was pouring across the swollen river. Again, however, Pacific Lumber saved the day. Without waiting to be asked, John Campbell ordered the dispatch across the bridge of several of the company's tank trucks full of water, allowing Rio Dell's fire department pumpers to extinguish the conflagration.

When the city council convened Tuesday evening, it was lost on no one that PL had saved Rio Dell's bacon. Nonetheless, the council was split over how to deal with the petition. No one was a fan of Hurwitz's but the city's legal counsel said flat out that he would refuse to handle any suit the city might file and the city manager was 100 percent opposed to any action against PL's new ownership. Bertain's most significant ally was the city's mayor and, thanks to his influence, the petitioners succeeded in getting the council to agree to take their request "under advisement" and meet in special session the coming Thursday to act on it, one way or another.

When the mayor reached his home that evening at close to 10:00 P.M., the dark sky in the direction of the freeway bridge was lit with the glow of floodlights being used by the repair crews and the wind carried the smell of charred wood. The mayor figured he'd just been part of the busiest day in Rio Dell's less than 100 years of history.

Then the phone rang and the day continued.

The voice on the line belonged to the city's fire chief. He was down at Mingo's Tavern, where he'd run into John Campbell. The chief said Campbell was furious about what the council had done about this lawsuit thing and some kind of trouble was brewing which he thought the mayor ought to know about. The PL boss had been drinking and was saying that he was going to cut off the city's bloody goddamn water. The chief thought the mayor better get down here as soon as he could.

The mayor was at Mingo's within fifteen minutes.

John Campbell lit into him when he arrived. What kind of rank disloyalty was fucking Rio Dell up to? PL saves their ass from the fire and the flood and they respond by taking this piece-of-shit lawsuit Bill Bertain cooked up under advisement? Under advisement? They should have thrown the whole bloody thing out the window, that's what they should have done.

The mayor tried to explain that it was only proper that the council give the requests of one hundred and fifty constituents the serious consideration that taking the issue under advisement implied, but John would hear none of it.

It was betrayal was what it was. How would Rio Dell have liked it if he had taken it under advisement when the goddamn town was about to burn down? Would that have been proper? Rio Dell would have been a pile of charcoal if PL had even hesitated. And this was their reward? He ought to cut off this goddamn temporary pipe they were going to start laying as soon as it crossed the river into Scotia. Maybe he'd just take it under advisement until Rio Dell got good and thirsty.

The mayor listened patiently, hoping this situation would turn out all right if he just let PL's executive vice president vent his considerable anger. And, sure enough, as Mingo's closing time approached, Campbell began to back off. Assuming a quieter voice, Pacific Lumber's executive vice president retrieved his previous threats and allowed that Rio Dell would get its water, just as PL had agreed earlier in the day. His feelings were hurt but Pacific Lumber would behave with a neighborliness that bloody Rio Dell apparently lacked.

The city's mayor thanked him and finally felt free to leave.

Outside, the sky still glowed in the direction of the freeway bridge, setting off fleeting rainbows in the fragments of mist blowing across the street. The sound of the mighty Eel carried through the night, as it slashed past the wreckage, running as fast as it could to reach the ocean and disappear. The radio was repeating reports that the river, still below its banks at Scotia, had at last begun to recede.

Two days later, the Rio Dell city council rejected Bill Bertain's petition.

The path was now clear for Charles Hurwitz to swallow PL whole.

22

The Pacific Lumber Company's last moments as an independent enterprise were spent in the offices of a Portland, Maine, law firm. Simon Jones Murphy, who'd begun his lumber barony as a hired hand in a mill on the state's Penobscot River, had first incorporated the company here in 1905, and here, on February 25, 1986, a little more than eighty years later, it ended. The occasion was billed as a special meeting of Pacific Lumber's shareholders but only Gene Elam, PL's in-house counsel, and a lawyer representing Maxxam were present. The three men spent the meeting tabulating the voting proxies cast on the only item on the agenda, the merger into Maxxam. Eighty-two percent of the shares were cast in favor of merging and, before adjourning, Elam officially proclaimed the deal done. Pacific Lumber was now another one of Charles Hurwitz's wholly owned subsidiaries and all the company's remaining untendered stock would have to be sold to him at $40 a share.

The following day, while Gene Elam was flying back to California, Warren Murphy tied off the legacy he'd inherited from old Simon Jones Murphy and the three generations who'd followed in Simon's footsteps. He'd planned to become the next Murphy to run the company since the day his father's lifeless body was carried off the company plane up at the Hydesville airstrip, but instead, Warren was now resigned to being the last of his family to ever work for PL. He knew there was nothing left to do but leave, even though the thought brought him nothing but pain. He'd held out for some four months, but it was now time to resign and bring his fruitless resistance to a graceful end. He thought rockets ought to have been shot off to honor this passing of the guard, trumpets blown, or drums beaten, but, as he took his last walk down Main Street before the final whistle, there was only the hiss of trucks braking at the log deck, the whine of the first cant being lopped off down the road at Mill B, the clatter of conveyors carrying redwood bark—all familiar, all the same, only sounding a little more hollow than before.

Warren didn't even bother stopping at his own office when he got to work and, instead, went straight to John Campbell's.

Campbell looked up with a mild expression of annoyance at the intrusion. Yes? he asked.

John, I've got to quit.

John's expression changed immediately. When he spoke, it was in a tone of voice that at least echoed the closeness the two of them had once shared.

I understand, he said. I'm sorry it's come to this, Warren, but I believe it is the best thing you can do.

Warren had no dispute with that. It was the best thing. His only worry was that he was living in the company's house. It would take him a while to find a new place to live.

Campbell waved off Warren's worry. He could stay in his house as long as he wanted. He would have to move out when he'd found a new place, but he should take his time. No pressure.

Warren thanked him. He truly appreciated John's attitude about the house and was pleased that the moment was at least framed in the sadness it deserved, rather than being mired in anger and retribution. When Warren returned home and told Sharon about the conversation, they both agreed that it was a surprisingly decent thing for John Campbell to do.

That impression lasted until the next day. Then the postman delivered a registered letter addressed to Warren Murphy from the Pacific Lumber Company. The letter, signed by one of Campbell's underlings, informed Murphy that since he was no longer in the company's employ, he and his wife had ten days in which to vacate the premises or face forcible eviction.

The letter made Warren Murphy so furious that he had all their possessions hauled off to storage that day and, by that evening, had relocated to the guest quarters at his family's ranch on Larabee Creek.

Warren Murphy never spoke to John Campbell again.

And though through himself, Warren expected that the ghosts of his ancestors—Simon, old A.S., and Stan—uneasy and violated by that son of a bitch from Texas, would be haunting this bend in the Eel for years to come.

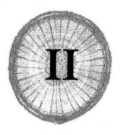

The Transformation

23

Charles Hurwitz couldn't help but feel just a bit smug. Standing on the landing gouged out of the hillside by his Pacific Lumber Company Caterpillars, he and his two adolescent sons, Sean and David, marveled at the panorama of steep helter-skelter ridges descending one upon another to the west, across Humboldt County toward the Pacific Ocean. Except for the random bald patches that marked previous logging episodes, every slope and crevasse, every watercourse and shoulder, every crest and every peak was matted with redwood forest, enormous and ripe for cutting.

In the foreground, the Pacific Lumber Company woods crew was a constellation of orange safety helmets, busily skinning the slope below. This, Hurwitz now knew, was called a "logging show." The rains were done and the 1986 cutting season was in full swing. The Cats grunted mightily, dragging downed redwoods along muddy skid roads, belching black smoke out their stacks, but the giant diesels were only barely audible—a mere dull rumble behind the high-pitched shrieks generated by the assault of four-foot chain saw blades upon tree trunks fifteen feet thick. Assuming the feller dropped it in one piece, just the single redwood being addressed down there now—to show the new boss how it was done—would be worth some $30,000 once it had been milled. And it, like all the millions of Hurwitz's other trees, had been had for a song. The first numbers from the Pacific Lumber Company's new timber cruise were flowing in and it appeared there was at least 2 billion, perhaps as much as 4 billion, more board feet of merchantable timber out there than Gene Elam and the old board of directors had assumed. Which, of course, meant Charles Hurwitz had paid $800 million for a property worth in excess of $1.8 billion—more than enough reason to be smug. Whatever else they might say about Charles, no one could question his ability to find a bargain and seize it.

But, of course, he still had to make that bargain pay for itself. His plan was to dispose of all of PL's holdings which weren't related to producing boards—selling off the farm lands, the office building, and the entire cutting and welding division—and to crank up lumber production as high as it would go. No one in the world owned even a fraction as much prime redwood as he did and he meant to take maximum advantage of that corner on the market. Upslope, to the north, he and his boys could make out along the distant horizon the scruffy ridgebacks that marked that advantage at its apex. There, among the latticework of the Coast Range, in holdings out behind Fortuna known to old-timers as simply "Salmon Creek," along the watersheds that drain into the bay and the Van Duzen off of Lawrence, Yager, Shaw, and Salmon Creeks and the Little South Fork of the Elk River, was a patchwork collection of virgin redwood stands that included the largest contiguous, old-growth redwood forest in the world still in private hands. Collectively, the virgin "Salmon Creek" holdings amounted to Pacific Lumber's mother lode. Once the company got chain saws in there, Charles Hurwitz expected to make money hand over fist and, along the way, show what idiots his doubters had been.

Needless to say, Charles would not be directing that onslaught personally. Nor would he be relying on Gene Elam. Despite the assurances of continuity Charles had given at the meeting in Scotia last December, Pacific Lumber's pencil-pushing c.e.o. would be gone by June, taking almost a half-million dollars in severance pay and accepting a gentle but unambiguous shove out the door. Instead of Elam, Hurwitz was counting on the big Australian, John Campbell, to transform the surrounding waves of *sequoia sempervirens* into cash flow. Charles and his Maxxam associates were reorganizing Pacific Lumber, leaving a national sales office in the San Francisco Bay area and moving all the other headquarters functions down to the MCO of-

fices in Los Angeles. There, William Leone, a manufacturing specialist
and longtime Hurwitz associate, was designated its c.e.o. John Campbell retained his executive vice president title and occupied the
perch in the organizational ladder immediately below Leone's.
Leone had never been involved in a lumber operation before but he
understood industrial organization and he was impressed with Campbell's obvious skill at managing operations out of Scotia. John knew
all the right knobs to turn and buttons to push and was relentless
once he'd identified an objective.

And John Campbell meant to live up to his new bosses' expectations—and then some. When the Pacific Lumber Company accelerated its operations that spring, his hand was quite visibly on its
throttle. He maintained the traditional Pacific Lumber Company
practice of employees addressing each other, from the lowest up
to himself, by their first names, so, around town, he was still just
"John," but that was one of the few company practices which continued unabated. Most of PL's policies for cutting timber, set half a
century ago by old Mr. Murphy, were transformed immediately
upon the advent of Charles Hurwitz's ownership. Clear-cutting was
now the company's preferred forestry technique and, in its first year
as a Maxxam subsidiary, PL would file as many timber harvest plans
with the state department of forestry—specifying company clear
cuts—as it had in the entire time since A. S. Murphy ascended to
PL's presidency.

The policy of setting Pacific Lumber's rate of cut at the level of
sustained yield was a casualty of the change in ownership as well.
John had told the audience gathered in the Winema last December
that the only increase being discussed was just 20 percent, but that
figure only referred to the extent of the increase set in motion before the buyout and attendant merger with Maxxam were finalized.
Now John was aiming to at least double and perhaps triple production. More than three hundred new employees would be added to
PL's Humboldt County operations before summer. A second eight-
hour shift was added at the factory in Scotia and at the second-
growth mill in Fortuna. Scotia's Mills A and B had their normal shift
increased to ten hours with mandatory overtime and plans were
drawn up to soon add a mandatory eight-hour shift on Saturday as
well. As Campbell had recommended, Hurwitz also began to gear
up for harvesting the mother lode out in Salmon Creek by purchas-

ing Louisiana Pacific's old-growth redwood mill along the Van
Duzen at Carlotta. Once it was readied, the Carlotta mill would be
double-shifted, just like Fortuna. The pace around PL was suddenly
dizzying. Lickety-split, as Kelly Bettiga put it, and, just like that, old
John Campbell had the whole goddamned place working like a
bunch of Koreans. The timber industry's last tortoise was joining the
hares.

Pacific Lumber's acceleration was at its most frantic out on the
hillsides, where the lumberjacks worked. At the Winema meeting
in December, John Campbell had declared that any increase in
woods activity would be handled by the company's existing woods
operation, but that declaration had also evaporated in the heat of
the production increase. As the spring cut commenced, PL was soon
deploying three times as many people out in the forest, but only a
fraction of the increase was achieved by expanding it own harvesting
crews. Three new gypo logging outfits were contracted to cover the
rest of the accelerated cut and, in addition, the woods crews were reorganized. Now, instead of working in a "set" of one feller and one
bucker, Pacific Lumber went to "single bucking," where the feller
was required to strip his own downed trees, allowing the company to
cover more ground more quickly. The woods crews also added a
mandatory Saturday shift, but that would soon be scaled back to
the old five-day week because, even with selling logs to other mills
in previously unheard-of quantities, the company's own log decks
were swamped in timber. State Highway 36, running along the Van
Duzen through Hydesville and Carlotta, hummed with new activity
as PL began nibbling at the edges of its Salmon Creek holdings.
Every ten or fifteen minutes, all week long, another log truck bearing twenty-foot lengths of freshly cut redwood rattled along the as-
phalt, hissing air from its brakes and scattering smoke off its tires.

Some of the old-timers on PL's woods crews were appalled. The
increase meant there were suddenly a lot of people out dropping
redwoods who'd never done it before. Buckers were promoted and
guys who had been running chop saws and routers down at the mill
were given chain saws and turned loose. And those novices were
now learning their craft on stands of trees fifteen feet across and
eight hundred or a thousand years old. The gypos had at least cut
trees before but, of course, they were unused to working big trees,
since there were so few of them to cut outside of PL's lands and, un-

til now, the Pacific Lumber Company had never allowed gypos into its old growth. In addition, the gypos were paid according to the board foot loaded on the truck and, as a consequence, often cut with both eyes on their paycheck. They just wanted the tree down as quickly as they could manage—so one gypo feller might well drop as many trees in an hour as a PL feller might drop in a day. Occasionally the gypos didn't even bother to cushion the redwoods' fall, but just let them explode on impact and then salvaged the portion of the wreckage that remained usable—an approach referred to out in the woods as "going for the guts." To the old-timers, this kind of mercenary massacre was an abomination.

To John Campbell, it was just a cost inherent in ratcheting the Pacific Lumber operation up to speed as quickly as was necessary. He correctly predicted that it would iron itself out, once everyone got in sync with what they were doing. In any event, such start-up sloppiness was certainly insufficient reason to sacrifice any of the volume or the speed for which he'd been pressing.

And none of that sloppiness was visible to Charles Hurwitz when he visited Humboldt County to inspect his company. He and his sons only saw the redwood harvest at its best.

There wasn't a more skilled feller in Humboldt County than the one addressing the demonstration tree below the Hurwitzes' landing and that feller had been advised that the big boss was up the slope watching. The trick was to drop the tree at an angle so that its entire length landed at the same moment, and this feller used every nuance as he sliced a deep notch across the redwood's innards. Then he stepped back from his cut, severing the scream of his saw in mid-shriek, and, in the sudden bubble of quiet, air seemed to gather around the still erect trunk. Soon it tipped, slowly at first, then accelerating as tons of timber accumulated momentum and battering its way through the morning sunlight, turning force into a blunt-edged noise that, though made by no more than the displacement of enormous volumes of sky, still gripped the ear and sucked attention toward the tree's accelerating arc. That surging force was cut short by an enormous thud, as sudden as the silence with which its fall had begun. The redwood landed all in one flat instant—no bounce even, just a thud and an immediate dead stop. Of course the tree's limbs crumbled, that was inevitable, but the trunk now lay on the ground in one, single, 220-foot-long piece, having taken its first giant Pacific Lumber Company step along the way to becoming $30,000.

Charles Hurwitz always evinced nothing but confidence in his company's ability to harvest its hillsides. Except for an occasional visit to Humboldt County, during which he and John Campbell spent a lot of time together, Hurwitz concentrated his own energies on cleaning up the loose financial strings left over from the takeover itself. That spring, two items dominated his agenda.

The first item was a final issue of Drexel high-yield bonds to set up Pacific Lumber's "long-term" financing and account for the adjustments he had made in his original financial strategy. Rather than make a quick sale of the cutting and welding division to generate immediate cash, Charles and Drexel had issued over the winter a string of debentures that were designed to be replaced by a bond issue. Or more accurately, two bond issues. One consisted of $615 million worth of zero-coupon notes sold at 43 percent of their face value, the other of $180 million worth of standard bonds, bearing interest rates close to 13 percent. Their collective principal would begin coming due in 1990, when the Pacific Lumber Company's annual payments on its takeover debt would rise to almost $83 million. After three years at that level, they would rise to $153 million in 1993, $220 million in 1994, and reach a crescendo of $294 million in 1996. Of course, Hurwitz had no intention of ever getting that far. He expected to refinance again several years down the pike when his debt could be rolled over at more genuinely "long-term" rates.

The most pressing immediate issue was selling this initial debt. And that was in Drexel Burnham Lambert's hands. Michael Milken was summoning the energies of his great financial engine to the task and it seemed well in hand. For this high-risk "long-term" funding, Drexel's leading subscribers would be a series of savings and loans and insurance companies, all of which needed an especially high rate of return on their investments in order to remain solvent. They all also had a special relationship with Michael Milken. Lead among those were the First Executive Corporation and its Executive Life Insurance Company and Executive Life Insurance Company of New York. First Executive was the fief of one Fred Carr, a former boy financial genius who'd come a cropper and then rebounded with the inflated dividends yielded by his symbiotic relationship with Michael

Milken. In Drexel's trading room above Gump's, a monitor over Milken's X-shaped desk ran endless stock quotations and next to it, Milken had mounted lists of First Executive's various portfolios. These he traded at will, only notifying Carr after the fact. When PL's new bonds were issued in July, First Executive bought $150 million worth. Over the following two years, when PL bonds began being traded on the open market, First Executive bought up more than $150 million more. And, of course, Milken moved the entire original Pacific Lumber Company bond issue easily, just as he'd promised.

The other item dominating Charles Hurwitz's spring agenda was finalizing the reorganization of Pacific Lumber's pension fund so that the company could swallow the pension's huge cash surplus. In its usual conservative fashion, the old Pacific Lumber Company had stashed a great deal more money behind its pension commitments than it was expected to need in meeting its obligations to pay benefits. To release that surplus, the new Pacific Lumber Company would have to go through a fiduciary process to guarantee all the potential benefits to date by purchasing an annuity from an insurance company. The annuity would then act as the sole underpinning of the Pacific Lumber Company pension plan. The cost of purchasing the annuity would be covered by the current pension fund and whatever monies remained in the fund afterward would be shuffled into the maze of Hurwitz holdings. No one was sure exactly how much cash the pension fund would yield—that would only be known in detail when PL received bids from insurance companies—but Charles expected more than $50 million, which he hoped to have in his hands before 1987. The Pacific Lumber Company was about to begin soliciting bids from insurers and ought to have completed the bidding by October. The rest, he figured, was just a matter of pulling off the final mechanics.

24

Charles Hurwitz counted on John Campbell to make sure he had the lumber production he would need to make his strategy work, and that role was a boon. It, more than anything else, would ensure that the isolation surrounding John in Scotia would ease.

John Campbell was now running a lumber boom town. Ever since the last months of the takeover, almost everyone in Scotia had been feeling rich. All PL employees had stock options as part of their wages, which most had exercised as they were able, and, that winter and spring, those who did had been paid $40 a share by Charles Hurwitz. For many families, that amounted to a total with four or, sometimes, five digits to the left of the decimal point, a princely sum at the timber industry's ground level. In addition, Hurwitz's escalation meant everyone began drawing overtime pay and the more than eleven hundred men who now worked for PL were bringing home as much as two hundred extra dollars a week. A lot of that new money found its way into Scotia. The rest spread a blanket of prosperity around surrounding Carlotta, Fortuna, Hydesville, Loleta, Rio Dell, and Pepperwood. The Pacific Lumber Company's Scotia garbage trucks were hauling off dozens of discarded appliance and furniture cartons from the alleys behind the company's bungalows and more than a few PL families were driving new pickup trucks.

The possibility that John Campbell's pariah status might recede surfaced that spring, when Leona Bishop came into the company offices to make a payment on her father's health insurance policy. Leona's father was a retiree who had spent most of his working life with the company. Leona's husband, Grant, pulled the green chain over at Mill B and her brother-in-law was a supervisor in the factory. Leona, who had once cleaned house for the Murphys out at Larabee Creek, had been one of Hurwitz's harsher critics back in November. When her husband Grant came home from the meeting at the Winema in December and told her how everyone had laughed when Hurwitz dropped his line about the golden rule, Leona had blown her cork.

You dumb-ass timber workers, she'd railed. He told you guys exactly what's gonna happen—he's got you right where he wants you and there's nothin' you can do about it. And you dumb-asses laughed.

Some five months later, when Leona came in to the front office to make her father's insurance payment, she passed John as he walked down the hall from his office. By then, in Leona's estimation, old John was so used to getting the cold shoulder that he'd made it something of a habit to refrain from looking anyone in the face. But he always issued a sociable greeting anyway.

Hello, Leona, John said, expecting no response.

He got two steps past her before his expectation was confounded.

Hi, John, Leona answered. How are you?

Campbell came to a dead stop. Typewriters around the office went silent, heads turned, and conversations ceased. A few people glared at Leona for breaching the invisible social wall around the company's executive vice president. Leona had done it impulsively, because she felt sorry for poor John, but she was not about to apologize.

John himself just looked stunned, one of the few times in anyone's memory that he had ever seemed unsure of what to say.

25

As much as Scotia boomed and as reliable as John Campbell would prove at turning Charles Hurwitz's *sequoia sempervirens* into cash, Maxxam's venture into Humboldt County had by no means broken into the open on its way to an uncontested score. Charles Hurwitz didn't yet know it in the spring of 1986, but he and his Pacific Lumber Company still faced more than half a decade of often desperate struggle over his plans to turn trees into money. Hurwitz's opponents would act both separately and in occasional concert, with several different and often conflicting motivations and objects, but their weight was felt and they did not back off, however unlikely their chances for success.

None of those opponents would prove more significant than two young men who first met that spring, on a gray day when the back edge of rainy season was just giving way to the cycle of sunny days and evening fog that would last until November. Charles Hurwitz was then contemplating the final steps of his company's restructuring when the two young men menacing his future met in a parking lot tucked into the middle of a block off Sprowel Creek Road in Garberville, pop. 1350, the principal metropolis among the highland watersheds of the Mattole River and the Eel, close to Humboldt's border with Mendocino County. The parking lot where they met belonged to a small ramshackle bungalow rented to the Environmental Protection Information Center. The lot was all gravel and mud and connected to the street by a short, rutted alley that emerged onto Sprowel Creek Road right next to Milt's Chain Saw Repair.

Darryl Cherney was inside the EPIC bungalow, and Darryl was losing it. He could not believe this was happening. It wasn't as though all this wasn't hard enough, anyway. He'd never figured a simple tree planting could get so crazy and complicated. And now his van was coming apart and he had no idea how he was going to get all of the dozen or so people who'd begun showing up out to Sally Bell Grove, their ultimate destination. This action was intended to hassle Georgia Pacific on its own turf once again, another infuriating jab in the side of the monster that was eating the forest—finely crafted with what was becoming recognized as the unique Cherney touch—but it would all be wasted unless he found something to replace that van. Invading a logging company's clear cut to plant trees. Too much, too fucking much. But that damn van! It comprised about 80 percent of Darryl Cherney's assets and was furnished with most of the other 20 percent, but it was still a piece of shit. After all those years in New York imagining this life for himself, now he was finally living it, and he was stuck with a 1976 Dodge that sounded more like a cement mixer with each passing day. This was the last irony of the apocalypse. No one could save Mother Earth without a new car.

While Darryl's head ran on at about one hundred and twenty miles an hour, Darryl's body moved around EPIC's tiny rented space at about eighty, ricocheting from person to phone to window to wall. This was, all the rest of the longhaired and barefoot in the room recognized, just the way old Feral Darryl operated. He was already a legend and he'd only been in town six months. It was as though the guy had caffeine in his veins instead of blood. He was high energy. And just plain far out.

And around here, that was saying something.

This was, after all, Garberville, capital of the hippie nation, nerve center of America's foremost marijuana-growing enclave. The Garberville hardware store sold miles of plastic irrigation tubing to barefoot, bearded farmers with dreadlocks and studs in their ears

who paid with handfuls of twenty-dollar bills and then disappeared
back into the Coast Range or toward the Lost Coast until harvest
time in the fall, when the traffic in pickup trucks along the area's extensive network of abandoned backwoods logging roads increased
geometrically.

Collectively, this tribe called itself the Mateel. Individually, a lot
of them called themselves by names like Oak, River, Moki, Baba, or
Harmony, none of which had been given them at birth. Their national vehicle was the backpack; their tribal colors, tie-dyed. They'd
begun coming here in the late sixties and early seventies, when the
scene in San Francisco's Haight-Ashbury fizzled and its true devo-
tees began to migrate "back to the land" and, along the way, discovered this dying logging hamlet surrounded by the second-growth
remnants of a forest that had been mostly logged out in the rush of
timber cutting that had consumed the area around the Humboldt-
Mendocino border during the 1950s. More waves of longhairs followed the first—homesteaders living close to the ground, dressed
out of the Salvation Army and used-clothing stores, fed up with urban civilization, and committed to getting simple and sustainable.
Some purchased their own little piece of land collectively, others as
individuals, and others just lived around with their friends. They all
ate lots of vegetables and brown rice. Some slept in lean-tos, some in
tents, and as their immigration gathered momentum, owner-built
houses began proliferating. Some of those homemade structures
were shaped into geodesic domes, some topped with weird backwoods minarets, others dug into the hillside. And, as word spread
and spread, more waves of immigrants followed. Thanks to the Mateel, no one thought Garberville was dying now.

Darryl Cherney, twenty-nine, considered his own presence here a
matter of simple magnetism. Just before last Thanksgiving, he was
driving south along the Oregon coast—aimless, drifting, almost two
months removed from his former life in Manhattan. He was writing
more songs than ever, borne along by the rush of being out on the
road at last, on his own. A half hour north, it was raining but the
night surrounding Darryl's Dodge was dry, though thick as porridge.
Then ahead, in the stab of his Dodge's high beams, a figure appeared,
walking very fast along the road shoulder, hunched a bit under a
pack with an Indian rattle sticking out of its back pocket. Darryl

stopped to give him a ride. His new passenger was a self-described "Cheyenne road man," a traveler for the Native American Church, moving up and down the coast, keeping his scattered flock's spirits uplifted and enlightened. He was called Kingfisher.

Darryl and the Indian watched the passing road in silence for a while and then talked all night.

Finally, Kingfisher just asked this scruffy white boy what he wanted.

Darryl told him he wanted to save the world, write songs, live off the land, and be self-sufficient.

Kingfisher considered for a moment, then spoke. You should go to Garberville, he said.

And here Darryl was, up to his ears in the struggle to save Sally Bell Grove, a classic patch of redwood old growth owned by the Georgia Pacific Corporation out in the Sinkyone, just over the line in Mendocino, adjacent to the Lost Coast where the last edge of the Coast Range dropped into the Pacific. EPIC had been in that fight for more than three years now and Darryl, the latecomer, was just a bit player in the effort, though already distinctive for the sheer volume of his manic energy.

The van, the van. What was he going to do about the van? He knew of a VW bug he could call on, but that still left him a car short. This smelled like disaster, and Darryl went back to racking his brain. Today's action could not fall apart now. It was too good a shot for that. Shaming GP right on in its turf, illustrating that the people who wanted to stop Georgia Pacific from making a mess out of the forest had to ignore the laws against trespassing in order to clean up the mess Georgia Pacific had already made. This small stroke of self-described public relations genius was now imprisoned by sticky lifters and worn-out engine rods or something. Of all times for that goddamn van to get temperamental.

Finally, Darryl couldn't contain himself inside anymore and pushed through the door and jumped off the top step and down into the parking lot. At that moment, a battered old Toyota sedan pulled in off Sprowel Creek Road and Greg King got out of it. Darryl immediately concluded that the Toyota was a gift from Providence, about to take him off the hook in the nick of time. Its driver was headed toward the bungalow and Darryl veered straight for

him. He didn't recognize the guy. He looked hip but didn't look
overgrown enough to be from the immediate neighborhood of
Garberville.

Cherney extended his hand to the stranger. Darryl Cherney, he
said by way of introduction. Glad to meet you. Can you drive a carload out to Sally Bell?

Greg King did a double take at this wild little guy with crazy eyes.
Greg, 25, was a reporter for an alternative weekly in Sonoma County
who had just won a local journalism association's award for his reporting about Sonoma's dwindling lumber industry. He'd stopped
here to get directions to the Sinkyone. He'd heard of the campaign
to save it and wanted to see the spot for himself. He knew nothing
about today's planned action and, at first, he didn't know what to
say to Darryl's request.

An hour later, the two of them and a back seat full of hippies
were headed west, on the road to Shelter Cove. Darryl rode shotgun
with his guitar in his lap. Everyone in the back seat had hoes and
shovels. Someone asked Darryl to sing his song about the Eel River
Flood, the one they'd heard on KMUD radio, but Darryl said he'd
sing it when they got out to the tree planting. Then there'd be
plenty of singing. Along the two-lane county blacktop on the way to
the trailhead for Sally Bell, he mostly just talked to Greg King.

Darryl explained to Greg how horrified he'd been when he arrived in Garberville and learned that 95 percent of the old redwoods had already been cut and that the lumber companies were
moving to finish off what was left. He'd first seen redwoods on a
family vacation as a teenager. Nothing in his life had ever moved
him as they did. He went back to New York City and dreamed of
them for years thereafter. Now, he personally felt the pain of those
trees as they went under the saw. When they cut the ancient forest,
they cut Darryl Cherney. And the scientific fact was that these timber corporations were indeed cutting all of us, not just a bunch of
trees. These were the lungs of the planet that were being "harvested." How will we breathe without them? If we failed to stop these
corporate clear cutters, the human race would eventually die an
ugly death. What gave us life was not lumber corporations, it was
Mother Earth. We had put a giant wedge of technology between
ourselves and our survival system and we were dying because we'd
severed ourself from our life support. We had to reconnect the

species or die. We had to protect what remained of the virgin forest so that, even if we wipe ourselves out, there will still be some building blocks left with which to reconstruct our ecology. This was a life-or-death drama and everyone had parts in it. And to think, Darryl chuckled, two years ago, in his incarnation as an ad-industry gofer, he'd been assembling ski contests for Equitable Life and writing flack copy for Capitol Records.

Life, Greg agreed, was full of irony. His own ancestors had been pioneer California loggers during the last century—prominent enough that the nearby King Range had been named after one of them.

Darryl said that blew his mind.

Greg was just as strident as Darryl about how the lifeblood of the ecosystem was being assaulted while the legal and political systems just sat by and watched. Or, even more likely, facilitated the rape. He'd seen it all down in Sonoma. The only winners in this cycle of destruction were a bunch of blind corporate fat cats who lived high, with no eye to how the human race was going to be able to last without an environment to nurture it. Greg sometimes wondered if the rise of human dominance was just the last act of a decaying planet and speculated that maybe humans were just parasites, gobbling up life itself. He wondered if, after consuming the rivers, the air, the land, the sky, and all the other animals, humans might not just devolve into a lower, more subordinate life form, the way dinosaurs became birds. What was for sure was that "civilization" was extinguishing all the earth's other species in a mad rush toward oblivion, all in the name of capital, growth, and "progress."

Right on, Darryl said.

When Greg's old Toyota and the Volkswagon caravaning behind it reached the trailhead to Sally Bell Grove, Darryl and the dozen other members of his tree-planting action got out and headed in one direction. Greg King hiked off in another. He hadn't come to plant, he'd come to see, and he headed straight into the old growth by himself.

This was by no means his first hike in the ancient forest and it was, as always for him, a step into the eternal. Even the ground underfoot was the powdered remains of a millennium of trees, one having finally toppled on its predecessor and then been fallen upon by the next and the next, century upon century, all the layers slowly rotting themselves into topsoil as deep as twelve feet in some spots. Greg had to boost himself up and over the latest in that succession of fallen trees, scrambling as bark peeled away under his step. In places, his feet broke through the forest floor, revealing a honeycomb of disintegrating redwoods. The best route through the old growth was often atop trees that had fallen within the last twenty years, forming short bridges across the most difficult spots. Greg looked for such avenues and kept track of landmarks along the way. In places, the going was solid and easy and he ascended the slope through ferns as high as his shoulders and sorrel that swallowed his boots. He tried to skirt the occasional tangles of huckleberry and salal but it wasn't always possible. Light sometimes broke through the canopy and splashed on a large patch of the forest floor, but mostly it sifted down through a grillwork of trunks and limbs, some stunted, others giant, some reduced to mere snags, a few twisted into corkscrews by their attempt to find a piece of light upon which to feed.

The California coastal rainforest, of which this was a last remnant, had been this way since the days of the dinosaurs Diplodocus and Triceratops. Greg thought of it as a taproot into time itself. This was the earth as it was meant to be. This was the tune with which civilization was supposed to harmonize. There was no need to "tame" such wildness, no call to treat it as just a resource to be consumed for the purposes of only one of the planet's species. This was the most precious of humanity's inheritances from life's past; its keeping, a sacred trust. And it reached out and touched him the way little else in life did. The forest was truly Mother Earth—the comforter, the sustainer, the source of all vitality. A walk through it was an embrace. The farther he moved into Sally Bell, the better Greg felt.

That, however, did not last.

Ahead, the dark bowels of the forest began to thin, then a wall of light emerged beyond it as the edge of the grove became visible. The looming brightness pulled him forward, accelerating his stride without his really noticing. It grew brighter and brighter and then Greg was out in the light, like a diver breaking the flat plane of a pool—instantly, the old growth was behind him and he was on dreadfully open ground.

Greg King's random path through Sally Bell had led him out the other side, into one of the Georgia Pacific Corporation's notorious clear cuts, emerging atop a precipitous three-hundred-foot slope that bottomed out in what had been a two-foot-wide stream. He'd seen clear cuts before but this one took his breath away. Fresh stumps were everywhere, salted with mounds of sawdust, scattered fragments, and the assorted piles of half-burned logging-show refuse known in the business as "slash." The slash had been torched as part of Georgia Pacific's on-site "cleanup." When the cleanup was done, Georgia Pacific left behind a slope that resembled the skin of a hastily plucked chicken. All the sorrel, all the ferns, all the salal were gone, as were all the trees. Another crop of redwoods would grow back from sprouts off the leftover stumps but a number of the stumps had been uprooted in the course of building beds to cushion the redwood felling. Those stumps were scattered about in random groups.

Last rainy season, when the Eel turned ugly and the city services of Rio Dell were washed out of existence, this naked slope had shed at least a foot of topsoil. That former forest floor was now deposited three hundred feet south, in the streambed. At places, the eroded silt had divided the watercourse into successive pools. At one location, toward the middle of the "harvested area," the entire slope had given way and several dozen tons of earth had slumped across the stream. The wall of solid light colliding with ground that had not felt anything like it for 20 million years gave off a brackish heat and mosquitoes swarmed around the puddles of water still cooking in the old tractor ruts.

There was one significant shred of dead tree left on the site, a twenty-foot length, broken clean in the middle and abandoned across the streambed. Greg King made his way along the edge of the avalanche and then up the devastated streambed until he reached the abandoned log. There, he sat, staring back up at Georgia Pacific's handiwork. Tears leaked down his face but no sobs cleared his throat. He felt an ache in his chest that seemed six miles deep.

Over and over, Greg King told himself that this butchery had to be stopped. Not just controlled, not just regulated, but stopped— altogether, in its tracks, and once and for all.

26

Had anyone advanced the notion to Charles Hurwitz that the Maxxam juggernaut was about to be impeded by two hippies who cried over cut trees and could barely keep one automobile functioning between them, no doubt he would have gagged in laughter. He was sailing along and, with Michael Milken's continued backing, already looking for his next acquisition. As far as Pacific Lumber was concerned, he was largely preoccupied with getting at the pension fund surplus and gave no thought to environmentalists. The lead bank in his PL bridge financing was impatient for repayment and Charles had already promised them the pension surplus whenever he could get his hands on it. This was not an altogether simple process, however. The federally empowered Pension Benefit Guarantee Corporation dictated a set procedure to be followed in the reorganization of a pension fund, requiring arm's-length transactions laced with fiduciary responsibilities, all designed to ensure pension stability. Getting at that cash would take some time. And, as would soon become the PL pattern, there would be unanticipated opposition for Charles to surmount.

In this instance, that opposition was generated by one Vincent Garner—Pacific Lumber's fifty-eight-year-old incumbent treasurer, chief financial officer, and overseer of its pension fund—though Garner was anything but an obvious candidate for the opposition role. He had not been a player in the resistance to Charles's tender offer and was no die-hard Murphy partisan. He'd come to Pacific Lumber when the only remaining Murphys were Warren and Woody and Suzanne and he had first been hired by the Cutting and Welding Division, so he was also outside the mystic fraternalism of the mill. He was just an M.B.A. from the University of Chicago with a history of financial analyst and consultant jobs. He'd been at the company for a little more than a decade—all of it spent at the San Francisco headquarters—and thought of Pacific Lumber as a very special place to work.

It was that thought that got him in trouble. In the hard-edged world of Wall Street sharks, Vincent Garner was a provincial Boy Scout. The assignment of overseeing the pension decommissioning fell to him because of his responsibilities as the fund's chief operating officer. He had not asked for it. And when he got it, he didn't question Maxxam's right to retrieve the surplus; he just insisted on approaching the task in the PL way, with the conservative finances, human loyalty, and top-of-the-line dash that had always been PL's special trademarks. That was simply the way Vincent Garner worked—for PL, for Charles Hurwitz, or for anyone else.

Charles Hurwitz, however, had his own way of doing things. He wanted unanimity in the pension decommissioning, making it much easier to cover Maxxam's collective legal vulnerability, and expected Garner to cooperate with his program.

When Vincent Garner didn't, he made what was perhaps the very last stand of the old PL.

At first, Vincent Garner saw no reason to expect that the pension decommissioning would be anything with which he would have a complaint, particularly since it would proceed under his immediate supervision. To handle the actual mechanics of substituting an annuity for the existing fund, he designed a two-stage procedure that would begin with the solicitation of "illustrative" bids from a short list of insurance companies. Those insurers, having analyzed the existing pension obligations, would return with an estimated price for a replacement annuity. On the basis of those illustrative bids, some of the companies would be asked to make binding formal bids. Then the company's new board of directors, chaired by Charles Hurwitz, would select among them. Garner's stated goal was to make sure that the pension fund was underwritten by a "high quality" insurer, with a track record that would generate a "high level of comfort," and, after some preliminary research on insurance companies, he produced the short list of those he thought suitable for including in a possible solicitation. It was a roster of the most prestigious names in the business, dominated by such firms as Aetna, Equitable, John Hancock, Metropolitan Life, and Prudential—all stalwart and well-established.

That there were other agendas operating besides his own first became apparent to Garner when he presented that list to his superiors at a June meeting in the Washington Street headquarters. The offices around their meeting room were all in the process of being packed up and shipped to MCO Holdings headquarters in Los Angeles. Each room now had an echo, and Pacific Lumber as Vincent Garner had known it was being dismantled. To track this changeover, a group of executives from both MCO and the old PL, Garner included, met regularly. On this particular day, Maxxam's chief financial officer had flown up from L.A. to chair the meeting.

When they reached the pension fund item on the agenda, Garner made his report and laid out how the bidding process would be conducted. Then he read the list of insurance companies that would be solicited.

Garner's remarks drew only one response. But that was from the chairman, Maxxam's chief financial officer. Without elaborating on why, Maxxam's c.f.o. instructed Garner to add the Executive Life Insurance Company, a subsidiary of the First Executive Corporation, to the list.

Vincent Garner had never heard of the Executive Life Insurance Company and was surprised at the instruction. He had expected the meeting to rubber-stamp his list but, recognizing an order when it was delivered, he wrote down "Executive Life" along with a note to include it in the bidding.

Garner also made a mental note to do some immediate research on this mystery company and, the next day, visited the periodicals room at the library, where he was surprised at how much had been written about Executive Life over the last few years. Most of the articles focused on Fred Carr, the fifty-year-old president of the insurer's parent company.

Carr's Executive Life Insurance Company now occupied a shiny new headquarters building just down the block from the Drexel junk bond shop run by Michael Milken, but Carr had not always been a Milken stalking horse. He'd been a prodigy by his own right in the mutual funds business during the late 1960s, described then by the *New York Times* as "one of the greats . . . a money manager's money manager." Carr's career in mutual funds had been cut short by the bear market of 1969 and a 1970 Securities and Exchange Commission complaint charging discrepancies in his record keeping. In 1974, he abandoned New York for Los Angeles and took over Executive Life, a tiny, nearly bankrupt Los Angeles insurance company. If there was a stroke of genius in Carr's venture into insurance, it was his decision to position Executive Life at Michael Milken's elbow. Afterward, its fortunes soared. Starting with barely $12 million, Carr used Milken's "high yield" bonds to build a rate of return on capital nearly four points higher than the industry average. Executive Life's assets were now almost $300 million and one of the financial products he successfully marketed to increase his company's pool of capital was a host of cut-rate annuities, most of which had yet to come due. Carr's parent company and its associated insurance operations were also the biggest collective purchaser of Drexel's final issue of Pacific Lumber bonds.

Vincent Garner ended his research more unsettled about this new entrant in the annuity bidding than when he'd begun and, at a July transition meeting in the Washington Street headquarters, he voiced his doubts.

Executive Life did not look like a very high-quality operation, he told the other executives. In fact, it looked a lot riskier than seemed appropriate.

No one else at the meeting had any comment on Garner's remark, so the subject went no further.

In August, the selected insurance companies, First Executive included, submitted illustrative bids. The procedure established by Garner required all the bidders to phone their initial estimates to Garner's assistant on the designated day. At the end of that day, only Executive Life had failed to make contact. Their illustrative bid came in several days later, after all the numbers from the other bidders had been disseminated inside the transition team. The Executive Life bid was also phoned in to the company's consulting actuaries rather than Garner's assistant. At $36 million, it was, however, substantially lower than any of the others.

When Garner raised the issue of Executive Life's violation of the agreed-upon procedure when he next met with Paul Schwartz, the executive at MCO designated to track the pension fund project, Schwartz cast his voice in the tone of a permissive uncle. Garner didn't want to exclude the best bid of all just on the basis of a technicality, did he? That seemed like throwing the baby out with the bathwater.

The Executive Life Insurance Company was included on the final list of five insurers asked to prepare formal bids, along with Aetna, Met Life, Equitable, and Prudential.

Garner nonetheless continued trying to raise alarms about Executive Life. This was, after all, his own pension he was attempting to guarantee and, even if it weren't, PL had always taken care of its employees better than anyone else in the business. Garner saw no reason to stop doing so now.

Shortly after the illustrative bids were received, he requested that Pacific Lumber's new c.e.o., William Leone, approve hiring a consulting company to rate the soundness of all the finalists in the annuity bidding. Leone agreed and Pacific Lumber retained the insurance consultants Conning & Company. Their ensuing report used three ratings in its evaluation: A, indicating average ability to fulfill its obligations; AA, higher than average ability; and AAA, high ability. The four other finalists were all rated AA or AAA. Executive Life was rated A. Conning's report noted that more than half of Executive Life's portfolio was held in high-risk corporate debt. Its parent company, First Executive, also dressed up its books by transferring liabilities back and forth between subsidiaries, creating an illusion of greater solvency than was, in fact, the case. This practice was currently under investigation by several state insurance regulators and the Internal Revenue Service. Vincent Garner also interviewed all the bidders individually and in those interviews, the other four companies all had respectful things to say about each other but all four had nothing but warnings about the operations of Executive Life.

Vincent Garner hadn't wanted this dilemma but he was now actively frightened of Executive Life and said so at another regular Washington Street transition meeting. This time, he attempted to bring even more force to his argument.

If the illustrative bid results held true in the final bidding, Garner pointed out, then Executive Life would be the low bidder. Even so, he, quite frankly, did not think they were a reliable enterprise, not the kind to be counted on over three or four decades. They were riding high at the moment, so they could underbid, but price wasn't everything.

Only Paul Schwartz from MCO responded. He noted that Garner's concerns were "known at the highest level of the organization."

Garner, however, wouldn't leave the issue alone. It was now well into September and, on October 1, the binding bids were due and a final decision would be made. Garner was convinced Executive Life was a disaster and knew his warnings were being studiously ignored. He also knew that everyone over his head wanted him to shut up and play along. Instead, Garner made one last attempt to derail Executive Life in a memo to Leone in which he recorded all the arguments against its selection. Garner also enclosed a copy of the Conning & Company report and Xeroxes of two magazine articles about Michael Milken that dealt heavily with his connections to Fred Carr. All of this material would eventually become evidence in court.

Garner received an answer almost immediately. "MCO and Maxxam have a high regard for the safety and security of Pacific Lumber's Employee Retirement Plan benefits," Leone wrote, and "MCO and Maxxam have and will continue to exercise their fiduciary responsibilities with you in making an informed decision. . . . I think you will agree that we have been diligent in obtaining the informed judgment of experts in the insurance field as to the ability of all . . . finalists to meet their obligations to retirees. The consensus indicates they are all 'top companies' . . . rated A or better by Conning . . . and are capable of doing so. . . . I trust you will complete the final aspects of our diligence by assuring that all data requested of those companies . . . is in our hands prior to October 1."

Leone signed his answer "Bill."

On October 1, a board meeting was convened in MCO's Los Angeles office to choose an annuity to replace Pacific Lumber's pension fund. Vincent Garner did not even bother to attend. He had previously committed to a convention of the National Welding Supply Association in Seattle on the same day, and, seeing no reason to change his schedule, flew there shortly after receiving Leone's answer. He figured everyone at MCO and Maxxam already knew his position and others from his office at PL would be down in Los Angeles for the meeting if they needed informational details.

The issue nonetheless dogged Garner's tracks. On the last day of September, he returned to his Seattle hotel room and found a message that Charles Hurwitz had called and wanted to be called back at a number in Los Angeles. Garner did so immediately. The ensuing conversation was not his first encounter with Charles Hurwitz, but it was the most extensive.

Hurwitz's charm made its obligatory appearance in his opening small talk, a somewhat ritualized warm-up process. Then he got straight to the point and his voice froze into sharp edges, wielded in parries and thrusts with tangible irritation.

He understood that Garner had "some concerns" about awarding the annuity to Executive Life. Was that right?

That was, Garner answered. He did.

And just what were those concerns?

Garner said he'd written them out for Leone and assumed that Hurwitz must have seen that memo, but he was more than willing to repeat them.

Hurwitz said nothing, offering no indication that he'd seen Garner's plea to Leone.

His concerns, Garner continued, could be summarized as covering two areas. First, as a carrier of annuities, Executive Life did not seem to be of sufficient quality and followed an investment policy that was not the kind upon which he thought Pacific Lumber should depend. There was also the issue of how the employees were going to perceive all this. He thought Executive Life's shakiness would give them considerable worries. They would also wonder about Executive Life's role in PL's bond financing and whether there'd been a quid pro quo involved.

Hurwitz interrupted. Fred Carr certainly knew a damn sight more about investments than Vincent Garner, he snapped. Carr was acknowledged as one of the most successful and capable investors in the country. Did Garner think he knew more about how to invest money than Carr did? And, as for the employees, he didn't care how they perceived all this.

Garner said he couldn't understand why Hurwitz wouldn't care what the employees thought. Hurwitz backed off a bit. Garner was right, he said. Perceptions were important. On that front, though, did Garner know that Prudential had also been a purchaser of PL bonds? No, Garner admitted, he didn't. That might reassure some of the company's employees, but it hardly changed his feelings about Executive Life.

That exchange essentially ended the conversation. All discussion of Executive Life now disappeared. Hurwitz stayed on the line for a while longer, returning to small talk about the weather and the welding convention, but both of them recognized it as ritual fluff.

The following day, the Pacific Lumber Company board of directors selected the bid for $37.3 million submitted by the Executive Life Insurance Company. The winner was more than $2 million less than its closest competitor. Approval by the Pension Benefit Guarantee Corporation was expected to be pro forma and, once the contract was consummated, close to $60 million of the Pacific Lumber Company pension fund's former holdings would be available for payment against Hurwitz's outstanding bridge loan. When the official contract was sent to Vincent Garner, the pension fund's executive officer, for his signature, he refused to sign, but that didn't even slow the transfer down.

A week after First Executive's selection, MCO's Paul Schwartz and an executive from the consulting firm that had been hired by Executive Life to assist in the bidding spoke on the phone. Both complained about the difficulties raised by Garner's continued opposition. It was unseemly for the managing officer of the pension fund to behave like that, but, in the end, it hadn't mattered. "I thanked Paul for all the help he gave us," Executive Life's consultant memoed in his files after the conversation. "Paul said it came down to a real dogfight at the end and many of the individuals [among Maxxam's inherited Pacific Lumber executives] still did not come to an agreement. This was a decision that was just forced on them by Charles Hurwitz."

Charles was, it seemed, almost as good at dismantling as he was at sniffing out bargains.

Five years later, the Department of Labor would sue Hurwitz

over the pension reorganization, but at the moment, it looked like another flawless maneuver in Charles's most recent series of maneuvers. By November, the Pacific Lumber Company's San Francisco offices were stripped and the building itself sold for a little over $30 million. That left the cutting and welding division to sell off, but, that accomplished, Charles Hurwitz figured to be finished, once and for all, with the leftovers from his Pacific Lumber conquest.

27

Charles Hurwitz misjudged those leftovers, just as he'd overlooked the hippies. Far from dispensed with, the last die-hard partisans of the old Pacific Lumber Company would also hound him, refusing to accept his coup as a fait accompli, despite all the evidence to the contrary. To them, Charles Hurwitz was still "that son of a bitch"; his takeover, a wrong that might still be righted somehow, some way.

Several dozen people would play roles in that effort to turn back history but its principal architect and agent would be Bill Bertain, the Eureka attorney with whom Warren and Woody Murphy had joined forces to make their failed court fight against the tender offer. Eventually, unseating Charles Hurwitz would become Bill Bertain's holy grail, for which he taxed his health to the limit and sacrificed his family's prosperity. By then, one of Charles Hurwitz's closest advisors was describing this log-town lawyer as "crazy," so obsessed with the 1985 takeover that "he even goes to sleep at night and dreams about getting us." Bertain didn't assume that stance immediately upon the completion of PL's merger into Maxxam, but the memory of being bulldozed out of court by Ezra Levin's firm did not sit well with the stumpy attorney and, for most of the spring and on into the summer, it provided the only discordant note in Bill's life.

He was otherwise an extraordinarily happy man, driving a new pickup truck and wearing a smile wider than he was tall. Right after the Murphy wake in Rio Dell, he married his sweetheart, Rebecca, and took the plunge into domesticity. He came late to marriage and she already had grown children from a previous marriage that had been annulled. They'd met at a Catholic church social where Rebecca played the piano and he made a point of being introduced to her. Their mutual religious devotion was one of the elements in their attraction. He found enormous solace in the church and had been active in Catholic antiabortion efforts ever since the Supreme Court changed the law. Bill and Rebecca honeymooned in April in the Mexican resort town of Ixtapa on the Sea of Cortez and, by late summer, Rebecca, forty-one, was pregnant with their first child and Bill was preparing to construct a family home for them on a lot he'd purchased out on the edge of McKinleyville, up the freeway from Eureka and Arcata, just beyond Humboldt Bay's northeastern shore. When looking back on those months a half a decade later, Bill would marvel at their quietude.

The only hint of what was to come was his increasing restlessness over that winter's failed effort to stop Hurwitz, a vague discomfort that was compounded by the sputtering end to *Murphy v. Pacific Lumber*, the legal challenge Judge Schwarzer had shoved down his and the Murphys' throats in February, right before the Eel began rising. Once the merger went forward, everyone involved in the case recognized that it had to be tied off, but Maxxam's attorneys were not content to simply have it dropped. They also wanted the Murphys to release them from any potential future lawsuits and sign a covenant promising never to sue Hurwitz or Maxxam again. If they didn't, Maxxam intended to take the Murphys back into Schwarzer's court and get not only a formal dismissal, but also an order requiring Warren, Woody, and their sister to pay the legal fees incurred by Hurwitz, Maxxam, and PL in defending themselves against the Murphys' actions. That could cost the siblings at least half a million dollars, and given Schwarzer's attitude, Maxxam's chances of getting what they wanted seemed large. In addition, the Murphys' San Francisco lawyers had already promised their clients' submission. Warren and Woody, however, were proud and still pissed off, though both knew paying Hurwitz's court fees would amount to throwing good money after bad. So they just dragged their feet, postponing any agreement that might satisfy Maxxam.

By the time spring turned to summer, this attitude provoked a series of increasingly threatening letters from Ezra Levin that Bertain, having now assumed all of the responsibility for the case, had to attempt to answer. Levin's pressure was relentless, pointed, and effective and Bertain eventually ran out of excuses. Following their attorney's advice, the Murphys finally shuffled up to the table, ready to eat their last crow. The document they signed pledged them and their heirs to forever discharge Hurwitz, Maxxam, Elam, the old Pacific Lumber board of directors, and a handful of other Maxxam subsidiaries "from any and all causes of action, damages, claims, liabilities, obligations and demands of whatever kind or nature, in law or equity, known or unknown."

Afterward, Woody went out into the woods with his new logging company, staying there from sunup to sundown, and Warren moved to San Diego to start his life over, running a small cabinetmaking business. Bertain returned to his practice, overlooking the waterbed showroom, but the taste of that humiliation remained in his mouth for months.

His first response was to become a fanatical reader of *The Wall Street Journal*, tracking anything to do with takeovers, junk bonds, and Drexel Burnham Lambert. Bill was looking to figure out just how that son of a bitch had done it, where he'd come from, and, above all else, just where along the way he'd stepped over the boundary of the law. He read, beginning to end, every story that fell within the play of his curiosity. He absorbed them, steadily increasing the weight of the figuring he directed at Hurwitz's move. He expected something would float to the surface and lead him forward, and he was right.

The newspaper story that finally did so concerned one Dennis Levine, a young investment banker who'd worked briefly in Drexel Burnham Lambert's New York office. Levine had been charged with using his insider access to planned mergers and takeovers in order to secretly trade in the involved stocks, making a small fortune quickly and in complete violation of securities law. In May, the *Journal* reported that Levine had cut a plea bargain with Federal prosecutors in New York and was prepared to turn state's evidence. Several more stories followed, speculating just who the former Drexel operator might incriminate. The name mentioned most often was that of Ivan Boesky, King of the Arbs. And, of course, any reference to Boesky caught Bertain's eye. He didn't know what the King of Arbs had been doing in the PL deal, but he doubted it could have all been aboveboard.

Part of Bertain's faith that the truth would surface was his sense of the surrounding situation. He could see a drift to the events he now tracked and it was running against the empire built by Michael Milken and the stock raids his junk bond shop had helped generate. The savings and loan industry—a key element in Drexel's ability to supply a seemingly limitless market for junk financing—was beginning to come apart at the seams. An escalating succession of failures were showing up on the doorstep of the federal authorities who, by law, were obliged to guarantee the great majority of the S&Ls' deposits. The uneasiness of government regulators with developments on Wall Street had also generated the Levine case and their Boesky investigation. Bertain was convinced those combined movements would eventually start squeezing secrets out of the woodwork, if, of course, he could afford to hang around and wait.

While the Levine stories were running in the *Journal*, Bill spent several weeks considering his first step toward renewing his involvement in the PL takeover case. He almost called the federal attorney in San Francisco on several occasions to argue for an investigation of the Pacific Lumber takeover, but kept holding back. Levine's turning evidence changed that line of thinking somewhat. Now he wondered, why San Francisco? The action on this question was obviously in New York. Bertain was worried about sounding like some sour-grapes kook out of the backwoods and worried that while he had a lot of information around the issue, he had no evidence of wrongdoing. These were, after all, just suspicions. But Bertain's handwringing was only a hesitation, destined finally to give way. In May, Bertain put in calls to Charles Carbury, the special assistant U.S. attorney in New York mentioned in the *Journal* stories, and Ira Sorkin, chief of enforcement with the SEC in Washington, D.C., also mentioned. Bertain left a message that he wished to discuss Ivan Boesky's role in the takeover of the Pacific Lumber Company by Maxxam.

Carbury called back within an hour.

Bertain began their conversation by admitting that he might be wasting Carbury's time. So, if he was, he had to apologize up front.

But he did think that the government ought to look into just what went on in the Pacific Lumber tender offer this last fall and winter. Carbury told him not to apologize. Most of the information the government was able to get in these kinds of cases came in over the transom from people the prosecutors had never heard of before. That was how they'd got Levine—an unsolicited tip from a stockbroker in Venezuela. So, there was nothing to apologize for. At the same time, it was obvious from his blank response to all mentions of Pacific Lumber and Maxxam that Carbury had no idea what Bertain was talking about.

Bertain spent the next hour filling him in.

He admitted that he didn't know what role Levine might have had or even whether he had any in it, but Boesky had been all over the PL deal, riding Hurwitz and Milken's flank, without making any real move of his own. Maybe Levine knew something about it. Whatever had happened, Bertain suspected it had violated securities laws. Bill would love to make the investigation himself but he, of course, had none of the resources Carbury had at his disposal. He no longer even had a case or a client, but he did have a dozen file boxes full of depositions and research left over from this winter's failed litigation. If he had to take a guess, Bertain would expect to find that Hurwitz and Milken and Boesky had been parking stock and making an end run around the 5 percent requirements enforced by the SEC. And, of course, Pacific Lumber's own 5 percent provisions. He then gave Carbury a detailed description of the old PL bylaws, of the timing of the raid, of Boesky's 5 percent interest in PL's shares over the course of the tender offer, of Boesky's fall phone calls, and of Drexel's affidavit in Schwarzer's court, denying all holdings of Pacific Lumber shares. Bertain allowed that all he really had were a handful of suspicions but, then again, suspicions were the currency of prosecutors.

Carbury asked him to send along any information he had and Bertain promised to put together a package of documents and newspaper clippings.

Bertain tied off the conversation with a plea. This whole takeover was going to be a disaster, he said. And while catastrophe in Humboldt County might seem small potatoes back in New York, out here it looked a whole lot more like the end of the world. He hoped Carbury would at least make it clear that these guys were not free to pillage the economy at the expense of places like Humboldt.

Sorkin at the SEC in Washington called Bertain back the next day and Bertain spent forty-five minutes filling him in. His plea was, by then, even stronger. The greedy and power hungry were taking everything now. That was like stealing from the mouths of our grandchildren, robbing their future. He hoped the SEC could do something about it.

Bertain had several more, much shorter, phone calls with Carbury and Sorkin over the course of the summer and into the fall. While he had no case yet and no client, he did have a strategy. He was going to imitate the bird that followed along after rhinos, feeding on whatever got turned over in the greater beast's ponderous meanderings. The only way this case was ever going to get made was if the government and the press began chasing it and doing the legwork that Bertain himself could not do. He was already spending a majority of his time digging through all the depositions from the unsuccessful state court cases against the tender offer, and he didn't even have a client he could bill. That had, in turn, created a sag in his cash flow at a time when he was assuming more debt than he'd ever had in his life. Borrowing enough money to build out on his lot in McKinleyville had been a big step and he'd ended up starting the house late. Now he was worrying about money and spending all his spare moments racing to get a roof on it before rainy season began. Rebecca was due in the spring and the birth was not going to be cheap, not to mention, of course, the child. Despite all that financial pressure, he still devoted himself to the Pacific Lumber takeover, sifting and sorting, making phone calls, reading articles, hashing it over and over and over. And billing no one.

In October, that didn't change, but at least he got a client. Realizing that he had to register a lawsuit soon, even if it remained inactive, or lose legal standing for violation of procedural time limits, Bill found Don Jose Thompson, a retired timber worker who was willing to proceed—though he couldn't pay anything—and filed *Don Jose Thompson v. Gene Elam et al.* The suit reframed a lot of the charges of the earlier Murphy suits, naming the familiar list of defendants including Hurwitz and Maxxam. It also launched some new legal tangents, accusing the old board of having ignored Article 10 of the old PL bylaws that instructed it to consider a larger impact than just the financial one on the shareholders. To Bertain, the Thompson suit was a foot in the legal door. He did not expect active litigation on it soon. It still seemed a sidelight, despite his obsession. He only expected to wait and see what kind of information developed out of the government probes.

The next link in that chain of discovery came on November 14, 1986, when the *Journal* reported that Ivan Boesky, the King of Arbs, had lived up to speculations and cut his own deal with prosecutors, agreeing to plead guilty to a crime, pay a $100 million fine, and, just like Levine, turn state's evidence.

Boesky's fall echoed up one side of Wall Street and down the other, all the way to Beverly Hills. One of Michael Milken's acolytes in the Wilshire Boulevard bond shop was in a meeting with Milken the day news of Boesky's turning evidence came over the Dow Jones. Drexel was pitching one of the largest S&Ls in southern California to buy more of its issues. The meeting was at 2:00 P.M. and news of Boesky's deal had been released at 1:00. Milken's face was the color of a sheet. He said little and left almost as soon as the meeting got under way.

Four days later, back in Eureka, Bill Bertain had what he would remember as his "vision."

It came at a time when Bill was inundated with worry. He'd gotten his roof on—beating the first raindrops of the fall by about five minutes—but he was still plagued with nerves. He didn't know what to do about all this PL stuff. It was eating his practice and he could not let it go. Who would stop these guys if he didn't? He couldn't walk away from a crime committed on his own doorstep. So he prayed and thought and worried and prayed, writing a few wills and doing some real estate law to keep some money coming through the front door, and then he prayed and thought and worried some more. Righting injustice was, after all, an obligation imposed by the teachings of Christ, not just a recreational option.

Early in the morning of November 18, Bill Bertain, tenth of the ten children of Louis Bertain, sat up in bed. He was completely awake in an instant. His mind was clear. There was nothing dreamy in his presence. He was poised out on the very tip of himself, knowing deeply. His certainty was absolute. If he kept after it, he could do it. God would take care of those who did God's work.

Bill walked down the hall from the tiny upstairs bedroom in his old house in Eureka. Rebecca was still asleep. The certainty followed along, enveloping Bill everywhere he went. He finally returned to bed, the certainty with him while he fell asleep. And it was still there when he woke at his usual 6:00 A.M. God would take care of those who did God's work.

Bill Bertain's only stop that morning on his way to the office was the newsstand for his *Wall Street Journal.* At the office, his first act was to read it, sipping the murky product of his Mr. Coffee machine. His cowboy boots were propped on the usual pile dominating his tiny office. When he reached the *Journal*'s page three, he threw his feet up in the air and brought them down on the floor, whooping and slamming his fist on the arm of his chair.

The story in front of him tracked the fallout from the Boesky plea bargain. This account said the King of Arbs was talking about Michael Milken, whose name almost never left Bertain's mind, and about Boyd Jeffries, a stockbroker of whom Bertain had never heard. SEC investigators were also serving summonses to a long list of Drexel executives. In the last of the story's seventeen paragraphs, the *Journal* reported that the SEC investigation was "concentrating on transactions involving at least twelve companies." One of those was "Maxxam Group Inc.'s acquisition of Pacific Lumber Co."

At last, Bertain crowed. The door to the inside of Charles Hurwitz's sneak attack was now open. Barely, of course, but it was a start.

28

By then, the hippies were mobilized.

That mobilization began with the second face-to-face meeting between Darryl Cherney and Greg King, this time in July in Piercy, the remains of a logging hamlet just off the freeway some ten miles south of Garberville. There had once been hundreds of people living in Piercy and six mills there cutting full bore. But that was around the time of the Korean War. Now, the gas station and the bakery, the last remaining businesses in town, were boarded up. The final vestige of Piercy's boom times was the Bridgewood Motel, down the old two-lane highway, on a short bluff over a bend in the Eel, where the roadway crossed the river on a steel girder bridge. The Bridgewood had a flat roof, thirty-eight units, and a swimming pool, generally untended but full of algae-ridden water. The motel no longer rented by the night, but only month by month, and usually had a dozen residents, all of them longhairs. Darryl Cherney was the Bridgewood's live-in manager. He and Greg King had been exchanging letters since they last saw each other.

They were an oddly matched pair. Darryl charged into encounters, looking to be the lead singer. Greg hung back some—more anxious, more watchful. Greg was the woodsman, at home roaming ridges with a topographical map, sleeping at whatever spot he found when the sun went down. Darryl was indeed now feral—

having shed his domestication and returned to a "natural" state—but, even so, he'd had a long way to come. Up until his early adulthood, years spent almost entirely on the west side of Manhattan, he was frightened of mud, most plants not located in Central Park, all bugs, snakes, and the entire outdoors—the saving of which was the chief subject of the songs he wrote and sang at Greenwich Village folk club hootenannies and the like. Darryl was the word artist, the pitch man, the hustler. Darryl's father was a high school teacher, his mother an office manager. Greg's father was a small-town banker, his mother an elementary school teacher. Greg was the researcher. Greg knew the forest and knew what all the specifications in a timber harvest plan looked like on the ground floor. Greg was the explorer. Darryl was the executive producer and lyricist. During the time since they'd last seen each other, Darryl had been supplementing the free room he received for watching over the Bridgewood with cash from some day labor at a car wash in Garberville and a stint of shovel work for a local hemp farmer. Greg had been carrying on his alternative press career. A month or so ago, he'd been approached by a Sonoma County logger on the empty dirt shoulder of a road out to the coast. The man was known for his harassment of hippies. And he was enormous. He pulled over when he saw Greg parked there. He just wanted to let Greg know that empty stretches of road like this could be dangerous. Especially if you fucked over loggers in your hippie newspaper. To Greg, this was all serious business. Darryl, on the other hand, once organized a pee-in to protest a call by Ronald Reagan for mandatory government drug testing, convincing several hundred people to mail urine samples to the White House. When the containers were all ruptured by the sorting machinery in the Garberville post office, much of that part of the county's mail smelled like a public toilet for several days. Darryl was informed of the disaster and shrugged sheepishly. When you were saving the planet, you won a few, you lost a few.

That July day at the Bridgewood Motel in Piercy, Greg and Darryl talked and talked and talked and talked. When the day heated up, they went around the bend in the Eel to a spot where the current had carved a swimming hole around a large rock in mid-channel. There they swam and talked and, when darkness fell, built a fire on the river bank and talked some more. Their exchanges covered the gamut of subjects, most related in some way to saving Mother Earth. Breaks in the conversation were full of splashing, eating, and Darryl's singing along with his guitar. Each of the two men brought a subject to their encounter that would define their campaign to come.

Darryl's contribution was the organization Earth First! He'd first seen one of its stickers—a green fist with its name, complete with exclamation point—glued to a windowpane on the day he first arrived in Garberville with Kingfisher. It was love at first sight. Founded in 1978, Earth First! was a loose conglomeration of people who endorsed its motto, "No compromise in defense of Mother Earth." Its founders, self-styled rednecked environmentalists, envisioned it as as hard-edged option to the bureaucratic compromise characterizing the more established environmental organizations. Their inspiration was an Edward Abbey novel, *The Monkey Wrench Gang*, about a group of "eco-warriors" who wage a guerrilla campaign to save the environment from the pillage of civilization. Earth First! advocated personal confrontation and whatever else it took, including "monkey wrenching" or sabotage, to defend the planet and *all* the species that inhabited it. In timber country, Earth First! was synonymous with tree spiking—driving nails into trees to foul any logging machinery used on them. The practice created a very active threat to the safety of lumberjacks and millworkers but finding someone to blame for it was next to impossible. Though the Federal Bureau of Investigation had already classified the group as "terrorist," Earth First! had no organization to speak of, no national headquarters, no national staff, just a loose group of identifiable founders and a national newspaper that came out every now and then. They considered themselves a movement of independent practitioners. Just a tribe, no hierarchy. They had one national rendezvous a year, modeled on those of early nineteenth-century Rocky Mountain trappers, but otherwise, everyone was more or less on their own.

Darryl had wanted to join Earth First! on that day he first saw their sticker, but he spent several fruitless months trying to find out how. At first, no one claimed to know anything about them. Then, finally, one of the dreadlocked regulars at the EPIC office allowed that they were "just a bunch of people who do things." When Darryl pressed and asked where he could find them, he was told "everywhere and nowhere." After several more weeks, Darryl learned how to subscribe to the Earth First! newspaper and did so. When he then asked how he could attend an Earth First! meeting, he was told just to call one. Whoever came would be Earth First!

Darryl liked the idea. These guys, he told Greg, are really pissed. Greg just nodded.

Greg's contribution was their focus on the Pacific Lumber Company. He had been vaguely aware of Hurwitz's takeover, but had only begun to really focus in on PL after reading an article that summer on the business page of the *San Francisco Chronicle*. The story reported on the new Drexel issue of PL bonds, identifying Pacific Lumber as the principal holder of old-growth redwood timberlands in the United States. Its new parent company, the Maxxam Group, was pledging expanded harvests to cover the costs of the financing. King soon obtained a copy of the bond prospectus and learned the actual extent of Pacific Lumber's holdings and that their cut was going to be at least doubled. With a little more research, he concluded this was going to be an absolute disaster for what little old growth remained in Humboldt County.

Feral Darryl agreed. He also thought these guys were a great target—a greedy corporation with two sinister *x*'s side by side in the middle of its name, run by a slick, mysterious Texas predator whose name ended in a *z*. There was a lot that could be done with that. The only thing lacking was a real effort to stop them. The Sinkyone fight was dribbling to an end, with the state about to purchase the old growth and a bunch of cutover property from Georgia Pacific for inclusion in a wilderness area, so there might be a pool of people to call on. To succeed, they needed to build something that was on the front page every week, week in, week out. They needed to make Maxxam and this son of a bitch Hurwitz into household names. They had to. Otherwise it was going to be an ecological massacre. No one else was going to stop them, that was for sure.

Despite Greg and Darryl's mutual enthusiasm, the only conclusion the two of them reached that day in Piercy was a "maybe."

The real conclusion came over the phone several days later. Greg called the Bridgewood from his tiny apartment in Sonoma.

Somebody had to do something about Pacific Lumber, Darryl repeated.

Greg thought for a moment. Then he said that it must be time for Earth First! to meet.

With that, the Humboldt County Earth First! Redwood Action Team was born.

By October, they'd held a conference attended by a couple dozen activists from all along the North Coast and announced themselves to the rest of Earth First! at the national rendezvous, where a couple hundred backwoods types gathered at Big Basin state park, in the Santa Cruz Mountains two hours south of San Francisco. Afterward, about a hundred participants in the rendezvous and about half that many folks from Humboldt and Mendocino met in front of the Pacific Lumber Company headquarters building on Washington Street in the city. They staged some guerrilla theatre, sang, gave a few speeches, and regularly cut loose with a bevy of hellacious animal howls. The company locked its doors as soon as they showed up. Inside, the last of the shipping boxes were around the hallways. The remaining occupants made jokes about what would happen if those weirdos did their howling bit back up in Humboldt.

The Earth First! Redwood Action Team debuted in Humboldt in November in Arcata, home of Humboldt State University, with another rally featuring guerrilla theatre, singing, and a few speeches. The howls were considerably fewer but they drew and kept a crowd of several hundred. The less than sympathetic among their observers joked about what would happen if they ever took their act into real timber country. Arcata didn't count. The college town had fifteen different places to buy tofu. The meat-and-potatoes part of the county was where it all really mattered.

Darryl Cherney ran into that derision shortly after the Arcata rally in a telephone conversation with the editor of *The Beacon*, a notoriously pro–timber-industry weekly published in Fortuna. Darryl had called in his weekly ritual of phone calls to the press.

Why hadn't *The Beacon* even sent anybody to cover the Arcata demonstration? he asked its editor.

Come on, the editor chided. When are you guys going to have the balls to demonstrate in front of the mill in Scotia? He'd print that on the front page.

Get ready, Darryl said. That was what he'd called about. Earth First! was headed into the Pacific Lumber Company town on the third day of December.

The Beacon had a reporter there for that one.

The rally was staged at noon, at a spot down near the freeway, separated by a chain-link fence from the looming presence of Mill A, with PACIFIC LUMBER on its side. By doing the rally part of things here, Darryl pointed out, the television cameras would be able to get the mill in the background of all their shots. The local cameras were there and Darryl had also turned up a crew from the San Francisco PBS station, who were producing a fifteen-minute segment for *The MacNeil-Lehrer News Hour.* This was a big video break and Darryl was in a tizzy. Then, the night before the event, he came down with laryngitis. His voice was raspy at its best and this made him almost unintelligible. Darryl nonetheless went ballistic when it was suggested he skip his song at the end.

And sure enough, Darryl sang it, sounding much like a longhorn in labor:

"Where are we gonna work when the trees are gone?
Will the big boss have us wash his car or maybe mow his lawn?
I'm a man, I'm a man, I'm a lumberjack man
But I fear it ain't for long
Where are we gonna work when the trees are gone? . . ."

About seventy-five people had come down from Garberville and Arcata to listen to him and, when he finished, they marched up Main Street to the company offices and back, through the entire length of Scotia's business district. Almost all of them carried signs, some sang, others danced. Nobody in town had ever seen anything quite like this. They'd seen hippies, of course. Everybody'd been to Garberville. But to see so many of them, parading downtown, now that was something.

And, for the next few days, the townspeople of Scotia chattered with each other about it. Had they heard the singer who sounded like a gearbox somebody forgot to grease? Did they see that hippie girl whose titties were about to fall out of her shirt? And how about that guy with all those rings on his nose? The sign he was carrying said LOVE YOUR MOTHER. Can you believe it? There was another guy who was actually wearing a skirt. Did you ever see anything like it in all your born days?

It was early and the approaching war over the redwoods still seemed like an exotic new game from which nothing truly threatening could possibly arise.

29

John Campbell was the exception.

PL's executive vice president tried not to underestimate anything. He also knew there was a lot at stake. His army of fellers was mostly out in the residuals now, doing whatever work winter would permit, and, since the rains were light this year, they were making some genuine speed. The company foresters were also out in Salmon Creek, planning skid roads for use when John turned the fellers loose on the company's mother lode. In the middle of all this, these hippies had shown up out of nowhere saying PL was a bad guy for cutting its own property and that somebody ought to stop them. It was crazy, but crazier things had happened; this, John knew well. And this was no bloody time to let anything sneak up on him. While everyone else in town was laughing at the scraggly parade, the Pacific Lumber Company's executive vice president was trying to learn more about just who these people were.

His first face-to-face encounter with Earth First! was with Greg King in January 1987. The meeting was precipitated by a letter Greg mailed to several dozen industry leaders and state politicians in the aftermath of the Scotia demonstration. In effect, it was a warning. "A protracted, heated battle over PALCO's virgin timber will continue for as long as the company logs it," he wrote. King proposed negotiations to begin immediately on an agreement that would "save *all* of PALCO's remaining old growth forests." The option, he reminded them, was "*years* of litigation, protests, legislative debate, civil disobedience, and overall bitter conflict."

John Campbell responded with an invitation for King to come by Scotia and talk.

Their discussion lasted an hour.

Greg pointed out that PL's old-growth groves were the last significant remnants of the primordial forest that hadn't yet been protected. If they were leveled, all of the old-growth-dependent animal species, now making their last stand in this habitat, would wither and die in the narrow confines of the parks. All the remaining ancient forest had to be preserved. It represented a unique ecosystem that, unlike the trees, would not grow back. It was a balance of elements that had taken centuries to develop. Logging would doom it.

John thought the sacred air Greg draped over old growth was entirely misplaced. You know what old growth was? It was nothing but dying trees, a wasted bloody resource. Those ancient trees had long since stopped growing and were slowly moving down the death curve until they could no longer stand upright. There was no such thing as saving them. The only question was when to bring them down. Logging did so when they were still useful. And cutting them helped the forest; it didn't hurt it. Logging made room for new growth, for healthy young trees to thrive. Cutting trees was a boon.

With all due respect, Greg argued, Campbell was kidding himself if he really believed all that. The whole North Coast was strewn with the damage of past harvests. What little was still untouched ought to stay that way.

King was out of touch, John snapped. No one logged that way anymore. And PL, of all companies, had an impeccable record of stewardship of its land. On top of all that, the forest had remarkable powers of regeneration.

Look, Campbell continued, walking to the office window and pointing at the forested slopes on the other side of the freeway. That entire hill had been reduced to nothing but stumps, bald as a billiard ball, less than a hundred years ago. Now the trees were so thick you'd think it had been that way forever.

Greg King bridled. Campbell's tone was patronizing and insulting. He talked as though he knew more about forests and redwoods and logging than anybody else around.

For his part, John Campbell thought King was berserk. This scruffy kid and his buddies didn't just want PL to stop cutting trees, they wanted people off the land entirely. This Earth First! outfit was really a movement against civilization itself.

You know, Greg, John continued as he sat back at the desk. If you accomplish your goals, I'm going to have to start laying people off. His voice now had an edge and his exasperation showed. Where did Greg want him to start? Should he start at age 49 and go down? Or maybe 50 and go up? Would Greg come along with him to deliver the layoff notices and explain his position so they'd know why John was having to do this?

Greg objected. John had to understand. In anything of this magnitude, there's going to be some suffering. This was far more than a matter of employment. The survival of the planet was at issue.

John Campbell could feel his temper rising and, with a curt nod, announced that their discussion was over. He thought the conversation had gone nowhere and, for the first time, entertained the possibility that these Earth Firsters just might be dangerous.

King rose, shook Campbell's hand, and left. He thought talking to people like Campbell was a useless, if necessary, exercise. The real power, he knew, lay up the chain of command. And that was where he headed next.

30

On March 25, the Maxxam Group held a stockholders' meeting in the Starlight Room of the Miramar Sheraton Hotel in Santa Monica on the west end of greater Los Angeles.

It was a delicate situation for Charles Hurwitz. He was in the process of merging the Maxxam Group into his MCO Holdings, an in-house takeover. His principal personal holding company, Federated Development, owned 67 percent of MCO and 49.6 percent of Maxxam. Six of the ten directors of each company served simultaneously on both boards. The delicacy facing Hurwitz that March surrounded the fate of the Maxxam Group's minority shareholders. Several had made loud complaints and would eventually file lawsuits alleging that MCO Holdings' offer to the Maxxam Group of $13 worth of stock—three dollars over February's market price but at least $40 a share less than the worth of its assets—was shortchanging them. One of the examples they pointed to was the declared value of the Maxxam Group's Pacific Lumber Company. For the purposes of this merger, it was valued at $840 million, but in evaluating its worth for the purposes of depreciation, the company's hired consultants had estimated its value over $2 billion. In effect, the dissidents claimed, Hurwitz was being allowed to buy PL on the cheap a second time and they were not being allowed a share in Maxxam's previous windfall. Hurwitz was unruffled by the complaints. He understood that these kinds of ripples surrounded all deals. Here in Los Angeles, he intended to convince his shareholders to approve the merger. He was used to handling these situations and what he couldn't handle, Ezra Levin could.

The only ripple he hadn't anticipated was that Greg King would show up at the meeting as well. At 10:00 A.M., Greg and a handful of longhairs, comprising almost the entire Los Angeles chapter of Earth First!, set up a picket line outside the Sheraton.

Greg got his first glimpse of Hurwitz shortly after the picketing began, when the Texan and the head of Maxxam's New York office appeared at the Miramar's entrance, on the other side of the police lines. Greg noticed Hurwitz's suit most of all. He guessed it was worth more than his own car. King had no idea what Hurwitz was planning to do at this meeting. He figured that just Hurwitz's decision to have it at a gilt-edged place like the Miramar told him everything he needed to know about Charles Hurwitz and his like. Money was everything with these guys and that they had it allowed them to make their own rules. In truth they were no better than thieves, mobsters, stealing life itself off the hillsides and out of the watersheds.

Several Earth Firsters shook signs at Hurwitz, with slogans like "Stop Maxxam Chainsaw Massacre" and "Axe Maxxam, Not Redwoods."

Greg shouted. Mr. Hurwitz, he yelled, I'm Greg King.

Hurwitz snapped his head in King's direction.

The move startled Greg, but he kept shouting. Mr. Hurwitz, people in Humboldt County will really suffer from the cutting. If—

Hurwitz turned abruptly on his heel and disappeared into the Miramar.

A half hour later, Greg King followed him, but it wasn't easy. King was stopped immediately at the police line. He was carrying a slide show about the redwoods that he intended to project for the shareholders.

Nobody from the demonstration was allowed inside, the cop said.

Greg said he had to attend the meeting.

No way.

But, Greg grinned, I'm a stockholder.

The grinning hippie then produced a receipt from a stock brokerage, proving, indeed, that Greg King—which is who he was—

owned six shares of the Maxxam Group. The entire Earth First! Redwood Action Team—namely, he and Darryl and whoever around Garberville they could convince to donate—had pooled their money the day before he left and bought what they hoped would provide Greg legitimate entry.

The cop took Greg's receipt off to his boss and then returned after several minutes. Greg was waved through into the Miramar lobby.

From there, it was a long hallway to the Starlight Room. At the door, he was stopped again.

Nobody from the demonstration was allowed inside, the security guard said.

Greg announced he was a stockholder and produced his receipt. When that had no effect, he demanded to speak to the security guard's supervisor.

Eventually an elderly man with a heavy limp appeared. He was the supervisor. What did King want?

King wanted inside, but when the supervisor consulted the list of shareholders supplied by the Maxxam Group's New York office, it did not include any Greg King.

That must be because he'd only purchased his shares very recently, King pointed out.

The supervisor said he'd see about that, took Greg's receipt, and disappeared into the Starlight Room. When he returned, he reiterated that Greg wasn't on the list, but, in view of the receipt, he would be allowed into the meeting. He would not, however, be allowed to talk.

Once inside, Greg found a seat near the audience microphone, anyway. There were about thirty-five other shareholders present. With Ezra Levin in the chair, the meeting was grinding through a discussion of a merger resolution and King listened and listened and listened, hoping for an opening into which to insert himself. To Greg, the discussion was no more than monotonous business bullshit, all running together at the edges. When the resolution concerning the MCO merger had finally been passed—the new merged corporation would eventually be named Maxxam Inc.—and there was a momentary pause before the final item on the agenda, Greg stepped up to the mike to seize the moment.

His name was Greg King, he announced, and even though he'd

been told he could not address the meeting, he thought he'd do so anyway.

Ezra Levin interrupted and told him he was not addressing anybody. The meeting had an agenda to follow and King did not set that agenda. The company set the agenda.

Greg insisted on just thirty seconds of the meeting's time. He had traveled here all the way from Humboldt County, where the Pacific Lumber Company was about to wreak havoc.

Levin repeated that King would not set the agenda and he should sit down and stop his interruption.

To emphasize Levin's point, two security guards moved in on either side of King. One turned the microphone so it couldn't pick up King's voice. Greg then sat down and stayed that way. Just to make sure, the security guards stayed nearby until the last item on the agenda was dispensed with and the meeting adjourned. Then Greg made another move on the public address system.

Humboldt County was going to be devastated by the change in Pacific Lumber, he shouted into the live mike.

The audience was filing out, paying little attention. Some turned their heads to see what was going on, but not many. The major exception was Ezra Levin, who, seeing King still attempting to make his address, drew his hand across his throat in a signal to the security guards. Moments later, the mike went dead. Greg shouted that he would be by the door to talk individually to anyone who wanted. He then stood there while all the stockholders filed by and ignored him. Then he noticed Charles Hurwitz across the room, talking to a reporter.

When King got there, Hurwitz was telling the reporter that, in fact, nothing had changed in Humboldt.

King barged in and challenged that notion, citing the doubled cut. What Hurwitz was saying was a lie. In truth, if that cut continued, Humboldt faced environmental collapse.

The reporter looked back at Hurwitz. The Texan's expression was a constant flat surface, unruffled by the hippie's interruption.

Maxxam was aware of these worries, Hurwitz noted, and the company would keep its eye on them. Then, without changing his face, he walked off, across the Starlight Room and into the Miramar Sheraton's hall.

Not long after their Santa Monica encounter, Greg attempted to contact Hurwitz directly, sending a handwritten note to Maxxam's Houston headquarters:

> Dear Mr. Hurwitz, he wrote,
> I hope you have contemplated the results of Pacific Lumber's current deforestation. . . . Nothing would be more sane, apt, and fair than your right now calling a halt to the old-growth liquidation. . . . Think of your children and their children and others who must follow. Think of the animals crushed and killed and made extinct due to the deforestation. You are a very wealthy man: Why do you need the life of these forests to fill your pockets more? . . . *Please.*
>
> Greg King

Charles Hurwitz did not answer the note.

Even if he had, Greg noted, it would have been all words. King loved language—it was one of the elements that had drawn him to journalism—but now, in the midst of a campaign in which words were thrown about with abandon, they often seemed to lose their meaning, turning mushy and without substance. There were just too damn many of them, so they began to suffocate him, and, in the grips of that claustrophobia, Greg needed to get away, to escape into a silence where no one spoke. Usually, when such moods struck him, he headed into the forest by himself. He did so again almost immediately after his return from L.A., on Saturday, when the logging shows were closed for the weekend.

Exploration was always an additional object of these forays and his hike at the end of March was no exception. This time, he headed cross-country from Kneeland Road, one of the two-lane county thoroughfares that wound through the Coast Range behind Fortuna, linking tiny hamlets with names like Rosseau, Quarry, and Fulton— mostly wide spots in the road where an all-but-forgotten lumber mill had sawed boards for a few years in the old days. When he was dropped off on the road shoulder at sunup, Greg immediately headed into the bush, hauling a fifty-pound pack and following his topographical map. He was looking for two large parcels of old growth for which Pacific Lumber had recently filed timber harvest plans with the California Department of Forestry. Those timber harvest plans, registered with the CDF as numbers 87–240 and 87–241,

were about to be processed for approval and were located deeper
into the forest than Greg had ever been before. All he knew was that
even at some three hundred and fifty acres, they were still only a
fraction of a large Pacific Lumber holding that encompassed the
headwaters of both Salmon Creek and the Little South Fork of the
Elk River. Greg expected to see some splendid country but when
he left Kneeland Road behind, he had no idea he was about to
frame the principal battleground for the "*years* of litigation, protests,
legislative debate, civil disobedience, and overall bitter conflict" of
which his letter had warned in January. The four-thousand-acre
stand of primoridial *sequoia sempervirens* for which he was headed
would eventually wedge in Maxxam's throat like a dog hung up on a
chicken bone.

Greg King's excursion was, of course, trespassing. He intruded
on the Pacific Lumber Company's property when he crossed a brisk
knee-deep creek some ten minutes in from the road. The first of the
company's old-growth stands he encountered was one he had ex-
plored several weeks earlier. The Redwood Action Team made it a
policy to give names to such locations, so they would not just be
known by their THP number. This one had been named All Species
Grove. The floor beneath its titanic redwoods was overrun with
ferns and small vine maples strewn around twenty-foot-tall lichen-
covered rocks. Moss hung in long strings from yew trees and water
dripped everywhere, feeding a meandering pristine tributary of
Lawrence Creek. The harvest of All Species had already been approved by the CDF and would commence in a matter of days. Greg
thought it was one of the finest groves on the planet, a priceless treasure, but he didn't linger for just one more look. Moving west, he
found a logging road, cut in preparation for the fellers' entrance to
All Species, and followed it to a four-way intersection of similar
roads where he picked up another dirt lane and continued west,
passing through a recent PL logging show where the mud was knee-
deep and laced with streaks of bright red sawdust. Numbers 87–240
and -241 were somewhere in the old growth that began on the far
side of that killing field.

Inside this forest, some of the ferns were ten feet tall and the sorrel was near knee-deep. A fine mist, dripping almost invisibly from
the redwood canopy far overhead, filled the air and made every step
Greg took slippery. Salted here and there along his path were huck-

leberry bushes, thimbleberries, and salal, the wild grape. Greg camped among the ferns near Salmon Creek that night and, early the next morning, headed upslope to cross the ridge and drop down into the drainage of the Little South Fork of the Elk. Along the ridgeline, however, his plans went awry. Here, where the sun's penetration was greater than anywhere else, the undergrowth was a solid matted tangle of vines webbed in among tiny, impenetrable oak trees and huckleberry bushes. It took him two hours to traverse a matter of yards and the more he moved, the deeper in vegetation he seemed to bog down. In some locations he had to fling his body against the wall of leaves, often not budging it at all. Eventually, he abandoned his plans to reach the Little South Fork and just attempted to extricate himself however he could. After almost half a day of thrashing, he finally stumbled onto a skid road. The skid road led to a wider logging road, churned into slop by trucks and Caterpillars, and the logging road led into a PL clear cut that looked as though it had been made using high explosives and a flight of B-52s. Stumps and earth were strewn across a hideous moonscape. Greg identified this holocaust on his map as 86–199, two hundred acres targeted during the company's initial escalation. From the remains of it, he was able to find the way back to Kneeland Road.

Late that evening, Greg King was in a communal house in Arcata, eating tofu and smoking a joint with Darryl and several other Humboldt Earth Firsters. He enthralled them with descriptions of his latest venture into occupied territory. This place was positively surreal, he raved. And it just went on and on and on. The two THPs he was looking for were in the heart of the biggest hunk of old growth Greg had ever penetrated. Because of Salmon Creek and the Little South Fork of the Elk, he thought they ought to call it Headwaters Forest. And, Greg emphasized, keeping it intact might very well be the single most important thing they could do.

31

Saving Headwaters Forest was still only a vague aspiration, but even that glimmer would have seemed far more far-fetched if the Earth First! Redwood Action Team hadn't already made significant allies.

Perhaps the most significant of those as Humboldt's 1987 logging season got under way was Robert Sutherland, a.k.a. the Man Who Walks In The Woods, or to his friends, just plain Woods. The Man Who Walks In The Woods was the Mateel's leading eccentric genius. When he tooled into town from his home out in the Mattole watershed, driving an ancient VW bug, Woods né Sutherland, hirsute and hefty, looked more like old Badger from Toad Hall than like Perry Mason, but he was, in fact, an extraordinary legal practitioner. At forty—after having taught himself botany and become an acknowledged consultant on the plant species *ceonothus*—he committed to the fight over the Sinkyone, taught himself law, and then wrote the legal brief for *EPIC v. Johnson,* in which Garberville's tiny environmental organization won a landmark 1985 decision that eventually saved the Sinkyone and established a precedent for possibly overthrowing a great deal of timber law enforcement's status quo.

Woods lived out the Ettersburg Road, down seven miles of old logging tracks, far beyond the last power line and phone pole. His house was almost entirely windows and had been built by a deranged Vietnam veteran who was convinced people were sneaking up on him and, hence, wanted a clear field of fire in all directions. Eventually, the former grunt just turned the place over to Woods and split. Woods fit in easily in the Mateel but he was hardly a native. He'd grown up outside of Cleveland, the son of a Nobel laureate in medicine, and spent a good portion of his childhood roaming in the hardwood groves near his home. After dropping out of Western Reserve University, dropping out of a career as an artist, then dropping successively out of a job monitoring birds for New York City's Museum of Natural History, a long run as a hippie in the Haight-Ashbury, a brief career as a longshoreman, an intense apprenticeship in Zen, and a stint as the manager of a San Francisco apartment building, Robert Sutherland dropped completely out of urban civilization, moved to Humboldt, adopted the name The Man Who Walks In The Woods—which he sometimes abreviated as T.M.W.W.I.T.W.—and set up housekeeping in a tent on some friends' land out near the Lost Coast. His principal occupation soon became living up to his new name and he hiked constantly, exploring among the vast tracts of second-growth forest in southern Humboldt.

As natural as he felt in the forest, "back to the land" was not an easy transition: during Woods's first year in Humboldt his total income was $65 plus food stamps; his first residence and all his possessions were destroyed in a forest fire; and, when he built a crude shack to replace his torched tent, the shack was destroyed by a neighbor who, in the midst of attempting to sell his property to marijuana farmers, became convinced that in order to close the deal he needed the neighborhood empty and took a sledgehammer to Woods's handiwork. Still, T.M.W.W.I.T.W. persevered.

He felt a calling in this place and that calling was confirmed by a vision that visited him several years after he arrived. It appeared in two incidents in sequence, several months apart. The first was an extraordinarily vivid dream in which Shiva, the Hindu god of death and rebirth, appeared, standing in a perfect forest glen, framed by young redwoods and Douglas fir. The second half of Woods's revelation came on one of his long hikes, this time up the side of King's Peak, the four-thousand-foot anchor of the King Range, overlooking the Mattole out near the Lost Coast. When The Man Who Walks In The Woods crossed a ridgecrest just below its summit, he stumbled upon a perfect forest glen, framed by redwoods and Douglas fir, and quickly recognized it as the exact same one in which Shiva had appeared to him in his dream. Woods concluded from this coincidence that King's Peak was an atmic center of some sort, one of the few locations in the world where the universal soul identified in Hinduism welled up out of the planet.

Woods was also convinced that the planet would only survive if two things happened. First, human beings had to learn to control their nature so that they weren't constantly externalizing their desires and fears in a consumerism that was devastating every aspect of nature unfortunate enough to be identified as a "resource." Second, human beings needed to liberate their own wildness and, abandoning masses of unnecessary institutions—from paper money to excess clothing—find their identity within a biology that harmonized with their environment instead of fluttering at the mercies of the unceasing capital-driven demand to grow and grow and grow. Woods's botany had led him into the fight over the Sinkyone and he'd quickly become someone of great stature in the movement. He'd been the first to insist that no one be allowed to smoke reefer in the EPIC office and that the organization incorporate as a nonprofit institution and position itself to seize standing in the eyes of the organized bureaucracy that almost everyone in the Mateel had fled. Around Garberville, it was known that Woods understood how "the real world" worked and he was respected as a "deep thinker" and warrior for Mother Earth.

The Man Who Walks In The Woods first became involved in the struggle with the Pacific Lumber Company when he attended a meeting in January at the homestead of Gil Gregori and his wife, Cecilia Lanman, out on a low bluff overlooking the Mattole. Gregori had saved the purchase price of his homestead by working long days as a forklift operator and managing apartment houses on the side. He still oversaw a string of Bay Area properties, commuting south once or so a month, and spent the rest of the time turning his homestead into a farm, planting orchards and reclaiming it from the ravages of the hostile logging done along the Mattole around the time of the Korean War. Lanman was a former boycott organizer for the United Farmworkers Union and had helped found the school most of the young children in this part of the Mattole attended. Both Gil and Cecilia had been very active in the fight with Georgia Pacific over the Sinkyone and Cecilia, in particular, had gained a reputation for her fierce verbal confrontations with the Georgia Pacific underlings assigned to deal with them. The meeting at their home was called to discuss how to stop Pacific Lumber. Darryl was one of several who made presentations.

The drift of that all-day discussion was defined by the end of the fight over the Sinkyone: the success there had to be followed up and Pacific Lumber was the appropriate target. PL's change in their cut was now by far the most significant threat to the North Coast's old growth, which all of them were committed to protecting. Pacific Lumber, driven by some of the most naked capitalist greed of this century, was about to finish off everything that wasn't yet in a park. This was the timber industry's last great buffalo hunt. To fight it required a broad front of resistance: with direct action, in the political system, in the media, and, of course, in the courts.

And when it came to the courts, everyone deferred to The Man Who Walks In The Woods.

For his part, Woods liked what Greg King and Darryl Cherney were trying to organize. And he liked them, as well. He found both of the young men enormously sincere, though he occasionally thought the self-promotional aspects of Darryl a bit much. T.M.W.W.I.T.W. was also well prepared to launch a fresh legal strategy. In the last few months preceding the settlement of the Sinkyone dispute, he had developed a new brief, attempting to expand on the opening provided by *EPIC v. Johnson*. Since the Sinkyone fight had ended before he'd ever taken the brief into court, he was stuck with a legal argument waiting for a case to which to attach itself. He also thought the identification of the threat posed by Pacific Lumber was accurate. Its takeover by Maxxam and the subsequent change in the company's character might well mean the death knell for species like the marbled murrelet, the Olympic salamander, and the spotted owl. Woods needed little convincing.

But he still needed a case. And in order to get one, it wasn't sufficient to simply select an area and sue over it. The procedure required was quite specific. All timber cases had to be focused on a specific timber harvest plan and, in order to claim standing from which to sue, the plaintiffs had to have first participated in the administrative procedure by which the THP was processed. And all of this had to happen within an extremely limited time frame. Once a THP had been officially filed, the California Department of Forestry had thirty days in which to act or the THP became legal automatically. Usually, the THP was submitted informally first and CDF provided suggestions on how to bring the harvest plan into full compliance with the Z'Berg-Nejedly Forest Practices Act, the keystone of California's timber code. Upon formal submission, with the clock ticking, the public had the opportunity to make written commentary and the law required the CDF to respond in writing to each comment. Then CDF had to convene a THP Review Team meeting, at which the department was required to consult with representatives of Fish and Game and the state Water Quality Agency about the impact of the THPs in question. A second follow-up meeting was often required as well. The public was allowed to attend and participate in these meetings but rarely did. Usually the only "public" in attendance were representatives of the timber company filing the plans being discussed.

But that, Woods pointed out, was the way it was with all of California's timber statutes. The process was weighted to the lumber companies—only the submitter of the THP, for example, could grant an extension of the thirty-day time period—and only the lumber companies participated. Although Z'Berg-Nejedly was reputed to be the toughest timber law in the country, it was still pitifully weak and more than a decade of operation had mired it in a backscratching relationship between the industry and its overseer. It was foolish to expect anything from this procedure, Woods advised, but it was mandatory to participate if you wanted then to go to the courts to challenge the CDF's actions.

Woods's instructions were followed when EPIC took its first concrete steps to prevent the Pacific Lumber Company from turning Headwaters Forest into cash flow. On May 7, a CDF Review Team meeting was convened to consider 87–240 and 87–241, the THPs that had first drawn Greg King to Salmon Creek and the Little South Fork of the Elk. The meeting was held in a conference room at CDF's offices in Fortuna. In addition to the representatives of Fish and Game and CDF, seven members of the public were present—Greg King and six other EPIC partisans. Pacific Lumber hadn't bothered to send anyone. Greg had attended several Review Team meetings before and was cynical about the procedure, at best. But this would prove a very different meeting than any seen around

Humboldt before. The seven hippies seated at the table were part of that difference, but the heart of it was the behavior of forty-seven-year-old John Hummel, the wildlife biologist representing the Department of Fish and Game. Hummel's May 7 statements would soon become an open wound in the side of the timber industry's status quo.

The meeting began with an exchange between Greg King and one of the CDF foresters.

King asked if logging in these areas would have a significant cummulative impact on wildlife.

The forester didn't think so.

Well, King persisted, when the habitat essential to old-growth-dependent species disappeared, how would those species survive?

The CDF hemmed for a moment. Finally he just said that he didn't think there would be any significant cumulative impact. There was, he argued, plenty of habitat out there.

Oh? King asked. Just how much of the original old growth was left?

The forester said he had no idea.

Then King turned to John Hummel. Did the wildlife biologist agree with the CDF's view that there would be no cumulative impact on wildlife?

No one expected what happened next.

Like everyone else in the process, Fish and Game's participants had always played along. THPs were almost never rejected and never at the urging of Fish and Game and certainly never to protect wildlife. And, up to now, John Hummel had just been one more good old boy, always cooperating with the program, helping CDF and the industry scratch each other's backs. A former infantryman and missile industry worker, he had returned to school late in life in order to learn and practice wildlife biology. He was soft-spoken, clean-shaven, wore his hair short, and usually said little. He'd always swallowed his doubts about logging practices and tried his best to save what he could with little suggestions along the way, but now, in the face of a direct question for the first time, he was not about to lie. And, for the first time in a very long time, Fish and Game openly diverged from CDF's lead.

No, Hummel admitted, he did not agree. Deforestation would

inevitably lead to depopulation of the species. There was no question logging would have adverse effects on wildlife. When their habitat disappeared, a significant population decrease would follow. These species didn't have the ability to move to another spot. When these stands were leveled, the species couldn't just move into the second growth next door. Second growth would not support them, even if they could reach it.

King pointed out that on one of the required THP forms, the CDF forester had indicated that these THPs would have minimum impact on wildlife. He'd even speculated that "some wildlife may benefit." Did Hummel agree with that?

Hummel said he felt the statement was "inadequate." The notion that clear-cutting benefited wildlife was "rather weak." Turning old-growth forest into an open meadow would certainly benefit the deer population, but Fish and Game was not interested in producing more deer habitat. Fish and Game's policy was to support the diversity of species. And once you cut a stand down to ground level, that diversity would be threatened. Species were going to disappear. Others might take over their place, of course, but the species native to the old growth would be gone. In truth, logging yielded a net loss rather than a gain.

Hummel's dissent was unprecedented, but didn't immediately disrupt the standardized workings of the process. On May 14, the CDF office in Fortuna forwarded THPs 87–240 and -241 to the CDF district headquarters in Santa Rosa, the seat of Sonoma County. Everyone involved—Water Quality, Fish and Game, and the local CDF—signed off on the approval.

By then, Greg King had reported Hummel's comments at the Review Team meeting to Woods and T.M.W.W.I.T.W. knew he had a case. On June 1, the California Department of Forestry's district resource manager in Santa Rosa gave the two Headwaters Forest THPs final approval and on June 4, The Man Who Walks In The Woods, working with a Garberville attorney who—unlike Woods—was a member of the bar, filed *EPIC v. Maxxam* in Superior Court for Humboldt County. The case was scheduled to be heard in September.

In the meantime, EPIC was about to ask for a restraining order to prevent PL from doing any cutting in 240 and 241, but Pacific Lumber, preempting any immediate court fight, announced it would voluntarily adopt a moratorium on those THPs until the court heard the case. This, John Campbell pointed out, was the PL way. Their company had the best record of any in California when it came to taking care of their timberlands, and they were proud of it. Charles Hurwitz, Maxxam, and Pacific Lumber had nothing to hide. They would bloody well go to court and win.

32

John Campbell's response to Woods's lawsuit was just the tip of a massive escalating frustration inside Pacific Lumber. People there were used to being the good guys, and to find themselves now being cast in black hats hurt. They all resented it, and no one more than John Campbell. All they were bloody doing, after all, was logging on their own bloody property using the same techniques other companies had been using for the last two decades. Memos were exchanged inside Scotia's executive offices about how to counter this growing public image of PL as the despoiler of Humboldt County, but nothing seemed to work. Now they were about to be painted as the destroyers of wildlife and, for the moment, at least, blocked from harvesting in their mother lode. John Campbell could only fume. What a bloody travesty.

"Why does a small group of people take upon themselves the role of protecting the 'public' interest," Campbell eventually complained in an open letter to the *Times-Standard,* "even after numerous public agencies ... have debated the issues involved and decided that, under the law, approval of a timber harvest plan is appropriate? The actions of the elitist environmentalists have placed their own interest above the people. They should not dictate the appropriate balance between economic and environmental interest when it comes to timber harvesting or other legal economic endeavors. Earth First! and EPIC alike will cost all of us thousands of dollars and potential job losses. . . . The Pacific Lumber Company has a continuing relationship with the responsible environmental community which has resulted in many of the parks and reserves the general public enjoys today." Now all this was being distorted. The good people of Humboldt had best beware, he warned. PL was now the target of "a deliberate campaign of disinformation regarding our operations and harvesting methods" hatched by "a few radical environmentalists . . . and other extremists" in pursuit of "their selfish and unsubstantiated demands."

The battle was now joined. And only a few people in Scotia were still laughing. From the way old John was acting, these hippies were obviously for real.

33

Though he made no public statement to that effect, no one in Humboldt familiar with the players in this conflict had any doubt John Campbell considered Darryl Cherney the "extremist" architect of the "deliberate campaign of disinformation" that was plaguing PL. Darryl's skill at hustling the Earth First! Redwood Action Team's version of events to the media had already become legendary inside Pacific Lumber's executive circles. One company vice president, who'd begun his working life as a newspaper reporter, credited Cherney with a p.r. coup of which the swashbucklers who'd made public relations famous back in the fifties would have been envious. The guy should give courses in media manipulation. This vice president was convinced that Darryl charmed the reporters, who were basically his age, and then smoked pot with them and ended up virtually writing their stories himself. As proof, the vice president pointed to the fact that PL was getting killed every time they opened a newspaper.

Certainly Darryl worked at it overtime. He was an artist and one of his mediums was the telephone. When he had a receiver pressed to his ear with a reporter on the other end of the line, energy seemed to crackle around his matted head. He chatted, he laughed, he schmoozed, he passed on information, arranged for interviews, coaxed, cajoled, and sold the story of the last redwoods to every newsroom from the Oregon border to Mexico. He also worked the San Francisco bureaus of the national publications and representatives of every possible form of broadcasting. He had an exotic story from a faraway place to tell, a touching drama, full of conflict and striking scenery. And every media outlet wanted a story like that. To make sure they had repeated occasions to evoke it, Darryl Cherney also staged public theatre with regularity.

Earth First!'s major extravaganza that spring was a national day of protests against Maxxam on May 18. Humboldt was the epicenter, but the day also included a picket by fifteen Texans outside Maxxam's Houston headquarters, leafleting at the headquarters of the SEC in Washington, D.C., by several Earth Firsters dressed as trees, and another small picket outside of MCO Holdings' office in Los Angeles. At the Pacific Lumber Company's national sales office, now relocated to an office complex along an inlet on San Francisco Bay in southern Marin County, a dozen demonstrators barricaded the doorway with uprooted tree stumps. Their banner demanded "Pacific Lumber, Stop The Plunder."

In Humboldt, one hundred and twenty-five hippies gathered along Highway 36 in front of the Pacific Lumber log deck that fed the mill in Carlotta. When the company got word of what was going to happen, it shut the Carlotta mill down for the day and padlocked its gates. Inside the fence, a thin line of sheriff's deputies stretched along the length of the roadfront, consulting occasionally with PL officials wearing orange safety helmets. Behind them were enormous mounds of redwood trunks, cut to lengths of twenty and forty feet, stacked in wedges and pyramids, row after row after row, some stacks rising more than a hundred feet high. On the Earth First! side of the fence, the crowd milled. Most of them had either come out of the Mateel for the day or cut their classes at Humboldt State. Darryl was off to one side, giving interviews to the news cameras. While they filmed, he spoke of stopping the slaughter and made sure there was a clear line of sight behind him to the mounds of dead redwood. Farther down the fence line, the women's marimba band from out in the Mattole watershed set up their instruments and chimed in, giving the gathering an almost Caribbean air, despite chilly gray skies and waves of conifers dominating the skyline in every direction. Some people danced, others just waved their signs.

Then the action broke loose. Three women from the Mateel jumped the fence and sprinted for the log deck, catching both the sheriffs and the press by surprise. The former leapt in pursuit and the latter made a frantic rush to the fence line, hoping to capture the race on video. The women had a banner they planned to unfurl atop the log deck, but they reached the deck in a dead tie with the phalanx of sheriffs. One of the women was thrown against a log, another was forced to her knees, her arm wedged behind her back. All three were arrested but, while the law was distracted, three more Mateel women made another run for the deck, with much greater success. They climbed to the top of one of the pyramids before the cops could respond and danced across it, hopping from giant log to giant log until the sheriffs caught up to them. The next morning, the news segment on NBC's *Today* show ran a brief clip featuring the Humboldt County actions and, all over California, newspapers ran headlines like "Protest In The Trees; Last Virgin Redwoods Said To Be At Stake." It made John Campbell want to put his fist through the wall, but there was little he could do.

The Pacific Lumber Company and the "last" of the redwood old growth became a national story that spring. *The New York Times* came through, as did *The Wall Street Journal, The Philadelphia Inquirer, Newsweek,* and *Time.* In June, CBS News filmed a story as well. All of the media interviewed Campbell, who took them on a tour of the mill, pointed out the slope outside his window that had been logged bald earlier this century, and touted PL's forestry practices. All the reporters also made contact with Darryl Cherney. Darryl always gave them his best rap and arranged for surreptitious tours of a Pacific Lumber clear cut, guided by Greg King.

During June, CBS interviewed Greg standing on the edge of this man-made moonscape, with the sun sinking toward the Pacific over his shoulder. In the middle of filming, they were interrupted by a shotgun blast that seemed to come from the north, off PL's land. Three more shots followed in rapid succession, all from the same direction. Looking that way, Greg spotted a glint of light that he identified as a reflection off a pair of binoculars looking into the setting sun. He soon spotted a rooster tail of dust near where he'd seen the reflection and then a white pickup truck driving flat out down a logging track. The head of PL security was known for driving a white truck, Greg told the TV crew. Everybody else at the company drove an orange one. The truck disappeared from sight and the crew returned to filming. Ten minutes later, shots broke out again, this time to the south and much closer, on Pacific Lumber property. Looking that way, the crew saw the same white pickup truck parked on a logging road on the far side of the clear cut. King and the television crew quickly packed their equipment and left.

Despite this surge of national interest, summer was a particularly challenging time for Darryl Cherney's talents. It was hard to draw any kind of numbers to demonstrations when Humboldt State was out of session, so attention was more difficult to attract. And, like all stories, this one had its doldrums. Timber was only just becoming a beat at many papers and coverage was far from automatic. Each and every story on the subject still had to be coaxed and cajoled into existence. That, of course, was Darryl's job and, up in Humboldt, especially in the summer, it often meant doing a lot with a little.

One of the techniques the Earth First! Redwood Action Team introduced to Humboldt County as a consequence was the tree-sit. Earth Firsters had used tree-sits in other parts of the country before, but not here. In a tree-sit, one or two protesters can disrupt a logging show by "sitting in," up in the canopy of a threatened grove, and refusing to come down. Since actually pulling a protester out of the tree was prohibitively dangerous, the only limit on how long the logging could be impeded was the endurance of the sitter. Darryl Cherney and Greg King had concluded quite early in their strategizing that tree-sits would be a great way to call attention to what was going on every day out in the backwoods—assuming, of course, that they could convince the press to notice. A botched attempt at one tree-sit had been made during the anti-Maxxam week, but the first "successful" effort was made that summer by Greg King and one of his close friends, a woman who adopted the pseudonym Jane Cope for the purposes of the tree-sit. During August, they ascended into the canopy in a last-ditch attempt to save 87–427, 385 acres of redwood along the highest reaches of the Elk River's Big South Fork.

With the help of some fifteen others, Greg and Jane erected two three-foot by six-foot platforms some hundred and fifty feet up in adjoining trees, just in from the steadily receding edge of 87–427's treeline. It was Sunday and the logging show was shut down for the weekend. Each of the occupied trees displayed a banner. One said, "Free The Redwoods," the other, "This Tree Has A Job; Hurwitz Out of Humboldt." Greg also had a radio telephone connecting him to Darryl, who was prepared to work the press, setting up live telephone interviews with the tree-sitters once the confrontation was joined. That publicity mechanism began functioning on Monday, when, after PL's logging show had been cutting and hauling for almost an hour, a feller thought he saw something funny in the far treeline and walked over to investigate. The feller's jaw popped open like he'd seen a flying saucer.

Jesus, he blurted, you guys got to be crazy!

Soon the logging show was moved to the other side of the grove and sheriff's cars were accumulating on the nearby skid road. The PL security chief's white pickup was down there and a lot of assorted orange safety helmets as well. The standoff stayed that way for the rest of the work week. PL security kept a watch on Greg and Jane at night, eventually lighting their trees with a generator-driven floodlight. On Friday night, however, their vigilance lapsed. While the PL security guard sat in the cab of his orange pickup truck, listening to a preseason 49er game, entirely oblivious to anything else, Greg and Jane rappelled down to the ground, abandoned their equipment, and disappeared into the forest.

Darryl got a good laugh out of PL being left with egg on its face like that, but the episode had been frustrating. Besides some more or less automatic local coverage and a few live radio spots with San Francisco radio, the tree-sit hadn't generated much in the way of coverage. A three-hundred-thousand-acre forest fire was burning over near Mount Shasta, commandeering front pages around the state and blotting out the tree-sit almost entirely. Still, Darryl kept at it. The next week, Earth First! staged a march of some two dozen people on the CDF office in Fortuna, calling on masses of protesters to file masses of comments on every THP, thereby grinding CDF to a halt with its own paperwork. That plan got minor play all around northern California and then Darryl helped Greg and Jane ascend into the trees again.

Their second tree-sit was in 87–323, part of the once magnificent All Species Grove. This time, instead of perching in the treeline, to call attention to the imminent cut, they set up deeper into the grove, to call attention to what was being destroyed. When they were finally discovered, the company used one of its giant D-8 Cats to cut a road into the site. Greg gave several more live interviews on the radio phone early in the tree-sit but Darryl was again having problems breaking through the media's indifference. The two of them consulted several times a day. To counter that resistance, Darryl told Greg, he'd had a brainstorm.

What was that? Greg asked.

Darryl wanted to hype the two of them as Tarzan and Jane, up in the trees. It was a natural, he said, and the press'd eat it up.

No way, Greg insisted. He was not going to be hyped as Tarzan.

The two friends chewed that over until Darryl finally agreed to respect Greg's position. Then, Darryl hung up and proceeded to unleash the Tarzan and Jane hype anyway. And he was right about the press.

The next day, the *Los Angeles Times* ran a picture of Greg King shimmying on a rope between trees with a "Save The Old Growth" banner in the background. "Environmentalists Taking A Leaf From Tarzan's Tree," the headline read. "He's Tarzan and she's Jane," the story began, "and together the swinging pair have put themselves out on a limb over what they consider a pressing environmental issue." The day after that, Greg and Jane descended and turned themselves over to sheriff's deputies. They were charged with trespass and released on their own recognizance several hours later.

Leaving All Species Grove in the company of the sheriffs was a sad moment for Greg King. He knew he would never see it again. The redwoods that had sheltered the twenty-foot-tall lichen-covered rocks, the vine maples, the ferns, and the moss hanging in strings off the yew trees were disappearing every day—dropped by fellers, skidded by Cats, hauled to the log deck, floated across the pond, skinned, run through the sawyer, the edgerman, and the trimmerman, and then spat out onto the green chain as prime softwood boards. It was hard for Greg and Darryl not to feel disheartened. Despite the furor they'd stirred up, All Species Grove would be entirely reduced to hillside stumps and stacks of planks in

the Scotia drying yards within several weeks. To counter discour-
agement, the Earth Firsters reminded themselves that it was still
early in the fight. If nothing else, The Man Who Walks In The
Woods and EPIC—the combination that had been instrumental in
saving the Sinkyone—were only just now bringing their full weight
to bear.

34

E*PIC v. Maxxam* went to trial in early September and, though it passed with much less notice than Tarzan and Jane's sojourn in the last remnants of 87–323, it would eventually go a long way toward ensuring that Headwaters Forest didn't suffer the same fate as All Species Grove. The case was heard without a jury, by a visiting judge from Del Norte County, because all the Humboldt judges had excused themselves from hearing the case. The trial would be used to present evidence that the judge would then take under advisement. An actual decision wouldn't be registered for at least a month or two after the trial, perhaps longer. Still, the courtroom was packed every day. Hippies dominated the audience but that, PL partisans were fond of pointing out, was because loggers and mill hands had to work for a living and weren't free to attend court during the day. Still, delegations of self-styled "timber people" managed to occupy several rows of seats over the course of three days of trial. They wore baseball caps bearing the names of auto parts companies and an occasional polyester leisure suit. Their counterparts for the plaintiffs favored Birkenstocks and tie-dyes. The enmity between them was occasionally palpable.

The Man Who Walks In The Woods sat at the plaintiffs' table along with the attorney of record, Thomas Lippe of San Francisco. Lippe had recently abandoned a brief career defending large corporate clients from environmental laws and switched sides. Woods liked and respected him and vice versa. Their case began with the precedent of *EPIC v. Johnson:* in that decision, the courts had ruled that the timber industry, despite certain specific exemptions written into the Z'Berg-Nejedly Act, was not entirely exempt from the requirements of the California Environmental Quality Act. One of CEQA's applicable provisions mandated assessment of the "cumulative impact" to which any specific action contributed. The California Department of Forestry had made no such assessment in the case of THPs 87–240 and -241. Consequently, CDF's approval of the THPs was in violation of CEQA and, hence, invalid.

Lippe called a succession of witnesses to make his case, including John Hummel from Fish and Game and the CDF forester who originally assessed the two Headwaters THPs.

The forester provided the biggest laugh of the trial.

Lippe first led him through his assessment process.

Had the forester calculated the amount of soil that might be washed off the slope and into Salmon Creek or the Little South Fork of the Elk after a clear cut?

No, he hadn't.

Had he considered recommending any other style of cut than a clear cut, in order to protect the integrity of the hillside?

No, he hadn't.

Had he conducted any specific search for spotted owls? Or Olympic salamanders? Marbled murrelets? Tailed frogs?

No.

But he had concluded none of these species would be impacted. Was that correct?

Yes, that was correct.

During cross-examination, PL's lawyer asked the forester if he was familiar with all the species Lippe had mentioned.

Yes. He had seen photographs.

And had he seen any of these creatures out in these THPs?

No, certainly not.

Lippe returned to the same point during his redirect. The forester had seen pictures of all these species he had mentioned. Was that correct?

Yes.

When had he seen these pictures? the attorney for EPIC pressed.

The forester looked sheepish. A week ago, he admitted, in the office of Pacific Lumber's attorney.

At that, the hippies in the audience cut loose with an enormous belly laugh, halting proceedings until the judge could gavel order back to the court.

Needless to say, the laughter didn't include everyone in the spectator section. John Campbell was in the front row, surrounded by timber people, and his face was set as hard as a rock. His contempt for the Birkenstock crowd was apparent in his expression of indifference. None of these yahoos knew what it meant to have to make a living. Working people were who John intended to champion and, in the meantime, he was not about to let these dreadlocked dingdongs see him sweat. He knew they were watching him and he was, of course, right.

All the hippies were aware who John Campbell was and whispered about him when they passed in the hallway during recess. John made a point of flashing his ruddy, good-humored, Aussie grin at them all, even Darryl Cherney.

Darryl attended the first day of the trial as a spectator. All of the official functions of Earth First! and EPIC had long since been completely separated, at the insistence of Woods, in order to keep the court case from being tainted by the others' direct action. During a break in proceedings, John Campbell and Darryl Cherney ran into each other in the hall.

Hi, Darryl, John called out cheerily. How you doing?

Real fine, John, Darryl answered. I'm doing real fine. How about you?

John smiled even harder. He couldn't be doing better, he said. Everything was going just the way he'd hoped.

35

Darryl didn't take John Campbell's hallway bravado seriously and he was by no means alone. Whatever PL's executive vice president said, the current of events that fall seemed to be running against PL on more than one front. The company hardly had time to catch its breath after the EPIC trial before it was faced with an even larger public relations disaster, this time in the national spotlight. On October 5, the Oversight and Investigations Subcommittee of the House Committee on Energy and Commerce, chaired by Representative Charles Dingell of Michigan, held a hearing on the takeover of the Pacific Lumber Company by Charles Hurwitz and Maxxam.

Bill Bertain was probably the first person in Humboldt to know this hearing was coming. He'd been visited by a member of the subcommittee staff early in the summer. In the course of their initial encounter, Bertain passed on a lot of information and gleaned a little as well. It was from the subcommittee staffer that he first learned of Boyd Jeffries and the role Jeffries had played in the takeover. He also learned that the New York Stock Exchange had done a secret investigation of possible insider trading during Hurwitz's raid. In September, the staffer called back and told him the hearings would be in October. He also invited Bill and his former client, Woody Murphy, to testify. The other witnesses about PL would be John

Campbell and Charles Hurwitz and both would be subpoenaed if necessary.

Bertain accepted without hesitation.

Pacific Lumber first learned of Bertain's participation several days before the hearings, when the company was frantically gathering information about what was in store for Charles in Washington. As part of that preparation, Scotia's resident p.r. officer was dispatched to the Bertain Laundry, down by the river, to talk to Tom Bertain, one of Bill's four older brothers. Tom, the only of the ten siblings who'd made a career in the family business, had inherited it upon their father's death two months ago. The p.r. man asked Tom what Bill was going to testify to Congress about. Tom said he wasn't involved with Bill's business and recommended asking Bill himself.

The p.r. officer did so the next day. He'd known the youngest Bertain through his dad since he was a kid. At first, the man from PL acted like he'd just called to chat and catch up on Bill's life, but the posture didn't wash. Bill knew what he was after and since, judging by the echoes on their telephone transmission, the p.r. man had him on the speaker phone, Bill assumed there were others listening at the other end. When the subject of what Bill planned to say to the subcommittee finally came up, Bill told him to find another subject to chat about. The p.r. man got off the line shortly thereafter.

Two days later, Bill Bertain left home for Washington, D.C., carrying his typed opening statement in his old briefcase. He expected this to be a big moment in his life. Rebecca drove him to the airport in his pickup, with their baby, William, strapped in the car seat behind him in the king cab. Bill was running a little late but nothing serious until he arrived at the airport parking lot. There, he managed to lock William, his carry-on bag with his best suit, and the truck's keys inside the cab after he and Rebecca got out. Rebecca frantically called a locksmith while Bill kept William entertained through the window. Miraculously, the locksmith got there in time for Bill to make the plane, running frantically up the gangway with his good suit in tow. He survived the airport episode, but it was like an omen. Bill Bertain felt as if he was two steps behind for the rest of the trip.

36

Once in Washington, he also felt like a very small-town lawyer in a very big-town lawyer kind of place. Under different circumstances, his acclimatization might have been eased by the assistance of his local congressman but, on the issue of Pacific Lumber, that was not an option. Bertain had contacted Doug Bosco, the congressman who represented Humboldt and several other northern California counties, during the takeover itself. Bosco, a Democrat, had promised to help and issued a press release criticizing the takeover but, while the release was in the process of being circulated, Congressman Bosco had met Hurwitz for dinner in New York. Immediately thereafter, Bosco had withdrawn the release, sending his staff in Eureka over to the *Times-Standard* to retrieve their copy from the "in" box and ensure that it didn't circulate. That was Bertain's last contact with Bosco and, two years later, he was still on his own.

Bill was obviously nervous when he took the witness table at the next morning's hearing. Behind it, he seemed even shorter than when he stood up. Woody Murphy was sitting next to him and Woody testified first. His statement was short and embarrassingly inarticulate. Then Bertain took the mike. Bill would later describe his own testimony as a disappointment. He managed to get in a dig at Bosco for having abandoned the district in this affair, but, otherwise, he scored few points. Early in his statement, Bill reached a line referring to his father, Louis Bertain, who had operated Bertain's Laundry in Scotia for sixty-seven years until his death two months ago, and, for a moment, he thought he was going to be overwhelmed with tears, his voice caught in his throat, and he had to pause to compose himself. Once he regained his equilibrium, he denounced the new policies brought by Maxxam and recited a list of questions about the takeover that remained unanswered. The best line in his statement was one of the last, pointing out that he was a Republican who voted for Reagan and he believed that the free market was one of the highest of values but, he emphasized, it was not the *only* value. By then, Bill was feeling more comfortable, but none of the congressmen who'd bothered to attend seemed to be listening. Everyone was waiting for the PL side of the presentation, where the real action promised to be.

Of the two company spokesmen who followed Bill Bertain and Woody Murphy's brief appearances, John Campbell had by far the most limited role. And, while he played it close to his vest publicly, he made no bones to his confidants about his suspicions regarding this process. PL was about to be pilloried, he complained. As far as he was concerned, stomping on the innocent was an automatic function whenever the government got involved. When he was a boy in Australia, the government had forced his father to sell their farm for inclusion in a giant reservoir, earning the senior Campbell's unending anger and derision and leaving an indelible mark on his son. In front of the subcommittee, he meant to simply bite off a corner of the company's argument and hold it, and his opening statement only addressed the issue of whether or not the Pacific Lumber Company had changed its timbering policies as a result of the takeover. He testified that it had not. The change, he said, had occurred before the takeover, at a meeting of the board in Scotia in September, 1985. There, before anyone knew of any approaching tender offer, the directors had indicated they intended to move the company away from selective cut and the tradition of the Murphys. The decision was simply good business and amounted to no more than adopting the approach standard to the rest of the timber industry. All of Pacific Lumber's forestry experts, both in-house and consulting, recommended it.

That said, the rest of that day's hearing was devoted to Charles Hurwitz.

The Texan was his usual unruffled self in his usual dark suit. He had not come to Washington to apologize. He had done nothing illegal or improper. Furthermore, his acquisition of Pacific Lumber had been good for the company, good for its shareholders, good for its employees, and good for timber country. Hurwitz then proceeded to elaborate a rough narrative of the several months involved in its acquisition. His attention had initially been drawn to Pacific Lumber by the company's oversubscribed stock buyback in September 1984. He'd been expecting to purchase the AMF Corporation, but he'd been outbid, so in June 1985, he and his bankers, Drexel Burnham Lambert, had begun to get serious about PL. In telling the story of the rest of the maneuvering up to the tender offer, Hurwitz provided a minimum of detail but, knowing the subcommittee had questions about his dealings with Boyd Jeffries, he attempted to head them off in his testimony. First, he pointed out, the subcommittee should remember that under no circumstances, Jeffries or not, did his share of PL ever exceed 5 percent before the tender offer. Second, until he agreed on September 27, 1985, to purchase the PL shares in Jeffries's possession, he did not own or control them. And, third, he had been consistently advised by his attorneys throughout this process that his arrangement with Jeffries complied with the Hart-Scott-Rodino Act and all other applicable laws.

Hurwitz was right to anticipate the issues raised by Boyd Jeffries's presence in the takeover. His role was one of two principal areas of concern raised in the ten-page confidential staff memo with which each of the subcommittee members had been briefed. The other was possible inside trading by a member of Ezra Levin's law firm. The memo identified Hurwitz himself as "a Houston financier associated with 'greenmail' and takeovers [who] has, over time, encountered difficulties with various state and Federal regulatory agencies." It concluded that Hurwitz had "an undisclosed arrangement with Jeffries & Company to 'park' the Pacific Lumber stock until such time as the tender offer would be announced." If substantiated, such parking violated the Williams Act provisions requiring full accounting of stock purchases, the Securities Act provisions requiring accurate book and record keeping, and the margin rules governing stock purchases. Jeffries, the memo noted, had already pled guilty to similar violations involving trading he'd done for Ivan Boesky. It also noted that there were strong indications that Hurwitz had violated the Hart-Scott-Rodino Act as well.

The subcommittee's questioning of Charles Hurwitz following his statement lasted almost two hours.

The chairman, Charles Dingell, did the lion's share of the interrogation of Hurwitz on the issue of his relationship with Boyd Jeffries. Guided by his staff, Dingell obviously considered the fact that Jeffries sold his more than 500,000 shares of PL stock for $29.10 a share—$4 or $5 under market price at the time of the transaction—proof that the two men had entered into an agreement. Such an agreement might well buttress the case for a number of alleged violations, but Charles Hurwitz was not about to admit to it, no matter how hard Dingell tried.

Hurwitz repeatedly denied that he'd had any explicit or implicit agreement with Boyd Jeffries. Jeffries had bought the PL shares on his own speculative account. They had started to make a put-call agreement, but Jeffries had insisted on attaching terms to it that he could not accept, so no agreement was ever made. When Hurwitz finally bought Jeffries's stock, it was strictly an over-the-counter transaction.

Chairman Dingell found this explanation hard to believe. The going price for PL shares at the time of the purchase was somewhere around $33 or $34. But Hurwitz paid only $29.10. If there was no previous agreement, why would Boyd Jeffries or any other stock market player sell $34 stock at $29.10?

Hurwitz explained that he had talked to Jeffries earlier, when the stock was selling at $29. At that point, they'd finalized their price.

But that, the chairman interrupted, was an agreement that had never been signed, correct? Hadn't there been an unacceptable wording in those documents?

That was correct.

Then how was Jeffries bound by the agreement?

Hurwitz explained that he'd just called Jeffries back and told him they had a problem and that he would purchase the shares outright instead.

But the market was at $34 by then. Why didn't Jeffries charge $34? Had Hurwitz purchased the shares under the earlier agreement?

No, Hurwitz repeated, they never had an earlier agreement.

Chairman Dingell rubbed his face in exasperation. Well, if Hurwitz hadn't had an earlier agreement, how could he still buy the shares at $29.10? Why would someone as astute as Mr. Jeffries allow himself to miss out on almost $5 a share in profits if he was not bound by some earlier agreement?

Hurwitz started his patient explanation again. Several days before, he repeated, they had agreed on a price.

But there was never any contract signed on that price. Was that correct?

No, there wasn't. But they'd agreed on a price.

How could he get Jeffries to go along?

He just called him, Hurwitz explained, and Jeffries had said that was o.k. by him.

The exchange between Chairman Dingell and his prime witness went around like that for some twenty minutes, the chairman making no headway and Hurwitz giving no ground. Finally, Dingell gave up and relinquished the floor.

The remaining questioning of Charles Hurwitz cut back and forth, occasionally focusing on one of the takeover game's more newsworthy names:

Did Mr. Hurwitz know Ivan Boesky?

They'd met once.

What was Mr. Hurwitz's relationship with Michael Milken?

Milken was someone he had been acquainted with for the past fifteen years.

The only other noticeable trend in the last hour of Hurwitz's testimony was the broad range of subjects about which he either knew or recalled nothing.

Asked about the fraud and breach of fiduciary duty charges filed against him by the New York insurance commissioner in 1977, Hurwitz admitted there had been some allegations but claimed to have forgotten all the details.

Asked why Maxxam hadn't cooperated with the New York Stock Exchange investigation of the Pacific Lumber takeover, Hurwitz said he'd never even been aware there was such an investigation.

Asked for a description of Maxxam's agreement with Drexel to indemnify its bankers against any securities law violations, Hurwitz acknowledged that such an agreement existed but said he was not familiar with it.

Asked about the Federal Home Bank Board's warnings to his United Savings Association of Texas to curtail some of its burgeoning investment in junk bonds, Hurwitz said he was not aware of it.

Asked about his relationship with Fred Carr, Hurwitz admitted he knew Carr but said he'd had no idea that Carr had purchased some $160 million worth of Pacific Lumber's bonds until quite recently.

Asked about how an annuity from Executive Life was selected to replace Pacific Lumber's pension plan, Hurwitz said he'd be happy to answer any questions he could about the Pacific Lumber's pension replacement, but the congressmen should understand that he had been "very removed" from that entire process.

Bill Bertain watched Charles Hurwitz's performance from a seat in the first row of the spectator section, immediately behind him. He expected to at least see a bead of sweat trickle down the Texan's neck, but, after two full hours, he hadn't seen one. When Charles Hurwitz finally filed out in the crowd leaving the hearing room after the Subcommittee on Oversight and Investigations of the House Committee on Energy and Commerce dismissed him from the witness table, Bertain came within an easy reach of him. Bill figured this was the closest he would ever get to his nemesis, so he willed his eyes to drill holes in the side of Hurwitz's head. All to no effect. Charles Hurwitz struck Bill as the coldest son of a bitch he'd ever heard of.

Bertain lost sight of him when they reached the hallway outside and Bill was waylaid by a staffer from Congressman Doug Bosco's office.

Bosco's aide immediately made it very clear that he was distressed by the bad rap Bertain had given his boss when he was testifying.

Bertain felt the heat inside him flare. The people of Humboldt are being screwed over and over by this con artist from Texas and all Bosco could think of was covering his own ass? Bertain abandoned all diplomacy.

You bet he'd gotten on Bosco's case, he barked at the aide. If assholes like his boss had stuck to their guns, none of them would have had to have been in Washington today. The problem was the fox guarding the chicken coop.

With that, Bill Bertain turned on his heel and headed down the hall to fetch his bags and then outside to catch a cab for the airport. He hated to admit it, but it looked as though Charles Hurwitz had slipped away again.

37

John Campbell's explanation for Charles's escape from chastisement at the hands of Congress was, of course, that there was no call for any. Even Chairman Dingell, try as he might, hadn't been able to make anything stick. After the hearing, Dingell wrote the Federal Trade Commission recommending they investigate Hurwitz for violations of the Hart-Scott-Rodino Act, but the FTC declined. Dingell also wrote the attorney general, suggesting that Campbell himself be investigated for possible perjury under congressional oath, but the attorney general declined as well. In the meantime, as October became November, bringing strings of days when fog choked Humboldt Bay and clawed its way up the river past the mill, Campbell assumed the role of Hurwitz's principal Humboldt defender and repeated the gist of his Washington testimony at Rotary Clubs and fund-raising dinners, over the lunch counter at the Scotia Coffee Shop, or with a beer or three down at Mingo's in Rio Dell after work. When asked for an explanation of what had happened in D.C., he portrayed the subcommittee with its head up its ass and Charles's appearance as brilliant—a clear vindication for the rights of property. When asked about his own claim that the transformation in PL's timbering policies dated from Gene Elam's reign, he reaffirmed it and railed at how bloody little respect for the truth had been demonstrated by any of the company's adversaries. Whoever he made his spiel to usually nodded their heads in agreement. John was the company here and, with a few exceptions, the company still owned this elbow in the Eel, heart and soul.

Just to make sure everyone got the message, though, John mailed a letter to all Pacific Lumber's Humboldt employees. "For some time now," he wrote, "the Pacific Lumber Company has been the target of adverse publicity in both the broadcast and print media. The source of this publicity has been a radical environmental group. . . . The story being told is that the corporate raider, Charles Hurwitz, is pillaging the last old-growth redwoods to pay off junk bonds used to finance the takeover. . . . This is simply not true.

"It is very important . . . that you, our valued employees, understand the facts. . . . The company is not cutting 'the last' old growth redwoods. . . . At least 65% of the remaining old growth redwood is preserved in State and National parks. . . . Since the takeover, the Company has approximately doubled its cut [but] in the opinion of . . . qualified forestry consultants, the current cutting rate is not only appropriate in relation to the Company's timber inventory, it is conservative by industry standards. . . .

"The decision to change the Company's timber harvest policies was made before the merger. . . . A presentation . . . was made to the Board of Directors in April and again in September of 1985 outlining the proposed changes. The Board agreed in principle . . . and management instructed the forestry and logging departments to proceed on the new basis *before the tender offer was made*. The proposed changes are exactly what is happening today. . . .

"The Company has endeavored to give all of the above information to representatives of the media. Apparently, our story is too dull. It doesn't have the news value of the version put out by the radical environmentalists. It's a situation where our story, the good news, is no news. The other story, with all its distortions, is bad news and therefore good news for the media types. You are already familiar with the results. . . . Since the takeover, there have been no changes in the local operating management of the Company other than the resignation of Warren Murphy, who fought the merger and was party to several lawsuits trying to block the transaction. Turnover at the mills will remain minimal. . . . The Company remains dedicated to good forestry, the manufacture of high quality lumber, and to its loyal workforce. We have new ownership, but we remain—the Pacific Lumber Company."

38

While that letter was being mailed, however, yet another disaster struck. On November 10, the judge finally returned a decision in *EPIC v. Maxxam* and, from Pacific Lumber's point of view, it could hardly have been worse. The case built by The Man Who Walks In The Woods and the attorney Tom Lippe had carried most of the trial's major issues. In approving Pacific Lumber's request to log parcels 87–240 and -241, the judge concluded, the California Department of Forestry had run roughshod over the requirements for wildlife and water protection—intimidating Fish and Game and Water Quality representatives—and ignored any assessment of the THPs' cumulative environmental impacts. CDF's stated justification for its actions—that the timber involved was private property, zoned for timber production, and that there were plenty of old-growth redwoods preserved in parks—was specious. What happened in the processing of 87–240 and -241 was simply a "rubber-stamping" of Pacific Lumber's requests, without any attempt to live up to CEQA in either law or spirit. The THPs in question were illegal, and the company would have to refile and start the process over. PL's planned advance into the mother lode along Salmon Creek and the Little South Fork of the Elk was, for the moment, stymied.

Frustrating as that was, however, PL didn't slow for more than a beat. The rainy season spanning 1987 and 1988 was light, as the previous one had been, and it wasn't until January that the wet weather seriously interfered with the cut. Logging shows were still plentiful out in the company's residuals and among the isolated pockets of old growth it owned out around Shaw Creek and All Species Grove. Whatever the courts said about 240 and 241, there was an abundance of very large timber to cut through the rainy months and the 1988 logging season. And all of it had long since been approved by CDF. Overtime and double shifts remained in place at all the mills. There was even some talk around town that the cut had actually been tripled rather than doubled but John Campbell denied every such rumor that reached him. The company's cut, he repeated, was moderate and one of the most conservative in the industry. And every bloody forester they consulted said the same bloody thing.

The guys down at Mingo's continued to nod, but John was hardly sanguine. The wave of the future was now clear to him. If he was going to keep Scotia operating at the level Charles needed, his principal task as executive vice president had to be salvaging the company's reputation and political standing. Otherwise, the battle would go to the hippies by default and the judges and bureaucrats would end up staking the company out like Gulliver among the Lilliputians. Throughout December and into January, as the dry winter's occasional rainstorms stiffened and increased a little in volume, John was a man with a message, repeated over and over, in Humboldt and to members of the state legislature on an increasing number of visits to the capital in Sacramento. Timber's throw weight had to be mobilized.

The most visible of John's local recitations came just after New Year's, at the first mandatory meeting of all the company's employees since the day Charles Hurwitz had come to town more than two years ago. Hurwitz didn't attend this time, but Bill Leone, PL's Los Angeles-based president, did. As usual, the company meeting was convened in the Winema Theatre. The idea was to make sure that all the media denigrations of PL didn't infect the workforce, but none of the electricity that had characterized the last company meeting had attached itself to this one. The men filed in with little bustle or anticipation and a great deal of inertia. Everyone looked a little tired—a continuous year of fifty- and sixty-hour weeks had taken its toll. Their expressions were either indifferent or just plain bored.

When John Campbell spoke, he tried to impress upon them that, while the company had things in hand, the situation itself was serious. As he'd said in his letter, Pacific Lumber was under attack and there might just be enough judges out there on the other side to give the company some problems. It was hard to get the truth out. And the truth was bloody simple. PL was still the most responsible sawyer in the industry, bar none, and the way PL was managing its timberlands was just plain good forestry, whatever Greg King and Darryl Cherney and all their friends drawing welfare checks might tell the *San Francisco Chronicle* or *The New York Times*. PL was also still the best employer around. The annuity behind the pension benefits was just as sound as the fund it had replaced. Maxxam was continuing PL's Christmas parties for the kids and college scholarship program.

Kelly Bettiga listened two rows back and wondered if he was the only one there who wanted to scream. The Winema was like a bowl of tepid water. And when Campbell finally opened the meeting to questions, no one stood; no one advanced on the audience mike; no one even raised their goddamn hand. Nobody had a thing to say, like they were all fucking brain-dead. Old John was up there talking out of the side of his neck, spouting a pitch as long as Highway 101 and as shallow as a dinner plate, and nobody had a word to say? Not even a question to ask? This was definitely more shit than Shinola.

When Kelly Bettiga finally broke that silence, there weren't many in the audience who were surprised. That this Bettiga brother was an oddball was well known around the mill. The guy'd always been on the edge—when he ran with the surfers at Fortuna High School, when he came back from the war and started hanging out up at Humboldt State. The guy'd actually brought a book of Lenin to work one day, just to freak everyone out. Still, he wasn't a nobody. His granddad worked for the company, as did his dad and his mom. His uncle over in Ferndale was a well-known local painter and his brother had been the best football player ever to come out of Humboldt State and actually spent a couple years on the 49ers roster before he came home and settled back into the mill. Kelly himself had served honorably, steering an aircraft carrier in the South China Sea naval task force that leveled much of North Vietnam.

Kelly had also left Humboldt State and his night shift job and was now working a regular fifty-eight-hour shift running a chop saw in Mill A, standing at a work station and sawing bad spots out of fir boards. A lot of people liked him but most would still be the first to admit the hippie didn't have the good sense to stay out of John Campbell's way.

Kelly himself figured that all his family's Scotia status would probably help protect him if he shot his mouth off at the meeting. He certainly had no doubts that somebody had to. This was all getting to be too much. He'd heard about the deal old Hurwitz had finagled with the pension fund and he'd even sent away for copies of the *Congressional Record* of the Dingell subcommittee hearing. Kelly'd never accepted the takeover and, as far as he was concerned, Hurwitz and John Campbell were just setting the company up for a major fucking fall. When nobody raised a question, Kelly scanned the audience looking for someone else to say something and started counting to himself. When he reached eight, he stood up.

Leone, chairing the meeting, asked him his question.

Kelly decided to raise the most recent gripe to make its way around the grapevine at the mill. The subject was the company's system of automatic raises. The old PL had granted pay increases with the simple accumulation of time on the job, but now, under Maxxam, they'd become real picky. Raises were being withheld for the smallest of reasons, like too many absences or tardiness, and at break time, everyone bitched that the company seemed to be avoiding raises any way possible.

Well, Kelly said, rubbing his jaw and rolling his words around in his mouth, he was glad to hear the company was in such good shape and that there were no problems with the pension and all that, but he had a question about raises. He didn't know what old John and Mr. Leone had been hearing, but Kelly said he'd be glad to share what he'd been hearing. He'd been hearing that getting a raise around here was getting to be like pulling teeth.

Leone stiffened a notch and Campbell's eyes riveted on Bettiga.

Kelly continued. He said he knew the company had this golden rule that Mr. Hurwitz had come in and told them about two years ago, but he wanted to remind them that there was another rule that spoke just as true. That was that you got just what you paid for.

With that, Bettiga sat down.

Leone cleared his throat and asked if this was a personal problem the questioner had.

No, Kelly answered from his seat, it wasn't.

Campbell was chosen by Leone to respond and he gave a short speech about how PL's wages were more than comparable with the rest of the industry. Then Leone asked if there were any more questions.

Again, no one said a thing until Bettiga popped back to his feet. He'd followed this investigation of Mr. Hurwitz and the company by Congress, he said, and he was wondering if there was going to be more of these hearings and whether there was something else that was going to show up that they ought to worry about.

Leone gave this question to one of the company attorneys who'd accompanied him up from Los Angeles.

There was no congressional investigation, the lawyer answered.

No investigation? Bettiga blurted. What the hell did he mean? He had read about it in the newspaper and that made it sound like Mr. Hurwitz'd been hit with all kinds of shit.

Oh, the lawyer said, *that* investigation. It was a minor incident. Mr. Hurwitz hadn't been charged with anything. It was all over with.

Well, he didn't know about that, Kelly said, sitting back in his chair, but he guessed everybody would find out the answer to that question sooner or later.

Before there were any more questions, John Campbell took a moment to reiterate that the only reason any of this had happened was the hatchet job that had been done on the company by the environmentalists. He then launched into a considerable tirade against the Earth Firsters and their harebrained buddies up in Garberville. He ended the tirade by reminding everyone that while these guys were annoying, the company would soon simply brush them aside.

With that, Kelly was back on his feet. The environmental movement was something he thought he knew something about. He'd talked to a lot of these guys when he was up at Humboldt State and he'd studied them in his political science classes. And he thought John was messing with fire.

With all due respect, John, Kelly said—not waiting to be recognized or even framing his statement in the pretense of a question—but the company was not just going to be able to brush this all aside. He knew old John and Mr. Leone didn't like to hear this, but they'd better face it now before it was too late. PL wasn't going to be allowed to just mow down trees at will and if that's what they fought for they were going to get their asses handed to them on a platter. If they didn't find a way to make their peace with these environmentalists, this was going to become a statewide issue and then it was going to be a question on which Humboldt County was so goddamn outnumbered that even a couple of large blocks in Los Angeles had more clout than they did. And that was a fucking fight they'd lose. Just look at when the government took all that timberland for the park at Redwood Creek twenty years ago and there were all those layoffs at other companies. It wasn't the environmentalists who lost those jobs. It was the companies who cut so goddamn ugly that it pissed the city folk off. That blindness got the politics started and once it became politics, people like everybody here were going to take it in the shorts.

Campbell dismissed the warning with a wave of his hand. These guys were just the lunatic fringe, nothing more.

Maybe so, Kelly answered, but they're the goddamn future. And things were going to get a whole lot crazier around here if any of this went much further. And it was going to get that way a lot sooner than anybody thought.

Leone then interrupted and said the company had the situation well in hand. Did anyone *else* have a question?

No one did, so the meeting adjourned.

It would be another two years before the next company meeting was convened and by then, Kelly Bettiga, the hippie with the loud mouth and the job on the chop saw, would remind more than a few of his fellow mill hands of that time at the Winema, when he'd warned them—back when PL still might have headed this war off.

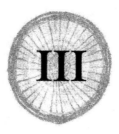

The War

39

In Humboldt County, among the little towns along the Eel, the Mad, the Mattole, and the Van Duzen, more than a few people would end up using May 17, 1988, to date when the war that eventually swallowed Humboldt really came into its own. Henceforth, the smell of battle was almost always in the air somewhere nearby. John Campbell had spent his winter making it clear that they were in the middle of a fight for the very survival of the logging industry, their own jobs included, and if they were going to run off and hide like a bunch of bloody hobbits, then timber country and everything it stood for were bloody doomed and so was PL. And the message got across. John expected everyone at the company to take up the banner in this jihad and for those who did, May 17 was their initiation. They didn't yet have much idea how ugly everything would get but they did know this was a fight they could not afford to lose, certainly not by default.

Little of Scotia's hobbitness remained by the spring of 1988. More than a third of the people now working for PL had been hired after Charles Hurwitz's raid and everyone in the mills, new and old, continued to work fifty-eight-hour weeks, so that life there had largely shed its bucolic storybook air and taken on a more glazed and bloodshot quality. Scotia was no longer lumberjack heaven, it was robojack village, always on overtime, grinding out as many boards as it could, and cashing its paychecks for satisfaction on its one day off. While enervating, the pace was a financial bonanza and what John said rang true. They'd heard all the Save the Trees bullshit before and they had few illusions about the message. Saved trees were lost jobs. They knew how many mills had been closed; a lot of them had seen firsthand what had happened to Louisiana Pacific's Humboldt operations when the state took their lands for the Redwood Park. Hardly anybody in the county worked for LP now and the people at PL knew that could happen to them, especially all the new hires who hadn't grown up safely ensconced in the Murphys' embrace. They wanted the boom times Charles Hurwitz had brought to town to last and May 17 announced that there were at least some people in Scotia and all the other fiefs in timber country who were ready to fight to make sure they did.

The occasion was a meeting of the board of supervisors at the county building in Eureka. On the agenda was a discussion of the department of forestry's recent denial of several timber harvest plans submitted by the Pacific Lumber Company. Timber people began showing up on the lawn outside at 9:00 A.M. and, by 10:00, some five hundred had collected. They wore workboots, frayed down vests, and baseball caps and they waited, sipping coffee out of Styrofoam cups, checking everything out. Most had never done anything like this before. Mingled among them were PL workers wearing their company's orange plastic hard hats. John Campbell had approved time off for any employee who wanted to demonstrate and more than a hundred did. Other sawmills had done the same, along with some ranches, dairies, and local businesses. The crowd carried stenciled signs saying "Save Our Jobs," "How Can You Replace $10–$16 An Hour Wages?" and "We Support Industry." A few men even brought along their chain saws and drew cheers by occasionally firing one up. Then came the trucks, almost three hundred of them—semis, vans, flatbeds, pickups, log trucks—all caravaning north up U.S. 101 where the highway passes through Eureka on the city's Fifth Street. Behind them, the morning sky was slashed with huge white columns of stink rising out of the stacks at Louisiana Pacific's pulp mill on the lip of the bay. When the trucks reached the county building, the crowd cut loose and the parade hung a left and began circling the block, rapping their pipes and laying on their horns. Some of those who were already inside the supervisors' chambers said you could feel the building shake. The men wearing trademarks of snuff companies and ammunition manufacturers on their caps chuckled that Timber Country was out in force, and, goddamn it, they were going to be heard or know the reason why.

The final element in the drama of May 17 showed up in much smaller numbers. Darryl Cherney, Greg King, and another dozen Earth Firsters were also in the audience inside the board's chambers for the THP "discussion." Darryl, for one, was scared shitless. He was sure everyone—absolutely everyone—in the room knew they were there and was looking at them. Darryl often felt encircled, but never more than now. He could feel strange eyes all over his shoulders and their malevolence raised a sweat on his forehead. He hadn't yet given much thought to just how ugly things could get, but, on May 17, he got his first strong hint of what it would feel like to wind up a target in somebody else's eyes. Under the circumstances, it was hard for him to concentrate on much but the issue of how to save his ass after this thing was over.

The portion of the supervisors' meeting everyone had come to hear was chaired by a twelve-year incumbent supervisor who was known behind his back as "the supervisor from PL" and had campaign signs strapped on several of the big rigs that circled the building. The "discussion" he chaired was, in large part, two speeches—one by the director of CDF, to address the specifics of the THPs in question, and the other by a professor from Humboldt State, to make an assessment of the economic impact of these THPs' rejection.

The CDF director cautioned that people were making too much out of the rejection. Clearly, given recent court decisions, the THP process was going to have to be modified to conform to law. This was just the initial shakedown. As soon as all the parties involved learned the procedure, things would run smoothly.

Darryl figured the CDF director just sounded bureaucratic, but the Humboldt State man made him squirm in his seat. First, the professor suggested that if these particular THPs—otherwise relatively run-of-the-mill among the hundreds processed for Humboldt County every year—were rejected, it would cost Humboldt residents somewhere in the neighborhood of eighteen hundred and fifty-two jobs—about half as many jobs as had been lost in Humboldt's timber industry over the previous two decades. Then the professor began laying into Earth First! and all the other environmentalists. They were the root of just about all of the county's problems and an abomination to the political process, an abomination to competent economic analysis, and an abomination to just plain old-fashioned, checked-flannel-and-suspenders common sense. The professor went on and on and on, escalating his diatribe with every minute. He only stopped when one of the supervisors asked him to stop.

The board's chairman then said he guessed they'd all heard everything they needed to hear and began to gavel this session of the board into recess.

With that, Greg King jumped to his feet. Wait a minute, he said. Weren't the supervisors going to take comments from the public?

A Fortuna city councilman who'd come as part of the demonstration jumped up in response. They weren't going to take any comments from an idiot like Greg King, he shouted, that was for sure.

The chairman then signaled adjournment and the room began to empty back onto Fifth Street.

The hair on Darryl Cherney's neck stiffened when he finally stepped outside. Like every emerging Earth Firster, he was immediately swept up in an eddy of Timber People, shouting questions, demanding debate, or just plain screaming. One man stood a foot from Darryl and declared that he was going to break Darryl's head open, then, his face beet red, he wheeled on his heel and left—only to return in a matter of minutes, pushing his way through the crowd to repeat his pledge. With that, he left again, then came back and said he hadn't meant what he said about Cherney's head but that he still thought Darryl was an asshole, scum-of-the-earth, bloodsucking lowlife welfare cheat.

When Darryl argued back, he argued that these people should be angry at Charles Hurwitz, not Darryl Cherney. It was Hurwitz who had ripped off their pension fund, it was Hurwitz who was going to cut so much that none of their jobs would last. It was Hurwitz who was part of the Wall Street elite who were ruining the planet.

Darryl's arguments made absolutely no headway. One entire family lined up for five minutes just to stare menacingly at him, toddlers included. Several others came by just to get a chance to shout at this Darryl Cherney they'd all been hearing about. Whenever the crowd around him seemed in danger of getting out of hand, Darryl pulled his guitar out of its case and began to sing. That was usually enough to drive away at least the front ranks. At regular intervals, he stood on his tiptoes, hoping to see over the surrounding Timber People and check what was happening with all the other Earth Firsters—each of them nearby, but each surrounded by arguers, swearers, screamers, and folks who only stared, just as he was.

Much to Darryl's surprise, they all made it through unscathed. As the crowd on the lawn gradually thinned, several departing Timber People even stopped by Darryl and had their picture taken with him. He grinned, patchouli and dreadlocks sandwiched between polyester pantsuits and Ben Davis overalls.

In the end, there were no incidents of violence: 0 dead, 0 wounded. Darryl began breathing easier when they were finally out on the freeway leading to Arcata.

The next day, photos of the loggers' demonstration and truck parade were all over front pages as far away as the *Los Angeles Times.* "It was wonderful that the working man had a chance to express their [sic] feelings," John Campbell told the *Redwood Record.* "I hope they will be listened to." Left unsaid was John's intention, approved by Charles Hurwitz, to make as bloody sure as he could that they were.

40

When Darryl Cherney in fact became a target and encountered a target's fate, he would share those crosshairs with Greg King, of course, but also with Judi Bari, a thirty-seven-year-old woman from Mendocino County who would be Darryl's partner in life and politics for the next two years. By May 17, 1988, Judi Bari was long since the love of Feral Darryl's life.

Cherney met Judi Bari at the Mendocino Environmental Center in Ukiah, where he'd gone to lay out a leaflet. He did the job so poorly that he asked around the center if there was anyone who could help him with his layout and was introduced to Judi. She was Darryl's height, a single mother with two kids from a failed marriage that had brought her to California from Maryland. She played the fiddle, she had dark blond hair with a natural wave in it, she had a great sense of humor. And she had politics. She had more politics than Darryl had ever had contact with before. Judi Bari had started as an organizer in the anti-Vietnam-War movement at the University of Maryland, which she dropped out of in order "to fight in the revolution," and ended up working in a grocery store, leading a rank-and-file movement inside the Brotherhood of Retail Clerks and staging a failed wildcat strike. Judi next went to work in a bulk mail sorting factory run by the U.S. Post Office, where she again organized a rank-and-file opposition to the established union leadership. This time, the rank-and-file movement she helped organize took over the local. Her ex-husband was another former radical labor organizer. After they'd moved to Mendocino County and divorced, she worked as a carpenter and then decided to throw in with the fight to save the redwoods.

Darryl went over to Judi's house for dinner. They played music, she on the fiddle, he on his guitar. They sang duets. And they talked and they talked, Judi a lot about the Wobblies, the Industrial Workers of the World, radical labor organizers whose heyhay had been before World War I. There had to be a way, she said, to do what the IWW had done so well back then, only this time not just for the workers but for the forest as well. When he left that night, Judi loaned him a book about the Wobblies. She had already captured his heart. In a matter of weeks after she and Darryl became a couple, Judi had become a major figure in the North Coast environmental movement, fiddling while he strummed and sang, speaking her mind with considerable skill and fervor. Darryl loved being with her.

Greg King was glad to have her on board as well. She knew how to organize and he hated all the hustle, all the demands, all the endless speed involved in turning out events. He much preferred the derring-do part of the cause and, on May 28, staged one of his most daring dos ever. At the time, Earth First! had three tree-sitters up in the last remains of All Species Grove, but they were drawing little media notice. To rectify that, the Redwood Action Team strung a banner saying "Save The Old Growth" across U.S. 101 early in the morning at a spot about halfway between Garberville and Scotia, just south of the turnoff for Rockefeller Forest and Avenue of the Giants, Humboldt's two largest tourist attractions. Greg sat up there next to it, on a traverse line, startling the increasing flow of motorists below. The original plan had been to stay there only long enough for a sympathetic photographer to take a picture that could be distributed to newspapers and wire services, but the photographer was late, so Greg just perched, a hundred feet up, waving to passing cars. Some signaled back, extending either thumbs or middle fingers out their windows. It was the better part of an hour before a California Highway Patrol officer showed up, pulled over on the road shoulder, and, using his loudspeaker, ordered King to take the banner down immediately.

Greg said that was impossible. Unstringing it was a two-man job and his helper was not around—though in fact his support team was hiding back in the trees on the other side of the road. And, of course, the photographer still hadn't arrived.

King's excuse bought him time. A second Highway Patrol cruiser drove up and then a maintenance truck from Caltrans and they all waited next to the flow of traffic slowing down to gawk at Greg King and the banner.

What the CHP officers were waiting for was unclear, but, whatever it might have been, the stalemate broke suddenly with the arrival of a battered Toyota pickup, driven by one of Pacific Lumber's tree climbers. The man was furious when he saw what was going on and passed under the banner screaming obscenities at King out of his truck window. Then he burnt rubber in an illegal U-turn across the highway, skidded to a halt across the road from the CHP assemblage, and jumped out of the cab, shouting and strapping on his climbing gear at the same time: These fucking Earth Firsters wouldn't know goddamn old growth if it fell on them. Their goddamn propaganda had gone too far. They get their fucking faces in the newspaper and play God with his job while people like him did the real work and paid for their goddamn welfare checks.

Then he started up the tree to which Greg and the banner were anchored with separate ropes. Using spurs strapped to the inside of his ankles and a rope anchored on his harness and looped around the trunk, the PL man climbed faster than anyone Greg had ever seen.

Greg yelled at the climber that he'd better stay away from his traverse line. If that were cut, Greg King would end up splattered in the spread-eagle position all over some unsuspecting tourist's Oldsmobile.

Stop your fucking sniveling, the climber yelled back. He could cut that goddamn banner down without putting a nick in the goddamn Earth Firster's lifeline. And the banner was going. He'd had it up to fucking here with all this propaganda.

That said, the climber increased his speed another notch, flipping his waist rope, grabbing a fresh purchase with each lunge of his spurs. He was soon almost three-quarters of the way there.

Then the California Highway Patrol stepped in.

Is he with you? the CHP officer loudspeakered to King.

King said he didn't know who he was, but he thought the guy was going to cut his lifeline.

Hearing that, the CHP officer sprinted across the roadway to the climber's tree and ordered him to halt and come back down immediately or face arrest.

The climber gave in. But grudgingly. He shouted at King on his way down that, unlike the fucking Earth Firsters, he couldn't get arrested. He couldn't afford it. He had a real job and kids to feed. There was no Welfare taking care of him.

King breathed a sigh of relief and then another, as he saw the photographer's car pull up.

Twenty minutes later, the pictures taken, Greg King voluntarily surrendered his banner and returned to earth. He was cited for illegally hanging a sign on a federal highway and released without bail. The photographs of the Earth Firster suspended over the freeway, a hundred feet in the air next to his billboard-sized slogan, ran in several California newspapers and a national magazine.

The next week, Greg was out in the woods by himself, looking over timberlands, still his favorite activity of all. His principal object of reconnaissance was some old-growth Douglas fir out along a tributary of Sulphur Creek, just upstream from where it flowed into the east branch of the Mattole's lower north fork. After climbing up to a 1,600-feet elevation, he moved along Little Rainbow Ridge to 2,500 feet and into the teeth of a north wind cold enough that he pulled a second shirt out of his pack before proceeding up the main body of Rainbow Ridge, elevation 3,500 feet. He'd hiked twelve continuous hours the day before and eight more today and his legs felt like lunchmeat. Walls of fog were now pouring past him. At the ridge-crest, he crossed a dirt road.

Greg started along the road for several minutes until, swerving around a blind corner in the fog, a pickup truck, driven by a local rancher who weighed some three hundred pounds, almost ran him down.

The fat rancher asked King what the hell he was doing up here on private land.

Greg smiled. Just hiking, he said.

The rancher next wanted to know his name.

Tom, Greg said.

Tom what?

Tom Jones.

The rancher repeated to this Tom Jones that he was on private land, leased from the Pacific Lumber Company, and he'd best tell what in the hell he was doing out here.

Just hiking, Greg repeated. He must have gotten lost.

What would this Tom Jones think if he called the sheriff?

Greg said that would be a shame since he was just a lost hiker. No cause for the law to get involved.

There was a different law up here, the rancher answered. He said they were going back down the road here to his friend Jack's house and see how Jack felt about all this. He said King better get into the truck.

Greg said he'd hop in the back.

Which he did, until the rancher started his engine and began to pull away. Then Greg bailed out, hit the ground running, and disappeared into the second-growth forest on the far side of the road. The fat man made no attempt to give chase. Humping along under his pack, Greg followed Oil Creek until he found an abandoned logging road. The next day, Greg made it back to his tiny room in Arcata.

There was a message waiting on his telephone answering machine. The voice identified himself as "a dirt bike fanatic." He said that Greg King would "die in the forest." The caller claimed to have captured King and King was history.

Greg King swallowed hard.

In the grainy background static of his answering machine, the twenty-seven-year-old tree lover could hear the unmistakable far-off sound of the shit beginning to hit the fan.

41

Famous as they were by now, not John Campbell, Charles Hurwitz, Greg King, Judi Bari, nor Darryl Cherney waxed brightest on Humboldt County's horizon as 1988 rushed toward autumn. That status belonged to one Patrick Shannon, thirty-seven, a freelance logger from Willow Creek out near the Hoopa Indian reservation, though Shannon would hold that celebrity only briefly.

Shannon's stature materialized almost instantly. When July began, Patrick was obscure and unknown and by the end of September, he was a major Humboldt County player, the author of an updated Ghost Dance Religion for loggers, who had convinced a wide and enthusiastic audience that, with his help, they could band together, buy the Pacific Lumber Company, and put it back the way it used to be. There was a mechanism for doing that and it was called an Employee Stock Ownership Plan and he, Patrick Shannon—as smooth a talker as most folks in timber country had ever heard, a native son who'd made his mark out in the big world of San Francisco and then come home where he belonged—was going to show them how to use it. He was, he said, a disciple of Louis Kelso, the man who invented ESOPs, and he had done this kind of thing before. Dressed in a coat and tie, thin and charming, never at a loss for words yet never talking over anyone's head, Patrick Shannon seemed something of a savior at the time.

Patrick Shannon himself told and retold the following story of how he'd come to this mission. It began with his ninety-year-old cousin, Wilma Bishop, he said, niece of his great-grandfather, Doc Bishop, whose own father, John, a Nova Scotian immigrant, had been a pioneer logger in Falk, now a ghost town up the Elk River. Patrick's grandfather had run Buck's Sporting Goods in Eureka and Patrick's father had been a logger all his life out in the inland pine and fir forests along the Trinity River. Two years ago, after his mother died—at the end of a decade or so down in San Francisco during which he saved the city's Yellow Cab Company and then failed as a trucking company entrepreneur—Patrick moved his family into the house in Willow Creek where he'd been raised. Out there, beyond the reach of the fog bank, where redwoods don't grow at all, he started a firewood business—buying small timber leases in the Six Rivers National Forest, felling and bucking all by himself—and drove Highway 299 into Eureka regularly to spend time with Wilma. She was ninety years old and, by this spring, she was dying. It was Wilma who asked him to rescue PL, Patrick explained. She said somebody had to do something and she knew what he had done for those cabdrivers down in San Francisco. His cousin, Grant Bishop, from Scotia, pulled the green chain out at Mill A and Grant's brother, Emory, was a supervisor up at the Carlotta mill. Patrick had to look out for Grant and Emory and all like them, Wilma said. She wanted him to promise he would. She wanted him to promise that he would put things right out at old PL.

Patrick Shannon told audiences around Humboldt that he had no real choice but to give Wilma her deathbed promise. She touched his heart. And she spoke the truth, he said. If he could help cabdrivers in San Francisco, he *had* to come home and help his own people.

Patrick's explanation to himself hardly needed articulation. He knew in his flesh that he had the gift and he believed that where others saw difficulty, he could see the possible.

Shannon's Yellow Cab miracle, a central pillar in his Humboldt legend, had been produced when he was only twenty-three. Around Humboldt, it lent him enormous credibility and made the dream he was preaching seem eminently possible. The Yellow Cab rescue had begun, he said, as a class project when he was a student at the University of California in Santa Cruz. Of course, he was no ordinary student. He had dropped out of Humboldt State several years earlier, was married with five kids, and was running a one-limousine tour service in San Francisco at night and on weekends. He'd founded his tour business with a limo rescued from a junkyard and ran it as an unlicensed scab when the regular tour drivers were on strike. One of the courses he was taking was an independent study project called "Organizing Corporations" and, three weeks before Christmas in 1976, when he learned that Yellow Cab was filing for bankruptcy, threatening a thousand drivers with unemployment, Shannon announced on the spur of the moment at a party that he was going to buy it and save those people's jobs. After a brief pause for more wine, he called the city's principal AM news radio station, repeated the announcement and, within minutes, his plan was on the airwaves.

The next day Patrick Shannon convened a news conference at which most of the San Francisco media were present. A series of meetings with drivers followed, along with negotiations under the supervision of the bankruptcy court, and the foundation of a drivers' cooperative that was able to borrow enough money from the Teamsters' Union to purchase the entire San Francisco Yellow Cab franchise. Ten months after the rescue, Shannon, the effort's principal spokesman and proselytizer, left all administrative duties there and moved on to found a trucking company. He never did graduate from UC Santa Cruz. The manager of operations who had done most of the nuts-and-bolts work to make good on Shannon's talk in the Yellow Cab rescue, James Steel, was somewhat blunt when approached by the local press for a comment on his former compatriot early in the ESOP campaign. "Let me tell you right off," Steel said, "the man is a bullshit artist. He did a lot of talking, but that's about it."

Nonetheless, folks all over Humboldt County began believing in Patrick Shannon that summer.

He started out talking one-on-one: hanging out with his cousin Grant Bishop and his wife, Leona, in their Scotia kitchen; looking up several old friends from high school; tracking down anyone he thought might be interested in an ESOP.

Pete Kayes was one of those Shannon approached. Pete was a blacksmith in PL's machine shop. He'd started with the company almost ten years earlier, handling logs out on the pond that fed Mill A. Before that he'd served in the Navy on nuclear submarines and earned a bachelor's degree in psychology from Humboldt State. During June, Pete had written a letter to the *Times-Standard*, saying that the employees at PL had been "kidnapped" by Charles Hurwitz. When John Campbell heard about the letter, he passed the word to Kayes that if he really felt kidnapped, John could surely set him free. That threat did not, however, change Kayes's attitude. And when Shannon approached him, he signed on. Pete was impressed by Shannon in general and his 800 phone number in particular. He figured Patrick must be a man of some influence and money to have one. He also thought the whole idea made sense. The only way the company was ever going to serve its people as the old company had was for the people themselves to own it. And it seemed apparent in every word that came out of his mouth that Patrick Shannon could pull off such a purchase.

Shortly after they first spoke, Pete Kayes helped Patrick rent the Hydesville Fire Department building for a series of August and September public meetings, escalating the ESOP recruiting effort.

The Hydesville gatherings drew about forty people apiece, filling all the Fire Department's folding chairs. And most who came arrived edgy. Some kept glancing out the window, to see if anyone from the company was out in the street taking down license numbers. They all agreed that attending would gain them automatic entry on John Campbell's shit list.

Patrick knew their worries, he told them. And, to be totally straight about it, this thing would never work unless the workers at PL were ready to overcome their fear of the company and speak up. If they didn't have the courage, then they didn't deserve to hold the stewardship of the forest any more than Charles Hurwitz did. Other workers—at Yellow Cab, at Avis, at North American Rayon—had stood up and it had worked for them. They owned their companies and, by God and with a little help from the banks, Pacific Lumber could add itself to the list. That was within their grasp. He had a plan and the plan would work. How the hell had Charles Hurwitz bought PL in the first place? Patrick asked. He had borrowed money, Patrick answered. And there was no reason people just like the people in this room couldn't do the same damn thing, because PL itself was the collateral, whether owned by them or that son of a bitch from Texas. They might be worried about losing their jobs for advocating an ESOP, but if Hurwitz kept cutting like this they were going to lose their jobs anyway. The forest was not infinite and his cut would far outstrip its capacity to renew itself. And once that timber was gone, all of Humboldt was going to follow it right down the tubes. You could take Patrick Shannon's word on that. It was time to save themselves or stop sniveling about what was happening. If they weren't willing to act, they deserved what happened to them. And if they were willing, he was with them all the way. When it was their company, he'd still be with them, pulling the green chain if need be, and doing his bit to make the company work.

For all his talk, Shannon's plan remained vague. He said the details of their actual purchase would all be worked out when they had a serious movement ready to put up or shut up. He said that he did know, however, that there were several large banks interested in providing financing and he'd already had some preliminary discussions with General Electric Financial. The simple truth was that if Charles Hurwitz could buy the company against its will, they could turn around and buy it from him. That was capitalism and it was time for Humboldt folks—folks who worked the Coast Range and along the Eel with their hands and their backs, the salt of the earth, folks like those right here in the Hydesville fire station—to get their own piece of the action.

When he opened the floor to questions, a mill hand from Carlotta wondered how they were going to convince Hurwitz to sell. Patrick said all they'd have to do was offer him a profit. That was the way people like Hurwitz worked. But even if that wasn't successful, there were other ways. Maybe they'd have to shut the company down for a day or two or six to make their point. But the important thing to know was that the workers had the leverage if they'd use it. They could be the boss and have the final word if they were prepared to seize the moment.

A feller from the woods crew spoke up toward the end of the meeting. He thought this guy Shannon was just wishing on the one hand and shitting on the other. And, as well-intentioned as he was sure Patrick was, the feller sure as hell didn't think he was ever going to be out pulling the chain under any circumstances. The way the feller saw it, even if the employees did buy the company, they'd have to cut more trees than Hurwitz simply to pay off the banks.

He didn't like what was going on with the company any more than anyone else at the Hydesville meeting, but he figured this was just a bad idea that wouldn't work in a month of Sundays.

Patrick admitted it would take imagination, but they would—this he could promise—they *would* buy the company *and* they *would* return it to sustained yield. An ESOP had tax advantages that Hurwitz didn't. An ESOP could gain special subsidies. And an ESOP would be smart enough to find a way to both make money and nurture the forest. Patrick knew this was possible.

And almost everyone who came to the Hydesville meetings agreed with him. He had reached out in the dark, Shannon later explained, and touched something alive.

Lester Reynolds believed even more than most. Lester had been with PL since 1956 and was now the lead mechanic for the mill's monorail system. He heard about the ESOP from Pete Kayes, one of his buddies in the company machine shop. After the first Hydesville meeting, Lester, even though he read poorly and spelled even worse, wrote a letter to the editor of the *Times-Standard* touting the effort. He also attended two more Hydesville meetings and when Patrick got to the part where he asked everyone to open up a $500 savings account—the amount each of the workers would eventually have to pony up to get the purchase rolling—Lester stood up, waved his bank passbook, and proclaimed that the process had already begun, yes siree. After three years, the deliverance they'd all prayed for was about to happen. They wouldn't be working for that son of a bitch Charles Hurwitz much longer. Their next boss was going to be themselves.

On September 28, Shannon convened an all-county meeting at the Eureka Inn. Volunteers had been building it up for weeks out of Leona Bishop's kitchen, calling employees, urging them to come, and people began lining up at the registration tables outside the Inn's main banquet room at 6:30 P.M. By 7:00, the room was full and the registration line still stretched across the lobby, so the adjoining banquet room was opened and soon filled as well. The reporters in attendance estimated the crowd at 350. Some of the veterans of the Hydesville meeting were there wearing hats with "ESOP" emblazoned on them and the mood was festive. Before Patrick Shannon even said a word, folks were celebrating the advent of a new day for old PL. The intimidation of those early meetings at the fire station had disappeared. Few seemed to care if the company knew they were there or not. This, they agreed, was the chance for which they'd all been waiting.

The buzz in the room hushed only when Shannon rose to speak. He didn't bother to introduce himself, talking as though everyone already knew him. They were all just neighbors here, he said, gathered to take control of their lives once and for all. With him at the table was a lawyer he had flown in from Tennessee who was an expert on labor law. Once the Pledge of Allegiance and an invocation by a local Catholic priest had been completed, Patrick turned the mike over to the lawyer. The lawyer said he had participated in a lot of employee takeovers and he reassured everyone that making a bid on the company was their right and advocating the ESOP was an activity protected by the National Labor Relations Act. The company had no right to punish them for it.

That, of course, drew a round of applause.

Then Patrick started in. One observer later described his speech as "rousing, bizarre, and idiosyncratic." Shannon had been reading Carl Sandburg's biography of Abraham Lincoln and peppered his presentation with stories of Lincoln's trials and tribulations freeing the slaves. They were here today to free the slaves as well, he said— free them from Charles Hurwitz and Texas money, free them from Drexel Burnham Lambert, from junk bonds, from Michael Milken and all the rest of the predators that had come into this county and seized its best company. Much of what he went on to lay out was the same as he had at Hydesville, mixing equal parts vagueness and inspiration. All the later newspaper accounts of the evening described him as "charismatic." He was interrupted for applause at several junctures. And this time, when he got to the part about the $500 savings account, Lester Reynolds stood up wearing an ESOP hat and a jacket on which his wife, Shirley, had stitched "SAVINGS" across the back. To rousing cheers, Lester turned a circle, like a model on a fashion show runway, and then sat back down.

For the question period, two mikes had been set up in the audience. One was designated for those in favor of the ESOP and one for those opposed. All the questioners came to the "in favor" one. Many raised the issue of convincing Hurwitz to sell. The company had already mailed all workers two letters from Hurwitz saying the company was not for sale, under any circumstances. Had Shannon talked to "Uncle Charlie" about this? one worker wondered.

No, Patrick admitted when the laughter died down, he hadn't. But if he were old Uncle Charlie he'd be shaking in his boots about now. There were five different investigations of him going on, Shannon claimed, plus Bill Bertain's lawsuits were waiting in the wings. Hurwitz might just be forced to make a distress sale. And if he wasn't, he might still have to sell if his employees took the power into their own hands and made him "an offer he couldn't refuse."

There was more laughter, then someone in the back shouted a question without coming to the mike. What was in all this for Shannon? he asked.

Patrick didn't skip a beat. He hadn't given much thought to a fee, he answered, but whatever it was, it would probably be in the neighborhood of 1 percent of the transaction and would be paid by the banks doing the financing, after the sale was complete.

Hell, someone else shouted, if he pulled this off, he should get something for it.

That comment was greeted with more applause and Patrick went on to the next question.

It wasn't until the last questioner that anyone stood at the "no on ESOP" microphone. This single exception scraped his feet nervously. It all sounded great, he said, but it would never work. This was all just "pie in the sky."

Patrick said everyone should give this man a hand for having the courage to say his piece.

When that was done, Patrick dropped the subject and began winding up the meeting. What had gone on tonight was, he said, "just a little short of a miracle," and now, it was time "to take the next step of fate."

A quick election was then held, in which sixteen members were chosen for a board to oversee the ESOP effort—including both Pete Kayes and Lester Reynolds—and then the hat was passed. These contributions would be used to open up an office in Fortuna and continue the effort, Patrick pledged. They were on their way.

Afterward, the crowd lingered in the banquet room sipping coffee for another half hour. The supply of ESOP hats was quickly sold and the volunteer lists were filled. When folks finally started straggling out, a number of them were laughing, slapping themselves on the back, and calling each other "boss."

Patrick Shannon stayed until the last one had gone, all a-tingle at what was going on. He hadn't a clue that his movement had just peaked.

42

Patrick Shannon was never more than an annoyance to Charles Hurwitz, but he was that. It irritated Charles to have some idiot from nowhere parading around one of his businesses claiming he was going to buy it, so one of the first responses Pacific Lumber and its parent, Maxxam, made to the ESOP movement was to circulate a letter from Charles Hurwitz stating unequivocally that PL was not for sale. Perhaps most annoying of all for Charles was that he had to give this bizarre movement even that much attention. His hands were more than full on far more important fronts. The corner on high finance that Michael Milken had controlled for the last decade was at last starting to collapse and a close Milken collaborator such as Charles Hurwitz needed to step lively to keep from being pulled down with it. By the time Patrick Shannon showed up, it was obvious to everyone in the business that the Pope of Junk Bonds was in deep shit, both legally and, an even more ominous portent, financially.

Much of the financial end of Michael Milken's collapse would grow out of the spreading catastrophe in the savings and loan industry, which, of course, also touched on the heart of Charles Hurwitz's alliance with Michael Milken and Drexel Burnham Lambert. Buying a savings and loan was the first deal Michael and Charles ever did, and Charles was by no means the only one with whom Milken did such deals. Milken recognized that the deregulation of the S&Ls in the early Reagan years had created a huge market of capital to tap for junk bonds and since the savings and loan industry was federally insured, it was essentially free money to use however the industry chose. Michael Milken immediately proceeded to build a network of allies who bought into the business cheap, used junk bond dividends to leapfrog into big-time finance, and created an automatic market for all the issues Drexel could generate. A *Wall Street Journal* column would later characterize these allies as a "spider web" of "deep pocket investors" who subscribed to all Drexel's "most difficult" deals. This web would include a virtual Who's Who of S&L bailouts: Columbia Savings and Loan Association, Far West Savings and Loan, and Lincoln Savings of California; CenTrust Bank and American Savings and Loan Association of Florida; and, of course, United Savings Association of Texas.

This USAT was the S&L Drexel and Milken bought with Hurwitz. Its eventual bailout by the Federal Savings and Loan Insurance Corporation would cost some $1.3 billion—the third most expensive such rescue in history. When the federal regulators finally took USAT over, they found assets that included real estate, junk bonds, an arbitrage operation that was wiped out in the October 1987 stock market crash, an interest in Houston Yellow Cab, and shares in two South American companies whose actual businesses were unknown to anyone in the USAT offices. One financier said it looked as though the company had bought "one of everything." Besides enough foreclosed Texas real estate loans to rank it as among the biggest landlords in Houston, what USAT had most of was junk bonds, some $650 million worth of "below investment grade" paper, 97 percent of the Savings Associations' securities portfolio at the time the Home Loan Bank Board had ordered USAT to cease purchasing such securities in the last half of 1987. It was controlled by the United Financial Group, of which Hurwitz was chairman of the board and, through a private corporation, a 23 percent owner. Drexel itself owned almost 10 percent of UFG as well, and both they and Hurwitz held stock options that would allow them to significantly increase their share in the holding company if that should prove necessary. Still, none of them individually was across the 25 percent threshold at which they could be held legally liable for USAT's squandered worth. There were those who would later claim that such an ownership was one of the prices Milken charged for his backing in the takeover game, but Charles was not one of those making such statements. Charles simply had no comment on the subject at all.

In March 1988, Hurwitz resigned as UFG's chairman, though he remained its biggest shareholder. By then, UFG's only asset, United Savings Association of Texas, had been under siege by bank investigators for almost a full year. By December, USAT was seized by Federal regulators, making all Hurwitz's UFG stock essentially worthless, but otherwise costing him nothing. At the time of his resignation, the UFG press officer explained that Charles was too busy "elsewhere" in his empire to give UFG the proper attention.

The "elsewhere" was another acquisition, even bigger than that of Pacific Lumber. While USAT slid slowly down the tubes, Hurwitz and the Drexel Burnham Lambert High Yield Bond shop just past Rodeo Drive were busy adding onto the Maxxam empire with one last collaboration before disaster overtook Drexel and its Los Angeles office. This time the target Hurwitz and Milken chose was Kaiser Tech—formerly Kaiser Aluminum, a fragment of the legacy of legendary California industrialist Henry J. Kaiser and the fifth largest producer of aluminum in the world. When Drexel and Charles moved on Kaiser, about the time the loggers' parade hit Eureka, the company was floundering after having been taken over by English investor Alan Clore. "The time," *California Business* noted, "was ripe for someone of Hurwitz's reptilian calm to make a killing." Losing money and facing margin calls, Clore began marketing his Kaiser holdings with such desperation that he spooked potential buyers. Hurwitz—backed with more Drexel-issued paper—then cornered Clore and bought him out at a price per share 30 percent under market. Next, he outmaneuvered a management attempt to block Kaiser's merger into Maxxam and, in a matter of four months, had become a magnate in the aluminum business and a member in good standing of the Fortune 500. His friend and lawyer, Ezra Levin, would later characterize Charles's performance in the run at Kaiser as masterful, a thing of genuine genius. The financial press rated the deal another "steal."

Charles Hurwitz was still ascending, even as his chief catapult fell away.

43

And Bill Bertain ground his teeth, read all the stories he could find, and watched helplessly. Much of his 1988 was spent wandering in the wilderness while the three-year anniversary of the takeover approached and, with it, expiration of the statute of limitations for filing any action in Federal Court against Hurwitz, Milken, Drexel, and the rest. Bertain intended to sue, but he knew he would have little hope of success until he could convince some big-city law firm to join him and bring resources sufficient to make a serious legal move against adversaries the size of the ones he was up against. Tired of doing nothing but keeping a foot in the door, Bertain made finding a legal ally his top priority. He tried firms all over the Bay Area, using his own acquaintances and connections and making some pitches cold, right over the transom. Whatever the angle of his approach, nobody was willing to take a flier on this little Humboldt County crusade, even for a healthy split of any eventual financial judgment. Bill made lots of calls and got lots of sympathy but no recruits.

In the meantime, of course, he was rapidly going broke and worrying about it. His crusade was generating as much as $10,000 a month in expenses, most of which he borrowed five and six hundred dollars at a time. His mortgage was becoming harder and harder to carry, Rebecca was pregnant again and due in October, and their savings were exhausted. He landed a little part-time legal work, but mostly he just worried over events from the fall of 1985 like a man picking a scab, usually strung as tight as a violin string inside. Bill Bertain was little more than a year's worry away from the onset of ulcerative colitis, featuring one- and two-week episodes of sometimes bloody incontinence during which he lost as much as fifteen pounds. When he prayed, he knew it was God's work he was doing, but he also knew his obsession was taking a heavy toll on him.

Still, he pressed on. After money and allies, Bill's foremost priority was still recruiting plaintiffs for his federal action. He knew his state court plaintiff, Don Jose Thompson, was game to repeat, along with his wife, Rose Olga Thompson, but he wanted more.

Then, not long after the loggers' truck parade that passed right by the window in his office overlooking the waterbed showroom, he got a call from Kelly Bettiga.

Nothing had been the same for Kelly after the company meeting in January. He'd put himself out front, mouthin' off to old goddamn John Campbell, so there was no camouflage left, no place to hide when the arty started falling, that was for goddamn sure. And he told anyone who asked that he was always prepared to back his shit up and would do the same goddamn thing again, bet your fucking ass. Almost everyone was surprised he still had a job, but Kelly wasn't. He'd figured on a standoff and that's just about what he got.

A couple of days after the meeting at the Winema, he stopped in at the Scotia Coffee Shop to talk to old Ruby, and John was there with a couple of his closest cronies. Kelly felt their eyes lock onto him as soon as he walked into the room and he eyeballed them right back. They were all laughing and looking at him like Who the Hell Is This Hippie Who Mouths Off at the Meeting? so Kelly walked straight over to their table.

How you guys doin'? he asked.

Then Bettiga turned his back and ate some pie at the counter without ever looking Campbell's way again.

And nothing happened.

Kelly was still putting in his ten-hour days plus Saturdays at a chop saw, where he stood and salvaged substandard Douglas fir boards. Wood that had too many knots or knots too big or a clear piece with a big knot on the end or other flaws came down to Kelly's division and they cut it to standard grades, if possible, and cut it into blocks that could be glued together into laminated wood if it wasn't possible. At break time, some guys avoided him because they were afraid of getting associated or because they just thought he was fucking crazy, but Kelly didn't get bothered being treated as weird and certainly was not about to back off. He'd made his play and, if anything, he wanted to enlarge on it. First, he had a meeting with his family and let them know he was going to get his shit down and he expected them to at least keep quiet if they didn't like it. This was important to him, real fucking important.

That said, Kelly made his move toward becoming really public and agreed to be a source for an article being written by a *Wall Street Journal* reporter about what was going on around Pacific Lumber. He met with the reporter in Arcata, having driven through a rainstorm one Tuesday after his shift. He was nervous at first, but once he got rolling, Bettiga didn't hold much back. He laid into everything and said Hurwitz was the worst fuckin' thing to happen to Humboldt County since the flood of 1964. The son of a bitch was just wreaking havoc. There was no goddamn way he could cut wood like he was cutting it and still have it all work out in the interest of anybody who was a worker. It was all bullshit and *The Wall Street Journal* could fucking print that and print his fucking name with it.

The reporter's mouth dropped a little at hearing this from a mill hand, but then the *Journal* never ran the story.

Bettiga was disappointed but undaunted. By the time he called Bertain, he had already decided to go even one step further and join a lawsuit against Hurwitz. He knew the Bertains from his childhood at St. Patrick's Catholic Church in Scotia. The family had one of the best names in the Eel River Valley.

Kelly began their conversation by thanking Bill for trying to save this thing when it was quite evident that most everybody else around the company wasn't going to get off their asses and say anything. Now, Kelly wanted to join in. He was ready to sue. The bottom line, he said, was that when the story was written about this place, Kelly Bettiga was not going to have anybody say that it was just full of a bunch of coward sons of bitches. He'd spent thirteen fucking months in the Nam, blowing the piss out of people over a bunch of fucking mud and swamp grass, and for this place to go out without him so much as a raising a whimper, life would have no meaning.

To die for somebody else's rice paddy and not be willing to risk getting fired from a goddamned mill job when your home was at stake was ridiculous. Sometimes you just had to fight and he was ready to do it, whenever the opportunity arose.

Bill said he thought that would be soon.

But Bill always procrastinated writing and, true to form, entered September, barely a month before the statute of limitations would expire, without having begun composing the necessarily lengthy legal complaint. Then, in the second week of the month, just as he was about to commence writing, his crusade got its biggest break yet when the Securities and Exchange Commission announced a massive civil fraud case against the firm of Drexel Burnham Lambert. The complaint alleged that between 1984 and 1986, Drexel's Michael Milken had masterminded a secret arrangement with Ivan Boesky in which Boesky traded in huge blocks of stock at Drexel's bidding, pushing forward their takeover projects and generating huge illicit profits. *Time* called it "Throwing the Book at Drexel." The suit listed violations of virtually every provision of the 1934 Securities Act. One of its prime examples was the takeover of Pacific Lumber Company by Maxxam, in which the SEC complaint cast Maxxam as one of the victims.

Bertain couldn't buy the analysis of Hurwitz as a victim in the process, but at least this complaint had kicked the door leading to Drexel and Milken wide open. So much so that Bertain was convinced that it would draw big law firms like flies and he launched into yet another round of visits to big Bay Area firms rather than start on the Federal Court complaint, figuring whoever he recruited could crank it out in no time. Unfortunately, however, he recruited no one, and in the second week of October, seven days before his absolute deadline, Bertain still had not written his complaint, was once again broke, and was strung tighter than ever. This was also the week before Rebecca was due to deliver, which he had promised to spend at home with her, so he began the week by breaking his promise and feeling terrible about it. Then he borrowed a word processor from a lawyer downstairs in his building and began staying at the office until 2:00 A.M. every night, cranking out the complaint. It named Drexel, Milken, Hurwitz, the old PL board, Salomon Brothers, and a number of others and asked that the company be returned to its state before the tender offer and the old stockholders awarded $750 million in compensatory damages and $1.5 billion in exemplary damages. Bill planned to file the complaint in Los Angeles, rather than San Francisco, because a number of the Drexel defendants were there and he hoped to avoid any chance of being assigned once again to Judge William Schwarzer.

Bertain's only break from frantic writing came on Wednesday, when Rebecca gave birth a week early to their daughter, Esther. Bill was there in the delivery room and spent the night at the hospital with his wife and his new child. He had planned to carry the virtually completed brief down to Los Angeles himself on Thursday, but the birth made that impossible. So instead of going himself on Thursday, the day before the statute of limitations ran out, he recruited an old friend to carry it down there on Friday, the last possible day. And—as was the case with much of the logistics arranged by Bill Bertain—that became an adventure.

It began Friday morning when the Arcata airport was fogged in, grounding all flights in or out. That forced the messenger Bertain had recruited to drive all the way to San Francisco, a five-hour journey, and catch a plane there to Los Angeles, where he was met at LAX by a friend of his in a sports car. By the time they headed for the Federal Building, the clerk of the Federal Court's office was only minutes away from closing and rush hour was in full swing. The messenger's friend drove frantically, sometimes the wrong way down one-way streets, sometimes up on the sidewalk. They and Bertain's complaint reached the clerk's office just as the door was about to be locked.

The Wall Street Journal ran a story the following Monday about the new lawsuit filed in the names of Don Jose Thompson, Kelly Bettiga, and several others—with a box on the front page and the actual story on page five—and in a matter of days, Bertain had been contacted by a Wisconsin law firm. Not long after Thanksgiving, the Wisconsin firm, one from Chicago, and one from Los Angeles all threw in with him.

Then, four days before Christmas, in the biggest securities fraud settlement in history, Drexel Burnham Lambert, once the hottest investment banking firm on Wall Street, pled guilty to six felony charges of securities law violations and agreed to pay some $650 million in penalties. They also agreed to cooperate with the ongoing criminal investigation of Michael Milken, essentially throwing the Pope of Junk Bonds to the wolves.

The Lord often worked in mysterious ways, Bill Bertain noted. The Lord often worked in mysterious ways.

Cecilia Lanman saw no mystery at all in the way PL worked. Charles Hurwitz's corporation turned ancient forest into money and trash—and the money left for Houston while the trash stayed in Humboldt.

And if that timber industry formula held sway, Cecilia expected the consequences to be dire: the marbled murrelet—a small sea bird that nested in the dead tops of ancient redwoods—might disappear, lost forever to life on the planet, and so might the spotted owl, the red tree vole, the fisher, the northern goshawk, the Olympic salamander, and the tailed frog. While they didn't add up to much when measured by their immediate impact on the lives of humans, Cecilia noted, these creatures were alive, had been around for quite some time, and if Pacific Lumber was allowed to strip their last islands of old growth, they would all be included in the leftover trash. The simple fact was that PL's planned old-growth harvest was a biological disaster that ultimately diminished the viability of all species and robbed everyone of the stunning variety that was at the heart of nature.

And Cecilia Lanman also made it quite clear that she meant to do everything within her power to stop it.

When Cecilia and her husband Gil Gregori hosted the January 1987, meeting at which a number of key players from the Sinkyone

fight had turned their focus to Pacific Lumber's accelerated harvest, Cecilia had endorsed the idea but sworn she would not get involved. She didn't want to jump right into another timber fight.
Instead, she felt herself pulled back toward life on their farm on a
dirt track off the Ettersburg Road along the Mattole, where their organic garden fed them and they'd planted orchards and repaired
erosion along the river bank and where she'd helped found the local school and raised their two daughters and where the whole
larger back-to-the-land settlement embraced them in a culture that
nurtured and loved her.

But, by the fall of 1988, that dream was tattered at best. Self-
sufficiency and organic simplicity had come to mean that all her
time was spent picking and pruning and canning and cooking and
making up for the absence of convenience with an abundance of
energy and it wore on her more than she'd ever imagined it would.
Now, Cecilia's marriage was broken beyond the point of repair, and
she'd moved closer to the civilization along Humboldt's paved
roads and thrown herself full bore into EPIC's campaign, which
had expanded to three active lawsuits and an ongoing process of
sorting through THPs and deciding which were worthy of throwing
their meager resources against. Holding it all together was too
much for The Man Who Walks In The Woods, and Cecilia—trained
as an organizer in Cesar Chavez's United Farm Workers national
boycott—shouldered an enormous load and, just as everyone had
expected, she carried it fiercely.

Among the folks of the Mateel, Cecilia had become something
of a legend during the Sinkyone fight. Others referred to her as
"the Velvet Hammer" and did so with enormous respect. Without
ever quite abandoning her poise, Cecilia would not hesitate to get
right up in someone's face if she thought the situation called for it.
During the Sinkyone, the story of one of her encounters with Gere
Melo, the Georgia Pacific Corporation's forester, was told and retold. She'd first met Melo on an inspection tour he hosted of some
Georgia Pacific land on which the company had promised to leave a
depth of trees along the cliffs overlooking the ocean, through which
a park hiking trail was then to be blazed. Instead, when they
reached Dark Gulch, the company had cut all the way to the beach,
violating the boundaries of their own THP. Melo laughed when she
pointed it out to him.

Cecilia never forgot that obnoxious laughter and, at one point in the ongoing fight over that part of the Lost Coast, she and Melo ended up face to face.

Cecilia was succinct and straightforward. She told Gere Melo he was slime, pure slime—looking right into his face, her blue eyes drilling through to the other side of his head, never raising her voice, managing not to sound mean, just enunciating as though she were stating a well-known fact that was beyond dispute. Slime, Gere. Not just any slime, but pure slime.

Cecilia Lanman made a lot of the timbermen with whom she dealt nervous.

Now that she was back in the fight, she didn't kid herself, either. They might be winning their court cases—in fact, EPIC would never lose one—but the structure of the law made them make a case for each THP they wished to challenge. PL, on the other hand, would file tens or even hundreds of THPs in 1988 alone. Three lawsuits, five lawsuits, ten lawsuits—it was all dwarfed by the lumber companies' deforestation machine. She knew they were losing the race, but hoped they could lose at a slower pace and win enough to maintain a corridor in which old-growth species could survive.

At the time Bill Bertain's suit was filed in L.A., EPIC was in Humboldt Superior Court, in combination with the Sierra Club, challenging the CDF's approval of 88–462, some 230 acres out along Salmon Creek, a slice aimed at the heart of Headwaters Forest. On Friday, October 21, both sides met at a hearing for a preliminary injunction to ensure PL did no cutting on the THP, even though the company was still maintaining a voluntary moratorium on all contested timber harvest plans.

When Greg King dropped by the courthouse on the day of the initial hearing on the case, he found Cecilia in the hallway, distressed in her typically defiant way. She explained that things had not gone that well in court. The Sierra Club had joined the case and the lawyer they supplied had insisted on pushing the judge to disqualify himself and that had ticked the judge off, initiating a running argument and ensuring that the restraining order request would not be ruled on that day. Cecilia wished that the Sierra Club counsel had just let the judge hear the case. Now PL, sensing an opening, had announced they were rescinding their voluntary moratorium and felt free to cut in any THP for which they had

CDF approval, challenged or not. In the absence of a restraining order, that might well mean disaster for 88–462. She suspected that the company meant to immediately begin cutting a road into the heart of Headwaters. It was Friday and she said she wouldn't be surprised if Hurwitz wouldn't have his company start cutting it over the weekend.

Greg was immediately as distressed as she was, but, he explained, there was nothing he could do. For the next week, the Redwood Action Team's resources were committed to blockading two gypo logging shows down along the Humboldt-Mendocino border. Cecilia, of course, was even more bound than he. In order to maintain the "clean hands" the court required from any litigant, she had to separate herself from any attempt to halt PL's logging by any means other than action by the court, so all she could do was hope the restraining order came soon.

By Tuesday, however, there was still no restraining order and Cecilia began picking up reports that trucks heaped with old-growth logs had begun rolling out of PL property at the end of Newburg Road in Fortuna. Short of trespass, there was no way to identify just where the logs were being cut, but she feared the worst.

Cecilia had no option but to grind her teeth and go on with EPIC's regular business, most of which meant participating in the timber harvest plan process. And, on Thursday, while still awaiting a restraining order on 88–462, she sat in on another of the regular team meetings at the CDF's Fortuna offices where new THPs were discussed. She brought her usual presence: unrelenting, well-informed, projecting a slight air of disgust that the subject even had to be talked about. How could they even be considering these THPs? EPIC had already sued over exactly the same thing and CDF had lost. In these arguments, she was always on top of her opponents' fallacies and never let one pass. And she always built a solid legal record, should she and Woods decide to target any of those in question.

After the Thursday team meeting concluded, Cecilia used a pay phone to check with the EPIC office in Garberville and learned that the court had just issued the restraining order for 88–462. After only a moment's hesitation, Cecilia and the woman with whom she'd driven to the meeting headed out Newburg Road in her old Volvo station wagon. She couldn't get those loaded trucks out of her mind and intended to drive onto PL's logging road and follow it to where it bordered on 88–462 and inform anyone out there that the area was now under court order. That was as far as she felt she could go and still maintain "clean hands" but she was determined to do at least that.

When the two women reached PL property, the gate leading onto the dirt logging road was open, so they headed up it. As they climbed on the lane and a half of dirt that rose from sea level to the crest of a ridge at some 1800 feet, the road was littered here and there with long shreds of bark and occasional lengths of discarded cable. The Volvo also passed several logging trucks—hauling ass in a cloud of dust, loaded to the gills with old growth—and Cecilia and her friend waved grimly at the suddenly slack-jawed drivers. Eventually, Cecilia noticed a rooster tail of dust behind them and the tell-tale outline of an orange PL Security pickup, but they kept driving until they came around a corner and one of the company's giant D-8 Cats was waiting for them. It dropped its blade across the road, the security truck skidded up behind the Volvo, and Cecilia was trapped.

When the security officer started reading her the riot act about driving a car on a private road, Cecilia warned him that if they were cutting anything up ahead in 88–462, they had better cease and desist because it was now under court order.

The security officer made it quite clear he could give a shit what she had to say. She was trespassing, pure and simple, and if she knew what was good for her, she would just shut up until he got his orders on just what to do about it.

Cecilia Lanman and her friend were detained out on the logging road for more than an hour before the Volvo was towed back to the gate where PL ended and Fortuna began. There, Cecilia was cited for vehicular trespass and released.

By the next morning, however, the traffic in old-growth logs exiting from Pacific Lumber property onto Newburg Road had shrunk to a trickle.

45

John Campbell held the high ground for Charles Hurwitz's Pacific Lumber Company throughout it all.

When Cecilia denounced the company for reneging on the public promises it had made about its logging techniques, Campbell issued a public statement maintaining that "Pacific Lumber has honored all of its commitments," despite ample documentary evidence to the contrary. When the *Times-Standard* published a report during Hurwitz's takeover of Kaiser Tech asserting that cash generated by PL was being used to help finance the deal, Campbell went on the public record denying any such involvement. Then, when PL's required public reports revealed that the company had been buying Kaiser stock for nine months leading up to Hurwitz's purchase, Campbell went on the public record again, asserting that PL's purchases were made in complete independence of Charles's plans and were not in any way connected to the move he eventually made on Kaiser. When Charles Hurwitz continued to be vilified around Humboldt as an outsider seeking a quick buck, John Campbell went in front of the Garberville Rotary Club and asserted that, "contrary to the doomsday headlines, Charles Hurwitz is not a bad guy at all." When the ABC Television program *20/20* ran a story implying that PL's cut had been tripled rather than doubled as he had claimed, a rumor circulated around Mill B that John had been so furious that he had punched a hole through a plasterboard wall. The next day, it was said, John showed up at work with a bandage on his hand.

Campbell's steadfastness did not go unnoticed by Charles Hurwitz watching from Maxxam headquarters in Houston and, when the company proceeded with an internal reorganization late in 1988—diminishing the role of the old MCO Los Angeles office—Bill Leone moved from the Pacific Lumber presidency to the presidency of Maxxam and John was promoted from Pacific Lumber's executive vice president and named Leone's successor. No one in town disputed that this promotion capped perhaps the most remarkable rise ever through PL's ranks. Barely twenty years ago, Campbell had arrived at the Arcata airport with Ed Carpenter's daughter in tow, back from Australia to throw his lot into a lumber business about which he as yet knew nothing. That first day, he had wondered out loud to the mill hand sent to fetch him and Cindy down to Scotia about just what his prospects might be in this place. Now, he'd risen to the presidency in less time than it had taken either old Mr. Murphy or his son Stan to do the same.

Campbell's promotion also marked the first time the Pacific Lumber Company presidency had resided in Scotia since the years immediately following Stan's death more than sixteen years earlier. John himself had no public comment on his elevation, leaving that task to Scotia's resident p.r. officer.

"It's nice to have the presidency back here [in Scotia]," the p.r. officer observed.

46

President or not, however, John Campbell was still surrounded by nemeses, and Darryl Cherney was foremost among them. Campbell had still not been able to turn the public relations tide Darryl continued to muster.

On the eve of John Campbell's promotion, Cherney was planning a demonstration he expected might be his most inventive one yet. The idea had actually come to him more than a year earlier but it wasn't until the end of 1988 that he'd found time and energy to organize it. The demonstration was a piece of street theatre intended to play on the classic horror film *Night of the Living Dead,* in which the dead rose out of graveyards and invaded the world of the living. Darryl called his demonstration "Day of the Living Dead Hurwitzes." In a burst of imagination, it had come to Darryl that Hurwitz was like a zombie who had invaded Pacific Lumber and the forest, intent on claiming them for the world of the dead. So this demonstration would be a funeral procession through Scotia to the PL head office, right outside John Campbell's window. The participants would carry black coffins marked "Economy," "Ecology," "Community," and "Security." And all of them would be wearing photocopied masks of Charles Hurwitz, made from a photograph in which the Texan's cold, dark looks seemed their most ghoulish. At the culmination of the demonstration, a young child would jump out of one of the coffins, symbolizing the death of the future. The point, Darryl explained to the press ahead of time, was that Charles Hurwitz was slowly turning Scotia into a ghost town.

Darryl did not hesitate to describe the idea as brilliant, but he was nonetheless worried. Something about the demonstration made him uneasy and he was dogged by a sense of dire premonition—so much so that he felt compelled to consult an astrologer about the demonstration's prospects.

The astrologer recoiled upon reviewing her charts. The Day of the Living Dead Hurwitzes was scheduled for a Thursday and that, she warned Darryl, was a great mistake. That particular Thursday was the Dark of the Moon, so it was imperative that the demonstration be moved to Friday. The Dark of the Moon was much too dangerous a time for such serious business.

Darryl cringed at her response, but the posters and leaflets were already distributed and he couldn't change the date. Later, he would cite this botched timing among the reasons for his disappointment with the day.

Though, he had to admit, it looked good when the forty marchers set off down Main Street. Darryl was there with Judi Bari. Greg King marched near them, carrying a rack of papier-mâché shrunken heads, plastered with Hurwitz's likeness. The whole crowd sang a ditty Darryl had composed to the tune of "God Rest Ye Merry Gentlemen": "God rest ye merry lumbermen, may nothing you dismay, remember Charlie Hurwitz has debts he has to pay . . . so watch him haul your redwood trees and pension fund away . . . Oh, tidings of hunger and fear, tidings of hunger and fear." Some demonstrators were dressed in black dress suits, like Hurwitz's, others wore Earth First! T-shirts. Altogether, the visuals were "great."

But the scene Cherney had envisioned when they reached the offices never materialized. Waiting for them there was a counterdemonstration twice the size of their own. Some were Pacific Lumber employees, some were employees from the Eel River Sawmill down the freeway, and others worked for Don Nolan Trucking—the area's biggest independent timber hauler. And they were all pissed. Their counterdemonstration generated more hostility than the Redwood Action Team had ever encountered. The yelling began as soon as the marchers came in sight and, when the two crowds came even with each other, objects were thrown at the Earth First! banners. Until sheriff's deputies intervened, pushing and shoving even broke out in several places. A few taunts urging him to step on over and fight were shouted at Darryl and Darryl shouted back that they ought to go to Houston and slug Charlie Hurwitz, that's who was going to cut them out of their livelihood. Someone yelled at Judi Bari that she and her ilk were all on welfare and she shouted back that she was a full-time carpenter and pretty soon her wages were going to be paying for the taunters' welfare checks, once Hurwitz had mowed down all the old growth and there was nothing left for Scotia to do.

In the midst of all this, the child jumped out of the coffin, but hardly anyone noticed, and those who did were shocked and screamed that it was sick, just plain sick. The child broke out in tears.

Sensing it was time to leave, Darryl got the march moving back down Main Street toward the freeway and, as they left, the taunts followed.

The next day's story in the *Times-Standard* was headlined, "Protesters clash in front of PL Co." and noted that by far the larger turnout had been generated by the timber people, not the Earth Firsters. The message Darryl had intended was hardly touched on.

Chastened, Darryl Cherney would never again schedule a demonstration for the Dark of the Moon.

Whatever the location of the planets, it was now abundantly clear to everyone involved that the situation in Humboldt County had become several notches more complicated. The company's side of the issue clearly had troops it could muster behind its position now and, remarkably, John Campbell was no longer the only one with a nemesis.

Now Darryl Cherney had one, too.

Her name was Candace Boak and the first demonstration Candy ever helped organize was the one waiting for Earth First! during the Dark of the Moon. Even in that throng, Candy was hard to miss—standing perhaps five foot six and weighing well over two hundred pounds. She was carrying a clipboard and asking every demonstrator she talked to just what they did for a living. The only one she found who had a "real job" was someone from the Sierra Club. All the others were students or had graduate study grants or described themselves as "land managers" or "contract farmers," phrases she took to mean they were living on someone else's property and grow-ing dope. Thirty-six years old, Candy was quick to point out she knew about life in the Mateel. She'd been something of a hippie herself once, a back-to-the-lander who grew her vegetables and wore her Birkenstocks, living out near Bridgeville behind Carlotta. She'd lived next door to people who were now Earth Firsters. And as far as she was concerned, they didn't know diddly about trees. Her hus-band, John, a gypo cutting pulp wood for Louisiana Pacific, he knew about trees. And the people at Pacific Lumber or Eel River Sawmill, they knew about trees. But people like Darryl Cherney and Robert Sutherland and Greg King and Judi Bari, they didn't know about nothing but politics. If there was really something so damn wrong with the planet, they ought to be down in Brazil doing something about it, teaching the natives the proper way to manage their land. Instead they were just stirring up shit where they didn't belong. Candy Boak had no use for any of them.

Candy had first been drawn into the timber issue earlier in the year, around the time of the big Eureka truck parade when she'd attended a meeting of a group called Women in Timber, where someone passed around copies of two of the local environmental newspapers. As she later told it, she almost passed out. This was what was happening out there? This was what they were saying about the logging companies and the people who worked in the mills? How could she have been so naive and paid so little attention? She set off to rectify her shortcomings almost immediately.

The first thing Candy did was to start monitoring classes held in Arcata by the Humboldt Outreach Program for the Environment, a program she would quickly identify as an Earth First! front: Greg King and Darryl Cherney taught "investigative journalism," Cecilia Lanman and The Man Who Walks In The Woods taught how to file lawsuits. Candy usually signed in on the class list using pseudonyms like "Georgia Pacific" or "Louise Pacific." She was, she said, dis-gusted. Who was Darryl Cherney, anyway? Some refugee from New York City who knew how to get his name in the paper. And Greg King? Just a guy who was good at trespass and propaganda. And Ce-cilia Lanman? She didn't know anything except how to be an orga-nizer. The guy they called Woods was just someone who liked to roam the hills naked. And Judi Bari? She was probably a communist.

Impelled by her disgust, Candy moved on to monitoring their

demonstrations and writing letters to the editor about what was going on. She and John were fixing up a house for resale in Eureka and she also ran an informal day care operation out of it, but Candy managed to find more and more time to give over to fighting Earth First! She eventually came to describe her strategy as "monkey-wrenching the monkey wrenchers."

In what would become her typical pattern, she unveiled that strategy against another of Darryl Cherney's personal projects. The occasion was Darryl's first tree-sit. Of course, this would not have been an easy moment for Darryl under any circumstance. Climbing trees was not his thing—not even close. During their first practice, when Greg taught him how to get up a tree and stay there, Feral Darryl, worried he might choke on his own fear, kept repeating the Lakota expression "It's a good day to die"—something he'd learned from Kingfisher, the Cheyenne road man who'd first brought him to Garberville. Darryl was prepared to go through this torment because he felt that if he was going to have anything resembling the appropriate standing within the national community of Earth First!, he had to have a tree-sit under his belt before the next rendezvous. He hated to look down, but he mastered the scaling technique sufficiently to join two others up in the heights next to a PL logging show off Redwood House Road shortly after the opening of the 1989 logging season.

By then, almost a year had passed since the last Earth First! tree-sit and Darryl expected that this one would draw a lot of attention. Again, however, Darryl's expectations fell short of the mark. Tree-sits seemed to be old news in a lot of circles and his attempts to generate more publicity were additionally thwarted by Candy Boak's "monkey-wrench the monkey wrenchers" campaign: Judi Bari was handling press relations for the sit, phoning news organizations with press releases according to the instructions Darryl called in on the radio phone he carried up into the trees. All transmissions on those phones could be received on an ordinary CB scanner tuned to the right frequency, so Darryl's strategy was easy to monitor and Candy Boak followed right along in Judi Bari's footsteps—calling news outlets, saying she was Bari, and canceling the release Bari had just announced.

Still, Darryl persevered and the tree-sit support group's most significant logistical problem became how to keep Darryl supplied with fresh batteries for his radio phone. From the time he mounted his platform, he was in a state of almost constant phone call: to call-in radio shows, to press rooms, to friends in Arcata, to Judi, to Greg, to dozens of others. All of it, of course, was being listened to like a soap opera by every timber person with a CB in the pickup. Stories about what old Cherney was saying up in his tree soon began to circulate all around Timber Country.

It didn't take Candy Boak long to come up with a plan for driving Darryl out of his tree, phone and all. It came to Candy when she saw her son at home, preparing a set of traps he was going to set out in the forest for game. Among his trapping paraphernalia, he had a supply of incredibly pungent skunk oil. She guessed that stench might just be what it would take to run Darryl out. So she and John drove their pickup up to a spot on the public dirt road overlooking the tree-sit and John set off with a bucket.

Darryl was on the phone with a television commentator in San Francisco, complaining that someone was out there monkey-wrenching their effort, when he noticed a figure approaching the base of his tree, carrying something. Darryl rang off in order to watch. The figure paused at the tree and donned heavy gloves. Then he removed a vial from the bucket and began to pour its contents around the tree's base.

The smell didn't carry up to his perch, but Darryl freaked anyway and frantically dialed the Earth First! command post in Arcata. Someone was attacking his tree, he shouted. He didn't know what they were doing but they were pouring some mysterious liquid all around the base. The pitch of Darryl's voice rose to the edge of becoming a shriek. They were going to light it on fire and burn him out, he screamed. They were going to burn him out. They—

Then the battery in Darryl's phone went dead.

Candy Boak, up the hill listening on her CB, was laughing so hard at Darryl's terror that she could be heard by everyone in the tree-sit. Her guffaws echoed up and down the slope. When John returned, they sped off in their pickup.

Meanwhile, down at the support demonstration on the public road, all they knew was that Darryl's phone was dead, and they were worried. So Greg King and a video cameraman jumped into Greg's old car and headed up the dirt road that ran by the tree-sit, drifting through corners until Candy Boak's pickup truck blew by going the other way. Then Greg and the cameraman skidded into a U-turn and gave chase, abandoning it only after they'd filmed the truck's license plate. As she drove off, folds of flesh hanging out the truck window, Candace Boak was laughing so hard she thought she might fall out of the cab.

47

By then, of course, Patrick Shannon's star was fizzling fast.

The fizzle had begun with a mailer, sent out from the ESOP's tiny office down on Fortuna Boulevard in late October. It was framed as a memo to "All employees, bosses, and managers of Pacific Lumber," and, authored by Patrick, it was blunt: "Too many PL employees are sitting on the fence," Shannon wrote. "They think that they are playing it safe. They say that they will go with ESOP as soon as Maxxam agrees to sell. It doesn't work that way. That's what's killing your chances. . . . When the offer is on the table, then Maxxam will decide . . . if the company is for sale. But if you don't have the guts to make the offer, you get what you deserve. Your job will be done in five to seven years. You'll work yourself right out of a job and you will have nothing left to pass on to your children. . . . You'll be standing in the unemployment line as soon as the old growth is gone. . . . The last word is commitment. Once you commit yourself, you are no longer a victim; your fate is in your hands. . . . Many bosses have been coerced and misguided by a false sense of loyalty to their paychecks to try and hold the ESOP down. [Actually,] any boss who is unwilling to work for ESOP and sustained yield is not worth his salt."

The letter drew two very visible retorts.

The first came in the middle of the night, shortly after the memo was mailed, when someone, playing on that last line about bosses being worth their salt, backed a dump truck up to the ESOP offices and dumped an entire load of rock salt in front of its entrance. When the regular volunteers arrived the next morning at work, they had to wade through a huge white pile. Shannon tried to laugh that one off by getting his people to bag the salt and auction it off at a fund-raiser, but most folks still figured the joke was on him.

The second response was a letter, this time from John Campbell to all of his employees. "At first," Campbell wrote, when "one of my fellow employees handed me the latest desperate letter of Patrick Shannon and the ESOP group . . . I was dismayed at the arrogance of the letter, but then I became angry. . . . This is no dream! This is a scheme, and a downright shameful one at that. . . . Here again, another group is trying to force their will on a very fine company made up of many, many fine people. I have 'had it' with Earth First!, the Sierra Club, EPIC, and now Patrick Shannon. . . . These are very dangerous times, for what they want is a divided PL family. They want discontent, they want employee against employee, friend against friend, family against family. That will help them achieve their goals. . . . What I think we need to do is stick together, support our Company, and get on with our jobs. . . . We all need to pull together . . . and we need to do that soon."

If that point was not clear in the letter, steps were taken to make it clear on the mill floor. Pete Kayes, an ESOP board member and one of Shannon's first recruits, bore the brunt of the message down at his job in the blacksmith shop. Kayes's boss in the maintenance department, overseeing not only Kayes's blacksmith shop, but the machine shop, electrical shop, and monorail shop—all of which were clustered together on the outskirts of Mill B—went through the area under his supervision and warned everyone not to talk to Kayes about the ESOP. In response, a number of the maintenance department employees went straight over to the blacksmith's shop on their next break, just to make it clear they weren't going to be told to whom they were going to be allowed to talk on their own time. Still, the number of people dropping by to talk with Pete slowed to a trickle over the next few weeks. The message also showed up in Kayes's paycheck, when he was dropped from the list for automatic raises. From the time he signed on with ESOP, Pete Kayes would never receive another raise. Within the year, he was working for a dollar an hour less than he figured he would have been if he had stayed away from Shannon and the buyback scheme. Pete's wife was irritated with him for having brought it all down on himself and wondered if he'd forgotten those days before PL, when he'd been working for dirt wages as a security guard over at Louisiana Pacific, but Pete was in no mood to back off. Finally, rather than "stick together and support our Company" as Campbell recommended, Kayes stuck his neck out even further and filed a claim against PL with the National Labor Relations Board, to protect what Shannon's lawyer had described as his legal right to advocate an ESOP.

While that claim awaited what everyone in the ESOP assumed would be positive action by the NLRB, Patrick Shannon's dilemma was only intensifying. He had initiated what amounted to an emotional Ponzi scheme, pyramiding hopes and expectations, and eventually he would have to deliver on some of them. But there was only one deliverance that would count and, on that front, he was stuck: he had no willing seller and without one, a purchase was impossible.

He tried to use the local political structure to force the issue open at the Humboldt County board of supervisors' last 1988 meeting several days before Christmas and, along with several supporters, appeared unannounced and asked to address the group. In an extemporaneous speech, Shannon claimed that the supervisors had a pressing public responsibility to involve themselves in what was currently happening out on Pacific Lumber's timberlands. He had done his best, given a paucity of certifiable information, to calculate just what the future held for PL and, by his estimate, the current rate of cut meant quite simply that some eight hundred of the company's employees would lose their jobs over the next sixteen years. By then, the company would just plain run out of lumber. The supervisors, at the very least, ought to hold hearings on the subject and determine how much timber Pacific Lumber had left and how much it had harvested over the last three years, and detail the specifics of the county timber tax it had paid over the same period.

The supervisors asked Shannon to make a formal request for these hearings in writing, which could then be discussed at their meeting in early January as part of the board's preset agenda.

He did so shortly after Christmas, in a letter that charged that "the timber harvesting policies of Pacific Lumber have created an atmosphere of trepidation and distrust among timber workers, the community, and special interest groups" and claiming that "ESOP management will adopt environmentally sound timber harvest practices that will insure the health of the timberlands and rekindle the local economy." The board put his request for a public investigation on its agenda for January 10, 1989.

In the meantime, Shannon also made a private written overture to Charles Hurwitz. Shannon's letter, mailed to Maxxam headquarters in Houston on January 3, asked Hurwitz for a meeting at which they might discuss a mutually advantageous proposition. Such a meeting could clear the air. "There have been grave misunderstandings regarding our proposal to purchase Pacific Lumber," he argued. "Pacific Lumber has responded emotionally and lacks the perspective to analyze the overall social, political, and economic ramifications of an ESOP buyout. Let's not be enemies. Our ESOP proposal benefits everyone concerned, including Maxxam and yourself by perhaps the greatest measure of all—economic profitability." Enclosed were copies of the ESOP's business plan and some descriptions of its plans for financing.

Shannon had heard nothing from Hurwitz in response when he and a half-dozen Pacific Lumber employees made formal presentations to the board of supervisors on January 10.

Shannon apologized for having so few PL witnesses, but claimed that the company had—at the last minute—canceled the time off promised a number of other employees. The list of witnesses included Lester Reynolds, dressed in his usual ESOP regalia. He was in his thirty-fifth year at the company, Lester told the board, and he figured that he and the rest of the company's labor force were just caught in the middle between this corporate raider who wanted to cut all the trees down and make big bucks in the process and all the environmentalists, who wanted to save every one of the trees, leaving them nothing at all to saw into boards. Another thirty-year employee followed Lester and said he was there because he was worried that his son and son-in-law, who also worked at PL, would never have jobs that lasted up to retirement time.

But Patrick Shannon was the one everyone was waiting to hear and Patrick did not disappoint. As usual, the words flowed out of his mouth like spring water. Mostly he talked about the way of life

Humboldt had made for itself up here among the giant trees and the future of that way of life. There was a war going on now, between the environmentalists and the logging industry, and that didn't have to be. In truth, if you scratched a logger, you'd find the soul of an environmentalist. The reason the county was rife with conflict was the blind policies of PL and the bottom line for the board was that they would be negligent in their duties if they did not investigate just what was going on out on PL's land and start acting in a way that would allow Humboldt County a future that worked.

In the supervisors' discussion, only one member of the board showed any support for ESOP's position. The most virulent of its opponents was a woman supervisor who had been a friend of Patrick's late mother. She went out of her way to note how lucky Humboldt was to have a man like Charles Hurwitz interested in it. He'd brought a boom to the logging towns in the south county and he was a nationally prominent businessman who owned lots of companies, even a bank. She had also been in touch with Hurwitz and he had sent her an answer to Patrick Shannon's letter of January 3, which—though addressed to Shannon—he requested that she read out loud to the meeting.

The woman's announcement brought Shannon up short. He had no idea Hurwitz had answered his letter and the recitation that followed was the first he had heard of its contents.

"Dear Mr. Shannon," Hurwitz's letter began, "I am in receipt of your letter of January 3. . . . I am concerned about the misinformation and the blatant falsehoods concerning The Pacific Lumber Company which appear to be circulating in Humboldt County. I believe that you and the so-called 'ESOP' group are partially responsible. Pacific Lumber does not intend to reply each time some irresponsible person starts a rumor. On this occasion, however, I wish to make unmistakably clear to the Board of Supervisors, the employees of the Pacific Lumber Company and the citizens of Humboldt County, that, contrary to rumors apparently started by you and your 'ESOP' group: THE PACIFIC LUMBER COMPANY IS NOT FOR SALE. . . . The Board of Supervisors, the employees of Pacific Lumber and the citizens of Humboldt County have my best wishes for a happy and prosperous 1989. [But], Mr. Shannon, we have no interest in meeting or carrying on a dialogue with you. We believe that your activities have given rise to discord and misunderstanding and continue to be a disservice to the Company, its employees and the community." The letter was signed "The Pacific Lumber Company, Charles E. Hurwitz, Chairman of the Board."

Shannon later described the letter as "rude," but its effect was telling and Shannon's fizzle now had a full head of steam. His pyramid began to collapse, attendance at ESOP gatherings began to dwindle, and, now, when he exhorted his membership to listen, his smooth words often rolled off the side of their heads like water off a duck's back.

As the 1989 logging season loomed, Patrick Shannon decided to reprise the meeting at the Eureka Inn with which ESOP had burst upon the scene. This time, he arranged to rent the gym at Fortuna High School, which would seat an audience of more than seven hundred. He hoped to draw such a crowd with a keynote speech by Dr. Louis Kelso himself, creator of the whole idea of Employee Stock Ownership Plans. The meeting was scheduled for the evening of April Fools' Day.

Only a hundred and fifty people showed up.

Dr. Kelso, now in his eighties, was long-winded and boring, but the audience listened politely. As usual, however, it was Shannon's speech that drew all the attention. Patrick had only figured out what to say during the hour immediately preceding his address—in what he would later recall as a flash of inspiration. He consulted none of the ESOP board about the proposal he had decided to make, nor had he even touched base with them so they would know what was coming.

Standing behind the mike, dressed in his usual suit, looking his usual thin and handsome self, he tossed out a bombshell.

He thought the time had come for the ESOP to go into partnership with Hurwitz, he said.

One ESOP member later recalled that the entire audience instinctively sucked in their breath as soon as the words cleared Patrick's lips.

Instead of buying 100 percent of the company, he continued, they should try to buy 30. Later, they could try to expand. The simple truth was that they had no other options. They couldn't force Hurwitz to sell, so they ought to make their peace with him and settle for just a piece of the action rather than all.

The hundred and fifty gathered in the Fortuna High School gym were as silent as early morning fog on the Eel. Lester Reynolds, Pete Kayes, and the rest of the ESOP board were in shock. Shannon sensed the reaction and kept talking, but the talking changed no one's mind. Everyone was too aghast to even stir. Eventually, a Pacific Lumber retiree stood up in the audience. He said his own father had gone on strike in '46, when old Mr. Murphy had busted the union, and he and his brothers and sisters had lived on cornflakes for months. He'd suffered through a lot and worked thirty years for the company himself. He'd signed on with this ESOP and opened his $500 savings account because of what he could see was happening to PL. And, he declared, Patrick shouldn't have any doubt about how he felt, nor should anybody else: it would be an icy day in hell before he'd ever strike a deal with the likes of Charles Hurwitz.

The retiree's statement received the biggest applause of the evening.

From that point on, ESOP sank like a rock. Its next regular meeting drew less than a dozen; the one after that, three or so. Then the NLRB ruled on Pete Kayes's case, deciding that ESOP organizing was not, as Shannon's lawyer had claimed, a protected activity and dismissing Kayes's claim. After that, Kayes pointed out, "everyone headed for the hills."

Barely a year after Patrick Shannon made his promise to his cousin, Wilma Bishop, and set off to save Pacific Lumber, the ESOP office on Fortuna Boulevard was closed and Patrick was back out in Willow Creek, cutting firewood again.

48

By the time the 1989 logging season opened, Greg King was convinced that his, Darryl's, and Judi's activities were being monitored by the Federal Bureau of Investigation. He figured it only stood to reason. The FBI had just completed an infiltration of Arizona Earth First! that produced a half-dozen multi-felony indictments. Indictments at the hands of FBI penetration were expected on Earth First! chapters in Montana and Washington State as well, all for various forms of "terrorism." And the Redwood Action Team was the most successful Earth First! campaign in the country. It stood to reason, he said.

And it did. Five years later, FBI documents released under court order would reveal that the bureau was certainly familiar with the Humboldt situation by 1989, something that would have been altogether impossible without its having become familiar with Greg King and Darryl Cherney and Judi Bari. The Houston FBI office had already begun investigating anonymous threats on Charles Hurwitz received at the Maxxam headquarters. The agency maintained an office in Eureka, where it also ran annual terrorist bombing workshops for local police from around northern California. For the last two years at these workshops, one of the regular features was a staged car bombing out on some cleared land provided by Louisiana Pacific. In this exercise, a car was blown up with a pipe bomb, then investigated.

By the spring of 1989, Greg King was also actively speculating in his diary about the possibility that the FBI might very well round them all up for some kind of detention without trial. He found it hard to conceive of the powerful financial interests they were challenging simply allowing them to proceed in the direction they were pursuing. He also was now convinced, thanks in large part to the Arizona indictments, that the organization was thoroughly infiltrated with informants and began approaching everyone with several degrees more suspicion than had been his previous custom. His diary entries now referenced contact with people identified as "alleged" journalists or "alleged" Earth Firsters whom he actively suspected of being police spies. He also talked a lot about these subjects to Cherney and Bari, so much so that they sometimes found it hard to take him too seriously on the subject.

At the summer Earth First! rendezvous, Darryl would invent a little ditty about his obsession: "Paranoid Greg, Paranoid Greg, he'll steal your reefer, hide behind your keg."

Greg laughed along with everyone else, but he still thought it best to know your enemy. That the government did such things and ten times worse was documented, and if they'd done it before, why wouldn't they do it again, and to them? He had occasional dreams of guns being pointed his way and, when he drove, he watched the cars in his rearview mirror more, with the occasional thought that he might be followed. Without being frantic about it, Greg saw the situation as consistently ominous and only getting more so.

Certainly along the North Coast it looked more and more like a war as the 1989 logging season proceeded: five smoke bombs were set off in Pacific Lumber's Bay Area national sales office by person or persons unknown and Timber People all around Humboldt County began flying yellow ribbons from their CB antennas, signifying Timber Country's right to exist. Dressed as animals, several dozen Earth Firsters invaded a hearing of the State Board of Forestry, condemning them for failing to preserve the forest's threatened species, and Eel River Sawmill just down the road from Scotia laid off thirty-six workers without warning, saying environmental restrictions had created a log shortage. Calling Charles Hurwitz "the Ted Bundy" of takeover artists, Darryl Cherney and the rest of Earth First! circulated a Wanted poster with the Texan's likeness, offering $5,000 to anyone supplying information leading to his arrest for crimes against Mother Earth. When Fortuna staged its annual rodeo parade, Support the Timber Industry signs proliferated and, around the same time, Darryl Cherney and Judi Bari began getting regular phone calls from Candy Boak, just to remind them that she was still out there. Person or persons unknown threw a dead deer in the swimming pool at John Campbell's house out in Redway and he found it there when he got up in the morning.

The war had already spread outside Humboldt County. By now, neighboring Mendocino County was engulfed in the conflict as well, mostly concerning the activities of the Louisiana Pacific Corporation. Judi and Darryl were directing a portion of their energies there, pointing out that the situation in Mendocino was desperate. A rally they organized in the mill town of Calpella that June was designed to illustrate just how desperate. Louisiana Pacific had a mill there, where an experimental program in making chipboard was being conducted. In Mendocino, virtually no old growth remained standing and much of the county's second growth was gone as well. In response to that situation, Louisiana Pacific had unveiled a program aimed at creating the board of the future. This product would be composed of wood chips, bound together into board sizes by epoxies and resins. Since all that was needed for their manufacture were slivers and fragments, LP—down to cutting eighteen-inch-diameter third growth on some of its Mendocino lands—had inaugurated an operation that was scraping the forest floor for brush and other scrap that could be reduced to chip. Their log decks at Calpella were dotted with huge heaps of wood debris.

Greg King arrived at the demonstration late, when everything was winding down. A dozen or so sheriff's deputies and Highway Patrol officers were still on the scene, separating the Earth First! demonstration from the mill gates. There was no organized counterdemonstration, but there were a number of angry Timber People looking on. The most fearsome of those was a logger who'd been hanging around the back of his pickup truck all day, firing up his huge chain saw every now and then and waving it threateningly at the demonstrators. That was usually accompanied by declarations of his intention to cut up some of these fucking hippie Earth fucking Firsters. He was in the midst of another such chain-saw manipulation when Greg joined the Earth First! group. Not having any idea this sort of thing had been going on all day, Greg approached the man as soon as he shut his saw down.

He motioned at the long bar on the logger's rig and pointed out that he wouldn't need a saw that size in this county. All the Mendocino trees that big could probably be dropped in a couple months. Once that happened, the logger would be out of a job.

The logger denied he'd ever be out of a job.

Greg said he was kidding himself and they went around like that for several minutes.

Then the logger told Greg to get out of there or he was going to bust him in the chops.

Greg told the logger he was crazy. There were a dozen cops here. He wasn't going to hit anybody.

At that, the logger turned away, like he was leaving, and then spun and planted his fist along the side of Greg's jaw, sucker punching him onto his butt.

Demonstrators rushed up, yelling at the logger. One of the Earth Firsters was carrying a six-foot-long redwood branch.

Greg's head was clear and he was furious. Leaping to his feet, he grabbed the redwood branch and bashed the logger across the chest with it.

The logger was stunned that the hippie had hit him back and made no move to follow up on his initial blow. During the ensuing standoff, he just stood there leaning against his pickup while Greg and the other hippies attempted to convince the police to file charges. Eventually, the logger sauntered off to the bar across the street, shouting antihippie epithets on his way.

That incident in Calpella got the summer of 1989's timber demonstrations under way, but the season was defined by another encounter in August down along the Humboldt-Mendocino border outside the hamlet of Whitethorn. What happened there was later described in the press as "the Whitethorn riot."

Whitethorn had a reputation as the heaviest place on the Lost Coast. The town itself amounted to a tiny grocery, a post office, a car repair shop, and a pay phone. Greater Whitethorn included the Sinkyone, Whale Gulch—one of the oldest back-to-the-land settlements on the North Coast—and a number of illegal methamphetamine labs ferreted out in the forest away from the eyes of the law. Because of the speed trade, the sheriff's offices of the two counties with jurisdiction around the hamlet reported regular discoveries of unidentifiable bodies dumped on the Whitethorn area's back roads.

Most of the corpses had suffered bullet wounds to the head, execution style.

Earth First! went down to Whitethorn that August when one of the local back-to-the-landers pleaded with Darryl to come down and help them deal with a small logging company run by a family called the Lancasters. According to what the hippie told Darryl, the Lancasters were cutting outside the boundaries of their THP, logging as late as 9:30 P.M. and on Sundays, firing weapons up on their land at all hours, and driving their logging trucks along the local dirt road at breakneck speeds. Darryl said it was a hard time, there were a lot of actions for Mendocino County scheduled for that month, but he was sure they could do something.

On August 16, Cherney, Bari, and King joined some twenty other Earth Firsters at a spot where the county road joined the dirt lane that ran up to the Lancasters' THP and set up a picket line. The original plan had been to set up a tree-sit, but the Lancasters' lumberjacks all stopped work when the demonstrators showed up, so they decided to blockade the road instead. When a logging truck finally came down from the Lancasters', the demonstration blocked the road and kept the truck stalled there for the next five hours. A good portion of the Lancaster family—including the seventy-five-year-old father, sixty-three-year-old mother, and two sons, twenty-two and eighteen—were already at the blockade when the truck was stopped, but things remained relatively peaceful. The older Lancaster son was sipping a beer and making small talk with Greg King and Darryl Cherney while his mother, father, and brother kept an eye on the hippies from the vicinity of their pickup truck. The tensest moments of the demonstration's first few hours came when a local speed dealer who called himself "Maniac" drove up to the blockade and wanted past. He was known to have an illegal lab operating in the vicinity and was very twitchy. He also had a pistol in his lap. Some of the locals were worried Maniac might get a little berserk when he was turned back, but eventually he just peeled away in his car, flipping everyone the bird.

Shortly after Maniac left, however, things got really weird. The weirdness started when Mrs. Lancaster's seventy-year-old brother, a woodcutter known to the local hippies as Logger Larry, came speeding down the dirt road in his pickup truck, forcing demonstrators to scatter out of his path and nearly hitting two of the local hippies' small children. When Logger Larry finally slammed on his brakes and joined his in-laws, a shouting match with the parents of the children began. During the conversation, a photographer with the Earth Firsters approached Logger Larry and started snapping photographs. Larry objected, grabbed a long-handled peavey—usually used for manhandling logs—and threatened the photographer. Then his sister grabbed at the camera and a tug-of-war began. Darryl ran to intervene and from that point on, so much happened so fast that both he and Greg remembered it as though it was going on in slow motion.

Just as Darryl arrived at the tug-of-war, the camera flew up in the air and over to the other side of Logger Larry's pickup, where Larry immediately pulled out an axe and beat it to smithereens. In the meantime, Mrs. Lancaster threw a punch at Judi Bari and Judi threw one back, setting the older Lancaster son into a screaming rage. He charged the melee, shoving Darryl to the ground along the way. His father would later explain that seeing his mother surrounded by hippies and in danger had made him crazy. While the Lancaster son was charging their way, Mem Hill, a fifty-year-old local back-to-the-lander woman, was trying to mediate the dispute, advising everyone not to get violent. They could talk this out.

Then the Lancaster son roared up and laid a forearm into Mem's face, sending her sprawling.

Mem Hill got herself up, complaining, and the Lancaster son drove a fist square into her face, splattering blood, breaking her nose, and knocking her unconscious.

A half-dozen hippies then jumped the son, pinning him to the ground until he seemed to have calmed down and was safe to be released.

At that point, Logger Larry, having finished off the camera, had armed himself with a piece of firewood and Darryl had fetched his guitar case to use as a club if need be. The situation stayed balanced for several moments and the enraged older Lancaster son maintained his cool until Greg King approached and began taking pictures of him. He then jumped on Greg and threw him to the ground. Greg jumped up and decked the Lancaster son and then everything started again. Logger Larry bashed one of the locals in

the head with his firewood log and the older Lancaster boy ran back
to his pickup and fetched a shotgun. As he did so, he swore he was
going to kill every one of these fucking hippies.

That threat was enough to cause the Lancaster father to intervene. He didn't want his boy shooting anybody, so he made him put
the gun back. Unsatisfied, the son returned and started another fist-
fight with several Earth Firsters. Then, with dust and fists flying in
the middle of the road, the eighteen-year-old Lancaster boy lost his
cool and joined the act. He too went for the shotgun. When he got
his hands on it, he fired it into the air several times, bringing everyone in the melee up short. Now that he had everyone's attention,
the eighteen-year-old announced that he too was going to kill all
these fucking hippies.

The gunfire was enough for Darryl, Judi, Greg, and the local hippies and they scattered toward the country road. Greg drove down
to Whitethorn and used the pay phone to call several members of
the press and, as he returned, at least ten police cars from the Humboldt County Sheriffs, the Mendocino County Sheriffs, and the California Highway Patrol roared up with an ambulance in tow. The
"Whitethorn riot" was over and both sides licked their wounds
while the cops decided that Mendocino had jurisdiction. The Mendocino sheriffs in turn dismissed the importance of the incident
and refused to take statements from any of the demonstrators, including the assaulted Mem Hill. They said anybody who wanted to
file charges would have to do so at the district attorney's office in
Ukiah, three hours' drive away.

Greg objected. What if that kid who threatened them with a
shotgun and vowed to kill them and whom the sheriffs refused to arrest decided to live up to his word in the meantime and blow them
away? he asked the deputy. What then?

The deputy shrugged. He couldn't predict the future, he said.

Greg just walked away in disgust.

After the Whitethorn riot, the August Earth First! actions in
Mendocino continued with another truck blockade organized by
Darryl and Judi, two days later, outside the town of Navarro. Both of
them considered it and the string of actions that had preceded it
successful. The next day, their summer campaign in Mendocino was
scheduled to conclude with a big demonstration in front of the
Georgia Pacific mill in the coastal town of Ft. Bragg and Darryl, Judi,

and another woman Earth First! organizer drove there in Judi's old Subaru station wagon. Both women had their children along, all four of whom were in the back seat or the car's rear carrying bay. As usual, the conversation among the adults was about their movement and how they could make it grow, interspersed with kidding and jokes and snatches of song. The road to Ft. Bragg wound through the second-growth forest, full of mingled redwoods, Douglas firs, and live oaks, all limp and dusty from the August heat, and, at times, Darryl and Judi and their friend just got silent and watched it pass.

When Bari's Subaru entered the hamlet of Philo, Darryl spotted a friend on the side of the road and, as Judi slowed the car, he waved.

At that moment, an unloaded logging truck traveling some forty-five miles an hour slammed into the rear of Judi Bari's station wagon, lifting it into the air and sending it sailing for a brief moment before it buried its nose into the side of a parked truck. There was hardly time for Judi to scream before impact.

Miraculously, though both the front and back of the car were crumpled, no one was hurt.

Judi was sobbing to her children and Darryl was checking to make sure he was all there when the truck driver ran up. The first words out of the driver's mouth were, "I'm sorry. I never saw the children." When the police arrived, he told them he'd been distracted until it was too late to stop.

Judi and Darryl accepted the story until they learned that the driver was one of those they'd blockaded at Navarro the day before. Then they asked the Mendocino sheriffs to investigate him and Louisiana Pacific—to whom he was contracted—for attempted murder, but the Mendocino sheriffs declined.

When Darryl called Greg and told him what had happened, Greg was shocked, but not surprised. He just repeated what he'd been saying all summer: things were getting heavy. Things were getting very heavy, indeed.

49

Whatever might go on in Mendocino, Pacific Lumber continued to mark the epicenter of the timber issue and the company continued to maintain a self-conscious posture of business as usual. Charles Hurwitz personally returned to Scotia to make that point during the summer of 1989. It was his first official "public" appearance in Humboldt County since the company meeting in December 1985, when he'd informed his new employees about the golden rule.

This time, the occasion was the dedication of Scotia's new cogeneration power plant, the one that Gene Elam had been consumed with planning while Hurwitz was stalking the company. After four years, the plant was finally completed and was ready to be presented to the public. It would burn the mills' wood waste to power a steam turbine, reducing the pollution levels from those generated by the previous power plant. And it would also generate some $6 million a year in income from the sale of surplus electricity and some $1 million a year in savings on the company's own energy use. The dedication ceremony was held in front of a select audience gathered at the ballpark down by the river. The event was invitation only and, while Earth First! showed up with a picket line, the demonstrators were confined to an area down by the freeway where the only look they got at Hurwitz was a brief glimpse of a passing car on the other side of a squadron of police.

Scotia had to have been something of a relief for Charles. There was a cloud over the acquiring business these days, cast mostly by the recent indictment of Michael Milken on ninety-eight counts of securities violations—including several specifically concerning his deal with Ivan Boesky in the Pacific Lumber takeover he'd done with Charles. And with Milken under indictment and cut off from any activity with Drexel as part of Drexel's own settlement, the junk bond market began a nosedive that would continue over the next three years. And Charles was, as usual, scrambling to make the most of the situation. None of that scramble was needed along Main Street in the town he owned. Here he could just be the boss and leave it at that. He arrived at the ballpark in his usual dark suit and was greeted with applause by the crowd there. Most of them were wearing their best clothes.

It was a warm day and the melody of the nearby Eel running shallow and wide provided a backdrop as he delivered the dedication's keynote speech from a prepared text and in a smoothly rounded, almost charming, drawl.

Hurwitz said the Pacific Lumber Company had never been stronger, nor had the future for redwood lumber ever looked brighter. This power plant was a symbol of Maxxam's long-term commitment to this place and its people. They were here to stay—to stay as a good neighbor, as a good employer, and as a responsible steward of the land.

His companies were, he repeated for emphasis, "here in Scotia and Humboldt County *to stay.*"

50

When Bill Bertain read those words in the next day's *Times-Standard* he felt like tearing the paper to shreds.

Not if he could help it, the lawyer told himself. Not, by God, if he could help it.

Whether he could or not was, of course, still an extraordinarily iffy proposition at best. In the immediate moment, Bertain had his hands full just surviving in order to fight—still living month to month, pressing his campaign with borrowed money, and worrying himself sick. It was all Bertain could do to hang on long enough to prepare the case for New York in conjunction with his big-time law firm partners, signing up shareholders to join the suit, borrowing more money to keep himself going, and persevering through colitis attacks. Whatever his condition, though, he was still endlessly available to help further any new grievances against Maxxam's takeover that surfaced around the country.

In the summer of 1989, after Charles Hurwitz had come and gone, a new grievance led to the last lawsuit Bill Bertain would file against Hurwitz, Maxxam, and the new PL. It was over the pension fund that Charles Hurwitz had stripped and sold off to the Executive Life Insurance Company. Executive Life was, of course, a long-time Milken fiefdom and no company was suffering more from the collapsing junk bond market than it was. Its portfolio was over-

loaded with Drexel high-yield issues and had already been identified by the National Association of Insurance Commissioners as one
of twenty-one California insurance companies in need of "immediate regulatory attention." Fred Carr, Executive Life's c.e.o., pooh-
poohed the notion and touted his company's strength, but, behind
the scenes, he had already begun to cook the company's books,
shuffling paper worth and liabilities back and forth between subsidiaries in order to pass muster with public auditors. A group of retirees and employees who had previously opposed Hurwitz's
takeover approached Bill for advice about what to do to keep their
pension from being carried down with Executive Life and he, already overworked, could not refuse.

He pointed out that the statute of limitations for court action
against Charles Hurwitz's original pension fund reorganization
would be reached in September and suggested that they find a law
firm of pension fund specialists to help them file suit. That was an
option these people couldn't yet afford, so, instead, Bertain helped
them file the suit themselves before the deadline was reached. Its
seven plaintiffs, momentarily represented by themselves, included
Pete Kayes and Lester Reynolds from the old ESOP board. The
group surrounding the suit called themselves the PL Rescue Fund.

When Pacific Lumber learned what this Rescue Fund was up to,
John Campbell mailed a letter to all PL employees and retirees who
were covered by the Executive Life annuity. To John, this was no
more than another eruption from the same set of Chicken Littles
who had followed Patrick Shannon around in a trance. They were,
he wrote, a "small group of former disgruntled employees, and a
few others who are unrelated to the issue" who were "trying to
use scare tactics to build support for their cause. They are doing
you a disservice by creating unnecessary worry and aggravation. . . .
The unfair allegation that Executive Life may go bankrupt is
unfounded."

Bill Bertain would later point out that this was far from being the
last statement John Campbell would have to make on the subject of
Executive Life. And each of the subsequent statements would
amount to a retreat from the assurances of its predecessor.

That, Bertain noted with his teeth set and jaw locked, was just
the Charles Hurwitz style of business.

51

Robert Sutherland, a.k.a. The Man Who Walks In The Woods, had Charles Hurwitz on his mind as well. He wrote Hurwitz in May 1989, asking him to save Headwaters Forest. Hurwitz sent no answer and Woods did not write a second time.

For Woods and Cecilia Lanman, Headwaters Forest and its three thousand contiguous acres of old growth were the final redoubt. There, the tailed frog—the last surviving direct link to the frogs that had populated the Jurassic period 200 million years ago—could still flourish, the marbled murrelet could still find thousand-year-old spike-topped trees in which to nest, and the Olympic salamander—brown on top, yellow underneath, and unfit for life anywhere else—could thrive around the shaded springs and water seeps. Here, the continuity of centuries was still unmarred, the wildness unbroken, its essence unmolested. Three thousand acres wasn't much in the context of the two million acres of just a century ago, but, Woods noted, it was the biggest parcel left outside the park system and the redwood parks that existed were simply not sufficient to ensure survival. As a consequence, EPIC's strategy, while aimed at preserving the totality of low-elevation coastal old growth, continued to be anchored by the specific effort to keep the Headwaters Forest intact at all costs.

In Woods's and Cecilia's judgment, the Pacific Lumber Company's strategy toward Headwaters was equally unequivocal. They were convinced that PL considered the contiguous character of this piece of ancient forest its greatest drawback. John Campbell and Charles Hurwitz knew EPIC would never have been able to muster this much fight for thirty separate hundred-acre parcels. Which is why, when PL set out to harvest along Salmon Creek and the Little South Fork of the Elk River, it filed its first THP in the middle of its acreage, rather than on the forest's edge. That THP had been blocked in the courts, but, as far as Cecilia and Woods were concerned, Pacific Lumber's strategy remained unchanged and, in the fall of 1989, as logging season was getting ready to wind down, the company made another push to commence that fragmentation.

The effort began well hidden from EPIC's view, both by geography and the intricacies of California's official forestry process. When it had first applied to cut in Headwaters, only to be stymied later in the court, Pacific Lumber had already been granted a separate application to build a road to service its future logging shows in that area. Company crews had begun building that road, PL's first full-scale intrusion toward the headwaters of the Little South Fork of the Elk, and had most of it completed before the road was blocked by the injunction in effect throughout the court case against THPs 87–240 and 87–241. But that case was now over and the road-building permit was still in effect, untouched by the court's rejection of PL's initial THP applications. The road permit had only a three-year life span, so, in August of 1989, PL applied to the CDF for a "minor" modification of the road-building plan that would extend its life for another year and would allow them to add an extra six hundred feet to its length. Such minor modifications were not subject to the public process that covered THPs, so EPIC was totally unaware of the extension. Unobstructed, PL pursued its construction without mercy.

Greg King later described this road extension as "a wide omnipresent swath into the forest heart." This particular construction even diverged from Pacific Lumber's usual tidy road-building standards. The first section of it, built before the court case, was typical PL: there had been no attempt to use any more than necessary of the permitted two hundred feet of allowable cut on the road's flanks, so trees were in place immediately off the road edge, and the underpinnings of the road were well compacted and drained. The section built after the company's defeat in *EPIC v. Maxxam*, however, pushed on down the ridge in an unsealed gouge to the east bank of the Little South Fork and then turned just above its headwater tributaries and ran along the narrow river's edge looking like little more than a heaped-up pile of dirt and debris that had been flattened on its top. The maximum two-hundred-foot width had been used throughout, so that the road was flanked by what amounted to a small, very ugly clear cut. Cecilia Lanman first learned of the road from a report by a pilot who'd spotted it from the air after it was a fait accompli. The rainy season then on its way would eventually wash more than forty centimeters of silt into the previously pristine Little South Fork of the Elk.

Throughout the fall and winter, Cecilia Lanman continued to hear reports about the road and accepted them with resignation. There was nothing she could do about it and she had her hands full dealing with another, more frontal, assault by PL against Headwaters. The company had filed two new timber harvest plans, 89–762 and 89–793, covering a total of 372 acres. When joined with 88–462, the THP now under litigation, this pair of proposed logging shows would bisect Headwaters Forest completely, north to south. On November 2, the new THPs were discussed at a CDF Review Team meeting in Fortuna attended by fifty EPIC supporters and three representatives from Pacific Lumber and to the surprise of most of the audience, instead of another rubber stamping in the traditional CDF fashion, the department of forestry declined to act on the THPs at the conclusion of the meeting, requesting that the company postpone their hearing to January, when they would be put on hold again, while the company did court-ordered wildlife surveys.

While Cecilia and Woods thought such victories significant, there was little celebration. They knew, hamstrung into fighting THP by THP, that their task was endless and were increasingly drawn to California's process of ballot initiatives as their only option for something other than an acre-by-acre reform of logging practices. Under California law, any proposal whose backers could collect some 600,000 signatures from registered voters over a four-month period could be placed on the statewide ballot and become law if approved. By the time Cecilia made her defense of 89–762 and 89–793, Woods was well into a complete rewrite of California's logging regulations that could be qualified for the ballot. Eventually, as the circle of North Coast activists who'd originally begun work on the initiative was widened to include more established groups like the Sierra Club and the Natural Resources Defense Council, the proposed timber law would be rewritten and rewritten again until it had been through more than fifteen drafts.

The end result was named the Forests Forever initiative and was a striking departure from any timber law on the books anywhere in the United States. In its final form, it would ban any clear cut—defined as taking more than 60 percent of the total timber volume—on an area larger than two and a half acres and banned any repetition of the cut on the same acreage for forty years. It would also require all proposed THPs to be surveyed for wildlife prior to approval and authorized the Department of Fish and Game to enforce wildlife protection. It required all commercial timber harvesters to follow a sustained-yield system that would limit their annual cut to the annual growth on their timberlands and would limit the harvest to trees that had matured and reached the peak of their natural growth cycle. Anyone cutting a logging road would have to maintain it to prevent erosion and, once it was no longer in use, restore the road to a natural state. No more than 20 percent of the trees flanking any watercourse with fish in it could be harvested over a twenty-year period and no logging whatsoever was allowed around springs and water seeps. Forests Forever also included a $750 million bond issue for the purchase of biologically significant pockets of old growth, the first of which would be Pacific Lumber's Headwaters Forest.

Forests Forever was, Woods noted, the big enchilada, EPIC's chance to go for broke, and, to the surprise of more than a few California political observers, it qualified for the state's November, 1990, elections with signatures to spare.

In the meantime, however, the pressure on Headwaters continued.

Three Earth First! trespassers in January, 1990, discovered a Pacific Lumber Cat scraping a new mile-long road along the crest of the ridge separating Salmon Creek and the Little South Fork of the Elk. It skirted the redwoods, so that none were cut down, and made its way through the open areas occupied by brush and tan oaks. The road's width varied but averaged about the breadth of a standard two-lane road and involved cuts into the slope as deep as ten feet. When confronted, PL said the road was actually a "trail" and explained that it was necessary in order to do the wildlife surveys required by the courts.

52

It was not like Charles Hurwitz to court visibility, but briefly, very briefly, as 1990 began, about the same time the Earth First! trespassers discovered PL's wildlife trail, he stepped out from behind the scenes and flashed through the spotlight focused on the issue of timber and how it was being cut.

Charles Hurwitz, of course, was anything but a public man. Even John Campbell, his principal Humboldt County booster, described Charles as "reclusive." But that description may have been too harsh. Hurwitz hardly led a recluse's life. He was visible enough in big-time Houston charity circles to garner a reputation as both dry and pleasant and he could be spotted rooting at an occasional Houston Rockets basketball game at the Summit arena. Basketball was a passion left over from his youth, when he was buck-toothed and not yet handsome, but drove a brand-new Chevy convertible and was widely liked by other Kilgore teenagers. In those days, no one expected he would climb the way he had. Now, while he might be inconspicuous by Houston standards—buying most of his trademark dark suits off the rack at his brother-in-law's exclusive haberdashery and driving a run-of-the-mill Mercedes convertible to work and back—he was worth some $150 million and ran a considerable empire out of an anonymous suite in a modest Houston office tower. His personal office there was spartan, almost devoid of furniture and decorated with a Plexiglas-framed print of a large fish swallowing a smaller one.

Charles Hurwitz's most visible indulgence was his recent move from a house in the River Oaks neighborhood to the Houstonian, a high-rise complex in a neighborhood known as Huntington, considered the apex of Houston's food chain. His apartment was described by *Houston Metropolitan* as "a cooly contemporary home of grays and blacks and whites [and] wood panelling burnished to a soft red glow." Charles's neighbors included some members of the Saudi royal family, President George Bush, and former Texas governor John Connally, now one of Charles's closest friends and business associates. Next year, Charles and Barbara Hurwitz and John Connally and his wife, Nellie, would co-chair the annual fund-raiser for the city's M. D. Anderson Cancer Center. The Cancer Center and the state of Israel were Charles's two favorite charities. Barbara appeared regularly on Houston's best-dressed lists—usually a direct function of circulation in high society—but the Hurwitzes were not regulars in the city's social scene and he wasn't much of a club member, except for the nearby Houstonian Athletic Club. Sunday patrons there often spotted Hurwitz on the exercise equipment, surrounded by a group of what one Athletic Club member described as "Charles Hurwitz wanna-bees."

Public or not, Charles was a man of not inconsiderable local stature—a function, as with most things in Houston, of his considerable wealth. Maxxam was now a national juggernaut. *Fortune* ranked it number 184 in its 1989 list of the nation's 500 largest companies—first in sales increase, fourth in profit increase, and tenth in percentage of return to its investors—and *Business Month* named Maxxam the nation's single fastest growing company for 1989, listing its interests as "lumber, aluminum, [and] real estate." The company's stock, selling around $10 a share when he was still digesting Pacific Lumber, was now around $40 and rising. The company's board, of which he was chairman, was about to reward him with a 1989 salary payment of $3.97 million, an additional bonus of $3.5 million, and $497,000 worth of stock options. That remuneration package was larger than those of the chairmen of General Motors, IBM, and General Electric combined.

But, with all his money, Charles continued to take taxis rather than limos, still flew coach, and confided to acquaintances down at the Houstonian A. C. that the institution of Maxxam itself meant little to him. He wasn't into making his business a monument to himself. If things got rough, he'd just spin Maxxam off and open another shop with a new name and go right on. He just loved to deal. He was at his best one-on-one over the phone or one-on-three behind closed doors. In front of large groups, his charm faded. Those close to him considered him shy and insisted that nothing along the course of Maxxam's rise had changed him. He was still considered "sensitive" and "human"—the kind of boss who remembered employees' birthdays, the kind of father who still kissed his grown sons. His close associates considered the evil image spread about him over the redwood issue nothing but a bad rap.

The antagonism was confusing to Charles as well. He hadn't anticipated it when he made his run at PL and it was an impossible element to turn into numbers. In his opponents' arguments, he saw fallacies at every turn: he was no enemy of Humboldt County. He liked the place. During his last trip out to dedicate the power plant, he'd attended the PL woods crew's annual picnic, shaking hands with all the lumberjacks who worked for him. They were people he thought he could understand. He also took some time off to spend a couple days up on the Trinity River, fly fishing with John Campbell and a couple of fellows from the Bank of America, with whom he was discussing refinancing PL's junk bond debt. He could understand those people, too. The people he couldn't understand were these crazy Earth Firsters who were constantly demonizing him. In private discussions, he expressed mystification at all the furor they'd managed to kick up and pointed out that most of the trees being cut were trees that no one even knew existed until he had the company resurvey the land. So why was everyone so upset?

Nor did he grasp the sacredness his critics attached to old growth. The way he saw it, old-growth trees were like old people. They just stopped growing and from that point on, they were taking up space that new, still growing trees could use to reach the sun. Cutting the old ones was just a business, albeit one that regenerated itself. He was like a farmer of the forest.

Charles made no secret of the fact he felt misunderstood, but he claimed not to resent the way the press had treated him over these issues. He just filed the distortions away with his general cynicism toward the media. Most reporters didn't find stories, he thought, they *made* them, and he had no interest in being grist for their mill. Unless, of course, there was something in it for him.

And as 1990 began, it seemed that there just might be. John Campbell, during his fishing trip with Charles and his visits to Houston every two or three months during 1989, mentioned that Charles's personal intervention in a public way at the right moment might be of great help to PL, particularly with the politicians in Sacramento. As a consequence, Charles decided to come at least slightly out into the open on the issue of redwood trees during the first months of 1990 and allow himself to be seen.

The first step in that public relations process was a guest editorial for the *Houston Chronicle*, headlined "Under the redwoods—room for business as well as beauty." It was written by the people at his headquarters whom he paid for such tasks and amounted to his first and only detailed declaration on the issue dogging Maxxam's Humboldt County subsidiary:

"Few forest product companies in recent years have been as subject to media attention [as the Pacific Lumber Company]," Hurwitz's article pointed out. "None has been more grievously misrepresented. . . . The basic dispute is between the economic survival of the region's timber industry and those who earn their living from it, against those who argue that preserving every redwood tree has a higher priority. . . . The struggle is over whether coastal redwoods, growing on privately owned land that is zoned exclusively for timber production, should be viewed as a renewable crop which is grown, harvested and grown again to produce a continual supply of lumber or whether the already enormous public holding of redwoods should be further increased until every single tree is protected behind walls of government regulation . . .

"Outsiders have examined this issue in great detail [and found that] the company's forest operations are conducted in strict compliance with California's forest management regulations. . . . We have taken an 'undermanaged company' and made it far more economically effective without paying a damaging environmental price. . . . Pacific Lumber is meeting its obligations to the work force of Scotia, to the community of Northern California, and to the protectors of the environment. We are improving conditions as we provide quality products."

The second and last step in that public relations process involved Charles's attendance at a private, but highly publicized, meeting with the three leading North Coast politicians in Sacramento at the end of January. The three—Assemblyman Dan Hauser, State Senator Barry Keene, and Congressman Doug Bosco—had pledged themselves to hammer out a compromise solution to the timber conflict by meeting with each side behind closed doors and bargaining concessions out of them with old-fashioned political headknocking. One of the politicians' announced goals was to settle things before, as Keene put it, "extreme results are dictated from the outside." Roughly translated, that meant they hoped to find some way of heading off Forests Forever before it was actually on the ballot. In their press releases, they referred to their effort as a "Timber Summit."

Their first announced meeting in this summitry was on January 29 with Charles Hurwitz, the now legendary owner of Pacific Lumber. Charles agreed to it at Campbell's urging. Hurwitz's attendance would give the whole process credibility and, John emphasized, it was in the company's interest to keep that initiative off the ballot. If that bloody thing got on the ballot and got passed, it would wreak no end of havoc with Pacific Lumber's operations. And Campbell thought these three could or should be courted. Hauser had killed the most recent antitimber bill to approach the Assembly floor, Keene was a powerful figure in the State Senate who had carried some pro-timber legislation now and then, and Bosco had been cooperative since he and Charles met back in 1985. They and the situation were worth Charles's attendance. This was not a public forum. The only thing public about it would be the fact of its occurrence and whatever they chose to say about it afterward.

Since the meeting, though private, had been trumpeted well ahead of time by the politicians involved, Earth First! sent an eight-person delegation to the capital on January 29 to demand a meeting with Hurwitz as well. Greg King was one of the demonstrators and they waited outside Keene's office in the Capitol for the Maxxam chairman to show up, distributing "Charles Hurwitz Wanted—$5,000 Reward" posters to whoever passed by. Among themselves, they referred to Hauser, Keene, and Bosco as "The Three Stooges." The Earth Firsters guessed Hurwitz's arrival must be close when a plainclothes security man started hanging around near them, listening as the longhairs discussed just how they could force Hurwitz into a meeting. Then a swarm of uniformed police began milling around nearby until the elevator arrived and the police quickly formed a wall between the Earth Firsters and an office door down the hall. Then, the ornate elevator doors opened and out stepped Hurwitz, followed by John Campbell and two others. The entourage moved quickly for the office where Hauser, Keene, and Bosco were waiting. Just as they reached the door, one of the Earth Firsters shouted, "Mr. Hurwitz." For a moment, Charles froze in the doorway, calmly staring at his adversaries through his round lenses.

This was the closest Charles Hurwitz came to an actual public appearance during the entire "Timber Summit" campaign.

After an instant, John Campbell gave his boss a little nudge, they all rushed inside, the door was slammed shut, and guards were posted to make sure they were not interrupted.

Bosco later described the two-hour conclave as "hard bargaining" in "a good-faith effort." Keene said only that "negotiations are under way" and that he had told Hurwitz that "time is running out." Hauser said his stomach "was still churning," the meeting went "well," and he and his two fellow lawmakers were still "very strongly united." Hurwitz said nothing at all.

When he was whisked out of the office, the Earth Firsters followed him down the hall, separated by the uniformed police, until he stepped into a private elevator, the doors closed, and he was gone.

Charles Hurwitz would return to Sacramento for four more meetings over the next few months, all of them devoted to brainstorming on how to stop EPIC's initiative and all of them not only private, but secret as well.

A week later his boss's well-publicized January 29 bargaining session, John Campbell announced that Charles Hurwitz's Pacific Lumber Company, "yielding to public and legislative pressure," had agreed to a two-year moratorium on all logging in Headwaters Forest. The deal, however, was conditional on its environmentalist opponents ceasing all opposition to harvesting on all the company's other timberlands. John told the press that he hoped this conces-

sion would "lessen all the hype" and allow everyone on the issue to
"get down to some meaningful dialogue." He also warned that this
was all conditional on the company being allowed to operate at will
on the rest of its property. If its opposition started blocking THPs
elsewhere, PL would consider Headwaters fair game and the deal
was off. Pacific Lumber's cards were on the table. If the intention of
the environmentalists was just to stop the cutting of trees, they had
a problem, but if they were prepared to be reasonable, they had a
deal. It was in their hands to save Headwaters. He awaited their
response.

Earth First!'s was graphic. In the early morning in the hamlet of
Alton, where Highway 36 ran into U.S. 101, some fifty Earth Firsters
captured a logging truck. Their original plan had been to occupy
John Campbell's office in Scotia, but word had leaked to the press
so they'd changed targets. After chaining themselves to the truck's
bumper and the cables securing its load of harvested old growth,
the Earth First! demonstration was serenaded by Darryl Cherney,
wearing a large, papier-mâché globe depicting the planet Earth over
his head:

> "Now Earth First! offers a reward," he sang,
> "Five thousand we will pay
> Whoever captures Charlie Hurwitz
> And puts that boy away."

EPIC's response, supplied by Cecilia Lanman, was more reasoned.

There wasn't a whole lot to the company's offer, she pointed
out. The courts were not about to let it into Headwaters anyway and
they knew it. Some concession. And EPIC was certainly not responsible for any problems Pacific Lumber had logging on any of its lands.
The problem was that the company kept submitting illegal THPs.
Charles Hurwitz should be reassured that if his company submitted
legal ones, it wouldn't have a problem.

53

By then, of course, Charles Hurwitz was back in Texas, where he had agreed to deliver a speech at the University of Texas Business School, his one truly public appearance during his period of increased visibility.

His son, Sean, was a first-year student there and was in the audience. The appearance, however, did not come off at all as Charles had hoped. While he was in the midst of explaining to the students how to manage rapid financial growth, some twenty-five demonstrators from Texas Earth First! rushed into the hall and began an organized disruption, waving signs and showering the room with "Charles Hurwitz Wanted—$5,000 Reward" flyers.

"Hurwitz must die," one of the Earth Firsters screamed before being run off in the hands of the campus police. "Hurwitz must die."

Charles Hurwitz's close associates would later say that he was shaken by his experience at UT Business School. Charles was very touchy on issues of family and Sean's presence in the audience while these crazies shouted about how Hurwitz should die made him feel especially threatened. Afterward, one of his friends noted, Charles seemed to feel vulnerable in a way he never had felt before.

Charles also seemed to have concluded that the controversy around Pacific Lumber had, for the first time in his life, made his own personal safety an issue.

54

Had Hurwitz said as much to Darryl Cherney, Darryl would likely have answered, "Welcome to the club."

By the time Charles visited his son's business school, Darryl and Judi Bari had been fielding threats regularly for months. Sometimes the threats came on the phone, sometimes by mail. Judi got one hand-delivered during the middle of the night to the front door of the Mendocino Environmental Center. It was a xeroxed picture of herself with the crosshairs of a telescopic rifle scope overlaid on her image. Darryl received a drawing depicting a longhair nailed face first to the side of a redwood tree, spikes through his hands and feet. The longhair was wearing an Earth First! T-shirt and his pants had been pulled down around his ankles, revealing a bare ass into which an unidentified, presumably endangered, feathered species had been stuffed. Both Darryl and Judi were sent copies of a leaflet announcing Earth First!'s "Nation Wide Tree Shit," complete with illustrations of two Earth Firsters up a tree on a platform defecating over the edge on the wildlife below. At the bottom was the instruction "for more information call Darrell [sic] Cherney," accompanied by Darryl's actual phone number. Judi also got a brief typewritten note advising her, "Get out and go back to where you come from. We know everything. YOU WON'T GET A SECOND WARNING."

Darryl and Judi compared their threats in their moments alone together and it often led to friction between them. Darryl worried that hers were scarier than his and that maybe that meant she was a better activist than he was. So he got defensive and she got offended and they fought. Though they maintained their unshaken public personae, both were regularly terrified and Darryl was, at moments, hysterical. At one point, he got so freaked out that he pulled over at a pay phone by the highway and began calling all his friends and saying he was going to commit suicide. He and Judi squabbled a lot now and, out of public view, their relationship was coming apart at the seams.

Still, Cherney and Bari organized. Two hundred Earth Firsters demonstrated at PL's Carlotta log deck, the log truck was captured in Alton, and fifty Earth Firsters, dressed as animals, marched through Eureka to Assemblyman Dan Hauser's local office, ripped the door off its hinges, and then made similar, if less rowdy visits on the offices of the rest of the Three Stooges—State Senator Barry Keene and Congressman Doug Bosco. Another Earth First! demonstration descended on the Humboldt State University Department of Forestry, where one of the members of the state Board of Forestry was on the faculty. There was also a crowd assembled in front of the CDF's Fortuna offices to protest the most recent road in Headwaters Forest and, while they picketed, several local Timber People threw eggs at them. Hurwitz's speech was disrupted in Texas and, down in Rancho Mirage near Palm Springs, where Maxxam had built a luxury real estate development and a Ritz-Carlton Hotel on what had once been bighorn sheep habitat, twenty-five Earth Firsters strung a banner declaring "Ritz Rapes Redwoods" and plastered the inside of the hotel with Earth First! stickers and Charles Hurwitz Wanted posters.

As pleased as Darryl was with the flood of activity, though, it still felt like a piecemeal effort and he wanted more. He wanted something that would crack this issue open once and for all and bring the full potential weight of the movement to bear in a monumental showdown with the timber industry.

He found what he thought might be that something shortly after Maxxam's compromise offer on the Headwaters.

Actually, Judi made the discovery and told him about it. One of her daughters got sick and had to be hospitalized briefly and while

Judi was hanging out at the hospital, she was visited by an itinerant political activist who called himself Walking Rainbow. Normally, she would have been too busy to give this Rainbow customer the time of day, but she had time on her hands so they talked. He'd been involved in social causes since the civil rights movement of the early 1960s. He suggested to her that the way to get a real handle on this redwood issue was to invite outsiders in massive numbers, the way the civil rights movement had done in Mississippi in 1964 with the Mississippi Summer Project. They ought to stage a kind of Mississippi Summer in the redwoods. Judi usually talked to Darryl on the phone three or four times a day and when they spoke next, she mentioned her conversation with Walking Rainbow and they both went for the idea. Within days, they had placed it at the top of their mutual agenda and what would be known as "Redwood Summer" was born.

It would prove an extraordinarily fateful decision for both of them, and for Greg King as well.

In the burst of inventiveness that followed their decision—revving Darryl up to his usual 110 m.p.h., bouncing between phone calls and songs and soliloquies aimed at Judi or at Greg—Redwood Summer seemed like a sure thing: hundreds, perhaps thousands, of committed students and activists flowing into Humboldt County, camping in the backwoods, and organizing into shock troops to save the forest. And, as they came, the media would follow them in, enlarging the issues exponentially and filling the news with tree-sits, truck captures, log deck occupations, picket lines, and demonstrations, turning Charles Hurwitz into George Wallace and John Campbell into Bull Connor and halting the devastation once and for all. Just as Mississippi Summer had broken the hold of racism on the south, Redwood Summer could end "speciesism." It was just as evil for one species, humans, to dictate life or death to all the others as it was to suppress a minority for reasons of color. They could catapult the movement they'd built here in this backwoods corner of California into a national hit. Darryl soon repeated to everyone that they could do this, they could do this.

Judi Bari officially announced Redwood Summer in the last week of February. It was agreed that she and Darryl would handle recruiting and publicity, while Greg King handled the woods end of things, but, in practical fact, they all handled everything. The first meeting they convened about Redwood Summer on the North Coast drew thirty-five people to Ukiah in Mendocino County. The second drew sixty in Garberville, both huge crowds by the standards of the Mateel. Stories about Redwood Summer were soon showing up in newspapers all around the country and Darryl's phone was in constant use. So was Judi's. The night after the initial Ukiah meeting, she even received a call from Candy Boak.

Candy said she'd come down to the Redwood Summer meeting. She'd been sitting outside in her car. Had Judi seen her?

No, Judi answered, she hadn't.

Well, she was there, Candy repeated. Then she began listing the names of the other people who had attended. Afterward, she signed off and hung up.

Candy Boak called Judi Bari again several days later.

This time she said she'd been down in Redwood Valley where Judi lived the other day, right by her house. She knew where Judi lived and she and her husband, John, were going to come by and visit her some day.

Great, Judi said, then got her off the line as quickly as possible.

For the rest of March and April and into May, Candy called Judi frequently, with similarly inane conversation. At the time, the fat woman's phone calls seemed just a nuisance—creepy, but just a nuisance.

Candy would later say she considered them great fun.

55

Darryl Cherney didn't talk much with Candy Boak on the phone, but he saw her face to face in late March, under an odd set of circumstances.

Their encounter came after Darryl had decided to clear his decks of unfinished business and do a ten-day jail sentence that had been hanging over his head for almost a year. The charge had grown out of the 1989 tree-sit that had launched Candy Boak's "monkey-wrenching the monkey wrenchers" campaign. Darryl decided to plead to misdemeanor trespass in exchange for ten days and get it off the books so it wouldn't be used against him during the summer. He and his tree-sit partner turned themselves in on March 20, after an hour-long demonstration in front of the court-house entrance on Fourth Street in Eureka.

Darryl told the crowd that the two of them were "prisoners of war in the fight to save the redwoods." The law, of course, was supposed to treat everyone equally, but their incarceration would put the torch to that myth. They wouldn't see any of the hundreds of violators of the state's forest practice regulations inside the slammer, they could bet on that. Instead, the law protected those people and made criminals out of the people who tried to stop them.

After the rally, Darryl, his partner, and twenty-five others marched inside the courthouse and up four flights of stairs, singing the civil rights anthem "Oh, Freedom" at the top of their lungs, including new lyrics about winning freedom for the land with a monkey wrench in their hand and going home to Mother Earth to be free. Outside the booking area, the others surrounded the two men turning themselves in with a human wall of linked arms. The sheriff's deputies tried to pry Darryl and his partner out several times, with no success, and then issued an official order to disperse, also with no success. Then, as tension mounted, Darryl parted the wall and offered himself and his partner to the law. The others filed out with another round of winning freedom for the land with a monkey wrench in their hand and going home to Mother Earth to be free.

Darryl was taken inside to a communal holding cell but was only held there for five days, just half of his sentence. The sheriff's department gave him no advance warning about his early release. They just rolled him and his tree-sit partner out of their bunks at 4:00 A.M. on Sunday morning and pushed them out onto Fourth Street. Darryl used the pay phone at a nearby Mini Mart to call the person in Arcata who had volunteered to drive in to pick them up whenever they were released, but there was no answer at the phone. It was cold, the fog was in and settling all over the street in a damp blanket, and Darryl was a little desperate. He had no fucking idea how they were going to get to Arcata, he told his partner. They might have no choice but to hitchhike.

Just then, Darryl heard his name being called out behind him, and there was Candy Boak.

Candy explained that she and John lived nearby and she'd been unable to sleep so she decided to drive down here to the Mini Mart and buy a Sunday paper. To Darryl, stranded at 4:00 A.M., she looked like a gift from God and he told her so. He was a deep believer in spiritual forces, he explained, and he knew from experience that the fates worked in mysterious ways. When he heard her voice calling his name and saw her car, he thought, "My ride has arrived."

Candy laughed, told them to hop in, and proceeded to take Darryl and his tree-sit partner to a nearby diner for an early breakfast. She was full of questions about Redwood Summer, running the gamut of subjects from ideology to logistics, and Darryl, slurping coffee, answered every one of them. Afterward, she drove the two hippies out to Arcata, then headed back through the fog toward her own home.

When Darryl told Judi about the encounter, he described it as an incredible coincidence.

Judi burst out laughing. Was Darryl out of his fucking mind? Coincidence? She couldn't believe his naiveté. Darryl was supposed to do ten days, he was being kept virtually incommunicado, then they release him after five days with no warning at 4:00 A.M., and who is the first person he runs into? Candy Boak? She'd virtually debriefed him on the subject of Redwood Summer by the time she left him off in Arcata. The woman obviously had prior knowledge of the release. Somebody had tipped her off and she used the opportunity to get what she wanted by manipulating Darryl. He might as well have talked to Charles Hurwitz or the FBI.

Darryl thought Judi was a little off the wall on this one and said so with no small amount of defensiveness.

Several days later, Candy Boak called Judi Bari again and said she'd given a nice long report to her timber group about her conversation with Darryl.

You see? Judi then prodded Darryl. You see? Some damn coincidence.

That was, of course, only one of Cherney and Bari's disagreements that spring. They fought all the time and on virtually every issue, over the slimmest of pretexts. Judi thought Darryl was losing it and she was rapidly becoming sick and tired of the relationship and that made Darryl lose it even more.

And throughout it all, the pressure of the threats continued, drifting in sporadically in the mail or left politely with Darryl's answering service.

One was a drawing of a hangman's noose with the inscription "Humboldt and Mendocino Countie's [sic] Welcome Dirt First To A Mississippi Summer."

Another asked, "What is it going to take to make you people realize that your demonstrations are dangerous? Is it going to take someone to get hurt or even killed? Loggers aren't going to full [sic] around. Alot of them are carrying weapons and we don't blame them either because they are only trying to make a living and

surpport [sic] there [sic] family. . . . We don't think that the loggers
should put up with your shit, they should just run you over if you get
in their way. . . . We must warn you, though . . . next time you try to
stop a logging truck remember that accidents happen!"

About the only thing Darryl and Judi didn't fight over that
spring was their politics. On this, they were still hand in glove and
directed mutual anger at common targets. One of those targets
that spring was Earth Day 1990. The event in the early seventies
that had birthed much of the current environmental movement
was being reprised for the first time in some twenty years. Among
other things, it had a host of corporate sponsors. In Humboldt
County, one of those was the Pacific Lumber employees' group
that had organized participation in the 1988 truck parade past the
county courthouse. Outside the Pacific Lumber offices in Scotia,
the company had also posted a banner saying every day was Earth
Day at PL. This pissed Darryl off no end and when he and Judi
railed about it, she suggested they declare a series of Earth Day
Free Zones, as a gimmick for taking a public shot at this co-opted
sham of an event. Darryl thought that was a great idea and began
writing a press release and, when he did, he had yet another inspiration about some fun he could have at Earth Day's expense. He
would put out a flyer for a fictitious rival event called "Earth
Night." Putting the press release on hold, Darryl designed a flyer.
It featured a drawing from a book about monkey-wrenching that
showed two shadowy forms carrying hand tools approaching a logging Cat in the dark of night. "Earth Night 1990," it announced.
"Go out and do something for the EARTH at night." With great
laughter, Darryl then mailed the flyer to his Earth First! mailing
list as a joke.

It did not, however, stop there.

Next, someone unknown secured a copy of the Earth Night
flyer, reproduced it—this time with Darryl's name and phone number on it—and mailed it to a list of logging equipment owners and
dealers throughout the state. For several weeks afterward, Darryl's
answering service was loaded up with messages from Timber People, all of whom had received this flyer in the mail: several said they
would be glad to kill him, others just offered to beat him up. One
described him as "a terrorist squirrel."

Several weeks after that, person or persons unknown, calling themselves "Earth Night Action," claimed credit for damaging three high-voltage power lines south of San Francisco.

To Darryl, it was like the echo of strangers' footsteps stalking him down a long, dark corridor. He now pointed out to everyone he talked to that something very weird was going on out there, though he didn't know exactly what.

56

And it just kept happening.

In an attempt to defuse the tensions provoked by their announcement of Redwood Summer, Darryl Cherney and Judi Bari staged an early April press conference at which they renounced the tactic known as tree-spiking. Nothing terrified Timber Country more than this form of sabotage, where large nails or railroad spikes were driven into a living tree so that when it was eventually cut and milled, the spike would destroy the equipment being used to turn it into boards. Two years earlier, a Mendocino mill hand had been severely injured when the saw blade he was running hung up on a spike and exploded into a hundred shards of flying metal. That incident was still talked about in mills throughout the North Coast, and most of those who talked about it assumed the spike had been driven by an Earth Firster. In their renunciation announcement, Darryl and Judi emphasized that while they still believed in monkey-wrenching, they wanted to monkey-wrench Charles Hurwitz and Maxxam, not the men in Mills A and B.

The Earth Firsters' renunciation nonetheless drew little sympathy in Scotia. Few, if any, timber people really believed Earth First! about much of anything and that innate distrust was only amplified when Darryl and Judi's announcement was followed the next day by a counterfeit Earth First! press release that was anonymously distributed among timber workers all over the county. Stacks of them were also left in Laundromats and individual copies were posted in bowling alleys and truck stops. "We, followers of the movement Earth First! of Northern California, do not agree with nonferal Darryl Cherney's recent statement advocating no tree spiking," it trumpeted. "We are in a 'war' with the north coast timber companies. Companies don't have rights, only Mother Earth has rights. We must save all trees. Mississippi Summer—Come one, come all to Humboldt County. We intend to spike trees, monkeywrench, and even resort to violence if necessary. . . . People of the north coast must stop raping the forests now. We have no time left." The release was signed Earth First! Arcata—an organization that did not exist—but it was printed on Earth First! stationery identical to the genuine article and sounded just the way most timber workers expected a genuine Earth First! press release would sound.

After its initial distribution, the phony press release was picked up and circulated to the media by Hill & Knowlton, the international public relations firm whose San Francisco office had been retained for Pacific Lumber by John Campbell.

John Campbell also personally involved himself in the spiking issue that spring. Shortly after Darryl and Judi's renunciation, Pacific Lumber's president addressed the Eureka Rotary Club. It was the kind of hail-fellow-well-met circumstances in which John excelled and this appearance was no exception. Everyone who had contact with John these days knew he was on a roll. He seemed to know just what he was doing and just how he had to do it.

The problem, Campbell told the Eureka Rotarians, was not environmentalism. Hell, everyone at Pacific Lumber was an environmentalist. Pacific Lumber supported Earth Day just like the Sierra Club. Pacific Lumber wanted clean air and clean water, just like the Natural Resources Defense Council. The problem was not whether to save the environment; the problem was some people's approach to that end.

Campbell then lifted up a foot-long piece of redwood log, revealing the half-sawed fragment of an eight-inch railroad spike embedded in the trunk. More than a few in the audience sucked deep breaths at the sight and everyone wanted a good look.

It was people who did this kind of thing that he couldn't tolerate, John continued. He didn't have to tell anyone in the room who those people were. They hadn't identified themselves, needless to say, but everyone here read the papers. They knew the people who advocated sabotage. This particular spike had been run through Mill B's head rig two weeks earlier, Campbell explained. And it was just one of three that hit the mill almost at the same time. Fortunately, no one had been injured in the incidents, but that was only a piece of good luck. The truth was that he could just as easily have been pulling body parts off his mill floor as spike fragments. This particular spike took fifteen teeth out of the head rig, a circulating band saw that was sixty feet long and sixteen inches wide. When the band was replaced, its replacement was damaged by another spike. Then the head rig next to the damaged one was shut down by yet another spike. All of these spikes were apparently driven into these trees shortly after the radical environmentalists from Earth First! were making their public renunciation.

Having raised the specter of terrorism on the mill floor to the Rotarians, John moved on to the subject of Forests Forever.

This initiative, he observed, was another piece of misguided radical environmentalism. If it became law, John warned, the state was going to take the best 3,000 acres PL owned and leave it with 193,000 other acres to manage with a forestry philosophy designed by some bloody Tarot card reader with a pillow between his ears. Pacific Lumber alone would be reduced to half its size, both in annual production and in employees. He didn't have to tell the men in this room what a disaster that would be for the businesses of Humboldt County. And all for no good reason. The truth of the matter was that if these radical environmentalists like Earth First! and Forests Forever would just back off, get out of the way, and let PL grow trees, the environment would be taken care of just fine. PL had been doing a bloody good job of that since before these kids were even born.

John Campbell's linkage of Earth First! and Forests Forever in front of the Rotarians was no accident. Nor was it just a personal rhetorical flourish. Rather, it was part and parcel of a strategy settled upon that spring by the coalition of timber industry organizations that had been gathered to fight the initiative and of which PL was a member. They were sure Earth First! would only lose if put to the people of California as a yes or no vote, so they intended to turn Forests Forever into a referendum on Earth First! That strategy was most obvious in the official ballot argument that Forest Forever's opposition submitted for the voter information booklet to be mailed to each California voter in advance of November's election. John Campbell couldn't have put it better himself.

This initiative was "simply TOO RADICAL an approach," the ballot argument alleged. "Not surprisingly, [Forests Forever] is SUPPORTED by persons associated with the RADICAL ENVIRONMENTAL GROUP EARTH FIRST!, notorious for driving spikes into trees, vandalizing logging equipment and harrassing [sic] timber workers and their families. . . . On [a] national television program . . . Earth First! leader Darryl Cherney advocated terminally ill people should strap bombs to themselves and blow up dams, power plants, and other structures they believe harm the environment. In fact several [Earth First!] members are currently under investigation . . . and federal indictment. . . . We must take steps to protect our forests, but not . . . drastic steps."

Needless to say, the coalition that supported Forests Forever— including the Sierra Club and the Natural Resources Defense Council—were as infuriated by the argument as they were helpless to do anything about it. Those more established environmental groups felt they had virtually nothing in common with Earth First! and had been among the first to denounce plans for Redwood Summer. It made Campbell chuckle to see them all scurrying around now, trying to escape from the onus of their buddies Darryl Cherney and Judi Bari and Greg King.

John considered pounding out the link between Earth First! and Forests Forever good strategy. And, John made a point of insisting, it was also the bloody truth. He saw these folks all the time. He knew Darryl and Greg hung out with Cecilia and Woods. He knew they talked strategy together all the time. He knew they rooted for each other. He saw them hugging and patting each other on the back in the hall outside the courtroom. He saw the same people in costume following Darryl up Main Street in Scotia, waving signs, and the same people sitting in the audience at the CDF headquarters in Fortuna and cheering on Cecilia when she went after another one of PL's THPs. They were all part of the same radical plan for the forest that would leave Pacific Lumber stripped and hobbled. One did physical sabotage, the other did legal sabotage, but the fruits of both their labors were the same.

The answer, John repeated to the audience at the Eureka Rotary Club luncheon, was to bloody well leave the forests to the people who knew something about them. This damn Forests Forever might very well cost a hundred, maybe even two hundred thousand jobs around the state. And it wouldn't accomplish much more than unemployment. It certainly wouldn't reform forest practices. It would virtually destroy them. There were much more reasonable options, he pointed out, much more reasonable options.

The particular "reasonable option" John had come to the Rotarians to promote was the second wing of the timber industry's strategy to defeat Forests Forever. The state's timber operators were putting forth their own initiative, "the Global Warming and Clear-Cutting Reduction, Wildlife Protection, and Reforestation Act of 1990." This, John argued, was real forestry reform.

As to just how good a strategy it was, however, John had his doubts. When the timber coalition's twenty-eight members had voted on pursuing this course, twenty-seven had voted yes and Pacific Lumber had voted no. Still, John campaigned for it as though he thought it the best thing since sliced bread.

The "real" reform he touted looked a lot like a relaxed version of the status quo. It "banned" clear-cutting, but defined clear-cutting in such a way that the ban could be avoided by leaving one mature tree per acre. It made no mention of the issue of the ongoing erosion that resulted from abandoned logging roads, and while it called for a state wildlife study to be prepared by a timberland task force, it included no set standards for wildlife protection. All that would be required was that wildlife preservation be given "consideration" in the THP process. Many of the other provisions were simply restatements of existing law. There was no mention at all of sustained yield or any other limit on the size of the timber harvest. It included a bond issue that would be used to control global warming by promoting urban forestry projects in which tree planting along city streets was the top priority. Its crowning provision was one the industry had tried to get through the legislature on four different occasions, each time unsuccessfully. This was called "the Long-Term Timber Management Plan." Under this proposed arrangement, a timber company could file a single THP for all of its timberland at once and, unless it secured an extension from the timber company, the undermanned CDF would have to act on that plan within sixty days or it would pass by default. In addition, the industry's initiative abandoned the current system in which approved THPs expired after three years, and allowed its Long-Term Timber Management Plans to last forever. The effect was to limit public review of the timber process to a few weeks every century.

Which was just fine by John Campbell. Come November, he pointed out, the people of California would have a choice between hysteria and reason, and God help us if they got suckered in by the dreadlocks and tree-spike crowd. Then no one would be cutting trees anymore.

None of the Rotarians at lunch that day raised their hands to challenge his assessment.

57

John received pretty much the same reception when he called a company meeting at the Winema Theatre during early April to discuss the same subjects. Even Kelly Bettiga, sitting way in the back, kept his mouth shut. He thought Campbell was a puke and he knew he wasn't alone in his feelings, but there didn't seem much point of acting like it in this situation. Campbell was the man now and everybody, like him or not, had to make their peace with that. John was blunt with his employees about the effect of Forests Forever. If this thing passed, he said, there were going to be layoffs. The company would have no choice. And there wouldn't be just a few layoffs. Eventually, he thought he'd have to let half the workforce go.

That drew muttering and foot shuffling out in the audience and caught the attention of everyone, including those who'd been staring out into space.

But, John continued, they all ought to be used to these kind of threats by now. They'd been hanging over PL's head ever since the Earth Firsters had first shown up. And, when this Redwood Summer everyone was talking about happened, they would be inundated with the biggest wave of disruptions yet.

But, John assured them, they shouldn't get anxious about it. The company had the situation well in hand. He'd hired an outside security firm to look after things and it was full of people who bloody well knew their business—former CIA and FBI agents. People, he repeated, who really knew their business.

This announcement drew a few chuckles and a lot of nudging among audience members.

John also told them that they should all remember that most of these people who would show up in answer to Darryl Cherney's and Greg King's and Judi Bari's calls to arms would just be college kids, looking for a good time. The problem was that their leaders might steer them into trouble. It was the leaders who were the problem. They were something else. Everyone here in the Winema today, he said, should realize that those guys are watermelons.

John paused for emphasis.

Those guys were watermelons, he repeated when he was sure he had everyone's attention. These guys were green on the outside, but on the inside, where it really mattered, they were red, through and through.

That drew cheers, particularly from the old-timers who still remembered what it meant to call someone a red.

After the meeting was over, John walked down to the coffee shop to grab a bite and, on the way, passing pickup trucks honked and gave him the thumbs-up sign. Some shouted for John to go get 'em, they were behind him all the way. John smiled in response. While he was in the coffee shop, one of the old-timers came in and presented John with a watermelon he'd just purchased at the grocery store. This drew a round of spontaneous applause from the rest of the diners. John thumped the melon with his knuckles and, with a grin as wide as his face, acknowledged the cheering with a beefy wave.

58

Darryl Cherney, the most recognizable of those "watermelons" to Pacific Lumber's employees, had been worried that the locals around the Mateel, particularly the dope growers, would be antsy about Redwood Summer and uncomfortable with a herd of outsiders clomping around in their woods, but, at the organizing meeting he convened in Garberville shortly after Redwood Summer was announced, none of those objections materialized.

The closest thing to an argument against the effort was raised by people concerned over Redwood Summer's potential impact on Forests Forever. If the timber companies' election strategy was to hang Earth First! around the initiative's neck, wasn't something like this, which would put Earth First! in the media foreground for the entire summer, just going to play into the companies' hands?

Not at all, Darryl answered. The timber companies were going to try to hang Earth First! on Forests Forever whatever Earth First! did. So why sit back and just accept the negative without also reaping Earth First!'s positives as well? That might be hard for the Sierra Club types to accept, but they had never been anything but nervous about Earth First! anyway—which was their problem, not Forests Forever's or Earth First!'s. If it hadn't been for the last four years of Earth First!'s efforts, the chances were that the Sierra Club and their like would never have even made a stand on the issue of old growth. Besides, Darryl pointed out, it was already obvious that if Forests Forever was going to have anything left to save, someone had to slow the timber companies down between now and the election. In response to word of the initiative, THP applications had multiplied geometrically. The companies were clearly planning a cutting frenzy in an attempt to anticipate the limitations that might be placed on them after November. Among other things, Redwood Summer would at least slow the logging rampage down.

Convinced that the Mateel locals were behind the project, Darryl, Judi, and Greg set out in March to recruit outside troops and build an organizational structure in which those volunteers could function. Announcements were mailed to hundreds of college newspapers and stories ran on both national newswires. Darryl also planned to organize, along with Judi, a major recruiting tour of California campuses late in May. A series of committees were also formed to oversee preparations for the expected influx. The plan was to use the volunteers against two distinct sets of targets. The first were highly visible locations such as the Pacific Lumber log decks, the Louisiana Pacific pulp mill, and the Georgia Pacific lumber operation down in Mendocino. These would be sites of major demonstrations, aimed not so much at disruption as at drawing the broadest possible participation and making a significant show of strength. The second set of targets would be individual "illegal" logging shows out in the woods, where smaller action teams would chain themselves to equipment, perch up in trees, and blockade logging trucks in a campaign of open and aggressive civil disobedience. Another committee was formed to select sites for these woods actions and yet another to oversee the training of all Redwood Summer personnel in the philosophy and techniques of nonviolence. Darryl, Judi, and Greg were all agreed on making everyone follow a pledge of nonviolence.

If there was going to be violence, the watermelons wanted it known, it wasn't going to originate with them.

They were, of course, well aware that speculation about possible trouble had accelerated even faster than Redwood Summer preparations. The thought of an invasion by thousands of longhaired Earth Firsters intent on stopping logging did not sit easily among the mill towns. In Fortuna, the mayor advised local citizens not to even talk to any Earth Firsters and several other figures in local government had spoken up for asking the governor to send in the National Guard to maintain order. Timber Country was already freaked and nothing had happened yet except announcements.

That panic was apparent in Darryl, Greg, and Judi's mail. Throughout the spring, death threats kept pouring in. By the middle of May, Darryl alone had received thirty-six. The most interesting among the April batch was sent to all three of them. It was neatly hand-printed underneath a homemade letterhead identifying it as coming from the "Stompers." Membership in the Stompers, a post-script to the letter indicated, was open to anyone who believed "in the basic rights of American citizens" and had "enough fortitude to get out and work for a living." The letterhead was flanked by sketches of hobnailed lumberjack boots. The main body of text was all threat: "We are Humboldt County employees of the Forest Products Industry," it announced. "We hereby give fair warning to the following *lowlife:* Darryl Cherney, Greg King, Judi Bari. Regarding 'Mississippi Summer' in the Redwoods. You three are the organizers and will be held personally accountable for injury to any of our fellow workers due to any act by members of Earth First! and including all imported scum. . . . Our justice will be swift and very real. We know who you are and where you live. If you want to be a Martyr, we will be happy to oblige. Our tolerance of your harrassment [sic] has *Ended.*" The letter was signed "Stompers."

Publicly, all three of Redwood Summer's principal organizers had the same response to the threats: they would not be deterred by such terror tactics, period, and the risk they represented was simply part of what they took on when they chose to stand up for their cause. Privately, however, each brought a personal nuance to their reactions and each reaction was different: Judi's changed the most over that spring. In the beginning, her fear was palpable. Shortly after announcing their plans for Redwood Summer, she moved to a house outside of Willits in Mendocino County and the anonymous threats followed her, as did the calls from Candy Boak. Eventually, the pressure prompted a pair of panic attacks, when Judi woke up in the middle of the night and was convinced she could hear someone climbing the ladder to her sleeping loft. She was also convinced that whoever it was intended to kill her. She was too scared to open her eyes and had difficulty drawing a breath into her constricted chest. When she finally did look, no one was there and she realized the sound she heard was her own heart, pounding as loud as footsteps. Eventually, however, she concluded that she just had to come to terms with the danger. Otherwise, the fear was going to dominate her life. She was through fretting, she told Darryl. She just had to accept that threats were going to be made against her and she wasn't going to let herself be transformed into a wreck by them. Henceforth, her policy would be to slough them off.

Greg took the threats in stride, as well. They were consistent with the barely hidden malevolence he expected from the powers that be. He now assumed that he was being watched, going so far on one occasion as heading off cross-country on foot in order to leave a suspicious pickup truck behind. He'd been having dreams of pistols pointed in his direction since long before the tide of death threats. By April, he was more disturbed by the simultaneous disinformation campaign than he was by the threats.

Darryl had no such equanimity or even anything remotely resembling it. Strangers writing and calling in to share their decision to blow his brains out left him frantic and twitchy. He made arrangements with several people to take over his various roles should he be killed or maimed and tried to ignore the danger, with no success whatsoever. He thought all the phony press releases and their like amounted to someone out there trolling for an assassin, trying to find the right bait to get some poor fuck whose elevator didn't reach his top floor to snap and reach for his deer gun.

Darryl religiously forwarded copies of the threats he received to the Humboldt County Sheriff's Department and, shortly after receipt of the Stompers letter, called in to see just what the sheriffs intended to do about the danger in which he and the others found themselves. He talked to a sergeant.

This was not just casual harassment or high school pranks, Darryl pointed out. When someone sent out phony announcements that Earth First! was going to spike trees, that made it very likely that some timber worker out there was going to want to kill Earth Firsters.

The sergeant agreed. He said that it was indeed very likely that somebody was trying to get Darryl and the other Earth Firsters killed. He thought Darryl ought to count himself lucky if the only thing that happened was someone beating the shit out of him.

Well, Darryl demanded, what was the Sheriff's Department going to do about it?

The Sheriff's Department was going to fill out a report, the sergeant answered.

That's all?

That was all.

Obviously unsatisfied, Darryl also took his worries to the Eureka office of the Federal Bureau of Investigation. The agent there was surprised to see him but seemed to know who he was. He said the bureau had no jurisdiction and Darryl left.

59

At the time of Darryl's surprise visit, the Eureka office of the Federal Bureau of Investigation was busy helping the bureau's Northern California Terrorist Squad stage its annual bomb school at College of the Redwoods, the junior college just south of Eureka. The classroom part of the week-long training for FBI agents and local police was held on campus. The field work was staged at a Louisiana Pacific clear cut north of Eureka and three cars were blown up, one by one, with pipe bombs located inside the passenger compartment. Then the site of the explosion was investigated before the next explosion was staged. The school participants were instructed by FBI Special Agent Frank Doyle, the Terrorist Squad's bomb expert, that this type of explosion, with the bomb inside the vehicle, was generally not the result of an attack on the occupants. Usually, it occurred when bombers were transporting bombs.

No explosions with the bomb placed outside of the passenger compartment were staged at the FBI's 1990 school.

60

By April, Greg King could sense momentum beginning to build behind Redwood Summer, but he was nonetheless in a very different state of mind than either of his organizing partners. Before they'd come up with the idea, he'd almost made up his mind to move on from what he'd been doing for the past four years. He was tired of living poor and repeating the same tasks and tactics over and over, as organizing required. He wanted something different. He also missed the old days, when there were just a few of them out in the forest. He thought their success had made everything harder to feel a part of and seemed to have dramatically increased the flakiness of the people drawn to their actions. He was also feeling more emotionally vulnerable than ever. His mother was down in Sonoma County dying of cancer and the expectation of losing her was a constant weight on Greg's mind. He'd only decided to stay around for Redwood Summer because it seemed the realization of the dream of making a mass movement that he and Darryl had articulated when they started out in 1986. Greg still thought such a movement was necessary but he was no longer sure he wanted to be part of it. He'd never been a joiner and was already uncomfortable just having to stand up for the other parts of Earth First! In this transition, Greg had decided to hang around, but only to take care of unfinished business.

One of those pieces of unfinished business was an action on Earth Day about which Greg had been fantasizing almost since the day he began committing aerial derring-do under the Earth First! banner. He'd been planning it off and on for almost two years.

This was to be the ultimate banner hanging. As Earth Day dawned, with the nation's attention focused on the environment, they were going to hang a banner over the Golden Gate Bridge, perhaps the single most recognizable structure in the United States. The banner they'd prepared read, "Save This Planet: 1. Defend Ancient Forests, 2. Ban Fossil Fuels, 3. Earth First!"

Darryl figured it had the makings of a photograph that would be printed in history books for decades to come.

Greg led his team of climbers onto the bridge at 3:15 A.M., when the middle two of its six traffic lanes were coned off in preparation for a reshuffling of incoming and outgoing lanes for the morning commute hours. Parking momentarily in that vacant middle, they unloaded all their gear from the cars and, splitting into two groups, scurried through the darkness to the sidewalks on either side and began mounting the four-foot-diameter cable that connected the towers and from which the bridge's roadway was suspended. By the time dawn rose in an orange sheet over Oakland and the blurry foothills across the bay to the east, Greg and the others, divided into two climbing parties, were perched on each side of the bridge's superstructure, two-thirds of the way up, some hundred and fifty feet above the roadway. Using flashlights in the dark, they'd already strung traverse lines to connect the two halves of their effort and upon which to hang the banner. The Earth Firsters had also sabotaged the locks on the elevators that serviced the top of the towers, hoping to prevent their use by anyone sent up to stop them. Greg had a cellular phone with him for bridgetop interviews with local media but, to make sure word was disseminated as widely as possible, Darryl was stationed up at the pay phone in the Vista Point area at the bridge's north landing, making calls. He'd brought along all his Earth First! files in the trunk of the old Datsun he was driving and was using it as a portable office.

Darryl was the first one the California Highway Patrol arrested. As soon as they discovered there were people on the bridge cables, the CHP called for a team of ironworkers to go up and bring the climbers down and its uniformed officers began a sweep of the area. By then, a local radio station was broadcasting live from near Darryl's perch. Time, however, was growing suddenly short. It only took the ironworkers a few minutes to melt the glue that the Earth Firsters had used to fill the elevator locks and mount the towers. Meanwhile, two of Greg's team were suspended on traverse lines over the roadway, just beginning the arduous process of inching the banner into position. It was perhaps one-third deployed when a group of ironworkers charged down the cable from the tower elevator station. They seemed extremely pissed off and, as soon as they reached the climbers' perches, began shoving people and threatening their traverse and safety lines. One of the ironworkers even began a wrestling match with Greg over the cellular phone. At that point, the action was called off by the climbers, worried that someone would end up splattered on the bridge below or toppled into the water.

Their banner was never deployed.

The entire group of Earth Firsters was reunited at the Marin County jail, where they sat, charged with various counts of trespass and property destruction, until they were bailed out that afternoon. All of the cars they'd used to get to the bridge, including Darryl's, had also been impounded. And all of Darryl's files had been seized as evidence.

Greg let out an audible groan when he learned that virtually the entire internal record system of Humboldt Earth First! was now in police hands.

And the news got worse. When Darryl rode with the tow truck driver to the impound yard to reclaim his car, he and the driver started talking. The driver said it was amazing who had come over to look at Darryl's Datsun and sift through all the files that were in the trunk. The whole thing had been searched top to bottom by the Oakland Police Department, even though they had no jurisdiction and the bridge action had taken place nowhere near their home turf.

When Darryl heard that, his heart sank.

It was well-known in Bay Area Earth First! circles that the Oakland P.D. was the principal local liaison for the FBI.

61

By then, Darryl was a mess.

He went over to San Francisco shortly after his release and met with Judi. Their relationship was now held together by no more than a few threads and when he stormed into the restaurant where they were to eat, she thought he'd gone crazy. Within a minute, he tried to turn the table over and began ranting paranoid fantasies. He accused her of working for the FBI or Charles Hurwitz or both the FBI and Charles Hurwitz at the same time and claimed she was trying to ditch him so he'd be easier to arrest.

She told him to get a hold of himself, but he couldn't.

They headed back north that night in separate cars and when they met up at Judi's house, they had what Darryl would later remember as the worst fight two people could possibly have without engaging in physical violence. Finally, Judi screamed at him that they were through, for good, and drove off. He got in his car and chased her.

Darryl went on in a similar vein for the next three days. His fear had driven him past frantic and Judi's rejection left him feeling totally alone and abandoned. He begged, he pleaded, he screamed, and he swore until Judi just couldn't put up with it anymore. In desperation, she called the Arizona Earth First! chapter and told them Darryl was going over the edge and asked them to take him for a week so he could mellow out. It took the effort of several friends to convince him, but Darryl finally agreed and went off to Tucson. He spent most of his week there on the phone, but, when he returned, he was no longer out of control and threw himself into organizing the May recruiting tour that he and Judi had planned to take. Their personal relationship might be over, but, he assumed, their professional relationship would continue.

Judi's assumption was somewhat different. She didn't think she could work at close quarters with Darryl, at least not now. He was too annoying—taking every available opportunity to tell her he couldn't imagine living if something ever happened to her—and working together was too difficult—they'd performed once together since the Golden Gate Bridge action and that had been the hardest performance she'd ever done. She needed more space than Darryl could bring himself to give her. As a consequence, she intervened in Darryl's tour organizing and limited their joint appearances to one, in Santa Cruz on May 24, 1990.

As it turned out, neither would make it that far.

On the evening of May 23, Darryl Cherney and Judi Bari both attended a meeting at a house in Berkeley, along the city's border with Oakland. They'd driven down from the North Coast in separate cars—she that day and he, several days earlier. The meeting was to finalize with a number of Bay Area environmental activists plans for four major actions during Redwood Summer. Darryl considered the meeting one of the most productive he'd ever attended. Afterward, he spent the night at the house in Berkeley and Judi, intent on keeping her distance, drove her Subaru station wagon to Oakland, where she stayed in one of the Bay Area activists' guest room. The next morning, Darryl caught a ride over to where she was staying. Judi thought it was important to be really nice to Darryl, since they were going to have to perform together in a couple of hours, but it was hard. They had one skirmish—it was now hard for them to be in the same room and not fight—but otherwise, the morning was reasonably mellow. They made breakfast and sat on the floor of the Oakland house and played music together until it was time to get under way for Santa Cruz.

First, however, they had to drive back to Berkeley to pick up their sound equipment, their banjo player, and Darryl's car. Judi drove, following another Earth First! vehicle whose driver knew the way back to the house where last night's meeting had been held, and Darryl rode shotgun with Judi.

Her Subaru was headed north on Park Boulevard when it happened.

At 11:55 A.M., as the car approached 34th Street, near Oakland High School, a bomb—eleven inches of galvanized pipe stuffed with gunpowder and sheathed in finishing nails—exploded directly under the driver's seat. The force of the explosion left burn marks on the surface of Park Boulevard, twisted the Subaru's entire front end, buckled its roof, and blew out the windshield. Fragments of the driver's seat and side window were sprayed all over the street. The mangled Subaru kept rolling for another block after the explosion, wobbling along until it came to rest against a parked car.

When Darryl regained consciousness, he discovered he was bleeding from a wound over his left eye, he had virtually no vision out of the eye itself, and his ears rang, but otherwise he was whole. At first he thought they'd been hit by a train. He tried to open his door and escape, but the door wouldn't budge. Then he turned to Judi. She was in agony and screaming at the top of her lungs.

Darryl reached over in an attempt to comfort her.

Sit still, he said. Everything was going to be all right. He loved her and everything was going to be all right.

Judi just kept screaming.

62

Darryl Cherney was the first one the paramedics extricated from the wreck. Judi Bari, still trapped in the Subaru, would have to be cut out of the wreckage. Darryl kept remembering a video he'd once watched about the "disappeared" in El Salvador who, as they were being kidnapped, would shout out their name to passersby so that their families could learn what had happened to them. Darryl did the same.

His name was Darryl Cherney, he shouted over and over. He was an environmental activist, trying to save the ancient forest from Charles Hurwitz. His name was Darryl Cherney, he was . . .

The paramedics just told him to shut up and get in the ambulance.

Darryl left behind a crime scene that was beginning to swarm with Oakland Police Department officers and FBI agents. More than a dozen of the latter would be on Park Boulevard within an hour of the blast. At least four of those agents were veterans of the 1990 Terrorist Squad Bomb School, as was the chief bomb investigator for the Oakland P.D. The FBI team was led by Special Agent Frank Doyle, the bomb school's instructor. Before even examining the wrecked Subaru, the FBI agents briefed the Oakland officers on Bari and Cherney, saying that these were the type of people who would be involved in transporting explosives. Both the driver and the passenger qualified as terrorists. An Oakland P.D. sergeant whom they briefed noted in his log that Darryl and Judi were "apparent radical activists with recent arrest for illegal demonstration on the Golden Gate Bridge" and "Earth First! leaders suspected of Santa Cruz power pole sabotage, linked with federal case of attempted destruction of nuclear power plant lines in Arizona."

As agents and policemen accumulated around the wreckage, the Terrorist Squad had to work out the details of jurisdiction, which it did almost immediately. An agent from Alcohol, Tobacco, and Firearms had arrived and at specific issue was whether Earth First! was on the FBI's official list of domestic terrorist groups and the case was a presumed bomb transport. If Earth First! wasn't, and Darryl Cherney and Judi Bari were probably not the bombers, then the case belonged to ATF.

Jurisdiction went to the FBI.

With that clear, SA Frank Doyle examined the Subaru. He could see the street through the hole under the driver's seat. Eventually the hole would be measured at two feet by four feet, with jagged edges curled outward by the force of the blast. Directly under Judi Bari, the seat had been destroyed and large parts of it embedded in her backside. After a short exam, SA Doyle told the Oakland P.D.'s bomb expert that the bomb had been behind the driver's seat, not under it, despite the fact that the area behind the seat was virtually unscathed. Doyle also hypothesized that the bomb had her guitar on top of it, further proof that this was a transport violation, not an attack. Like the area behind the seat, the guitar case had survived relatively intact. The Oakland P.D. bomb expert had been trained by Doyle and disputed none of his conclusions.

By 3:00 P.M., Judi Bari, still in agony as surgeons did their best to clean up her wounds, had been placed under arrest for felony transportation of illegal explosives and policemen had been posted at the door of her hospital room.

In the meantime, Darryl Cherney, also at Oakland's Highland Hospital, had no idea what was going on. He was taken to a room where a doctor sewed shut a gash over his left eye, treated him for a scratched cornea, and covered his eye with a bandage. Both of Darryl's eardrums were also broken and doctors eventually pulled several fragments of car seat foam out of each. Once the emergency room was finished with him, Darryl waited in the hospital for about an hour under the guard of an Oakland policeman until two men he remembered as "suits with heads balanced on top" came into the room.

One of them who addressed him as Mr. Cherney asked if they could talk.

Who were they? Darryl asked.

Instead of answering, they pulled out their identification and flashed it in front of his face.

Darryl had more than one eye covered and could barely focus with the other and couldn't believe anyone could be so dumb as to flash an I.D. to someone who could barely see.

You must be the FBI, he said.

One of the agents confirmed as much. Then he asked Darryl what his name was.

It was all Darryl could do not to scream. They knew what his name was. Who were they trying to kid?

Then the agent asked if Darryl had any idea who had done this to him.

Darryl responded with a list of possible suspects he'd been accumulating in his mind as he waited. The list started with Charles Hurwitz, then ran through Candy Boak and her allies and a number of other figures involved in the mobilization of Timber Country, including John Campbell and the Pacific Lumber Company. Before he could complete it, however, the agent interrupted.

Look, the FBI man advised in a stern voice, why waste time? They had ways of telling whether or not this was Darryl's own bomb that had gone off by accident, so why didn't he just confess, make it easy on them all, and get it over with.

Darryl didn't need to hear any more. He figured immediately that he and Judi were about to be railroaded. Darryl told the agents he wanted to see his attorney.

With that, the two FBI men closed up their briefcases and walked out of the room. Darryl never saw them again.

At 3:00 P.M., the police shipped him over to the city jail. There, he was locked into a windowless room furnished with a metal table and chairs. Darryl felt like he'd been sequestered in a bread box and he worried about Judi. All he knew of her was word slipped him by a nurse at the hospital that she was still alive and looked as though she would stay that way.

While Darryl waited, on through the afternoon and deeper and deeper into the evening, the Terrorist Squad convened a briefing for some thirty case investigators, half Oakland P.D., half FBI. The first report was by the squad's supervisor. He reiterated that Earth First! was a terrorist group and mentioned the Arizona indictments and the tactic of tree-spiking. Cherney and Bari themselves were suspects in a recent power pole bombing. Then Doyle took the stage and reported that the bomb had been behind the front seat and she put her guitar down on top of it so Bari must have known it was there. Later, another agent from the Terrorist Squad reported that he had a secret informant, a woman close to the leaders of Earth First!, who had told him "some heavies from up north" were coming down to Santa Cruz for some undefined "action." None of the Oakland P.D. at the briefing had much doubt that the FBI was convinced they had their perpetrators. No suspects other than Darryl and Judi had yet been investigated and none ever would be.

At 11:00 P.M., two plainclothes Oakland detectives finally returned to the jail and began Darryl's interrogation. They brought him a cheese sandwich on white bread and a piece of cake. He wolfed down the food and told them he wanted to see his lawyer. They said he would have a better chance of getting out of there if he just talked to them now without having to wait for some lawyer to show up. Darryl agreed reluctantly. All of their questions were about him and Judi and the interrogation proceeded a half hour on, followed by a half hour off, until well past 2:00 A.M. One of the cops noted at the end of one of their sessions that Darryl was hard to figure since he didn't act like the usual bombers they busted. Their interrogation report noted that he had spent a lot of time trying to actively convert them to his cause. At 3:00 A.M., the detectives passed the news to him that they were through with him and were going to send him over to the jail. He was under arrest for suspicion of possession and transportation of an illegal explosive device.

Darryl immediately lost his temper. He couldn't believe it, he screamed. These guys had no idea what they were doing. Why didn't they go out and look for the real bomber? Were they just too lazy to get off their asses and go up north and solve the case? Nobody in their right mind could actually believe that he and Judi had bombed themselves.

His protests to no avail, Darryl Cherney spent the rest of the night in a single holding cell and would stay there for the next four days before finally being released on $100 bail.

Meanwhile, Judi Bari was out of surgery and recovering in a hospital room under guard. The bomb had crushed her tailbone so severely that it sat at right angles to its natural position. It had also driven a spring from the car seat into her colon. Flying shrapnel had reduced extensive patches of her buttocks and pelvis to badly chewed meat, creating nerve damage extensive enough to leave her right leg essentially useless. She was still in extreme pain and drifting in and out of consciousness, but when her sensibilities finally returned she too was approached by the FBI. She refused to talk to them or the Oakland Police Department without her attorney present. From the beginning, she thought they were only interested in framing her and slandering Earth First!

With both suspects incommunicado, the FBI's version of the crime was given wide circulation early, when the audience was its most impressionable. On several occasions, Bari and Cherney were described as "terrorists" and word that they were the only possible suspects was disseminated among the media before Judi was out of surgery. Reports that the FBI had discovered a bag of nails in the car that were "similar" to those strapped around the bomb got wide circulation, as did an FBI search of Bari's house when they found more nails, this time out of the same batch as those on the bomb. Both "leaks" were phony. The nails on the bomb were finishing nails and the only bag of nails in the car were roofing nails, two remarkably dissimilar types. As for belonging to the same batch, the nails used in the bomb were manufactured in a batch of at least 100,000, similar nails could be bought almost anywhere on the North Coast, and, even then, the FBI had been unable to match them with anything from Bari's. Wide coverage was also given to a public affidavit from Special Agent Frank Doyle that the bomb had been located behind the driver's seat, not under it, and, therefore, had been visible to Bari when she loaded her car before heading out Park Boulevard. Despite the fact that this theory was contradicted absolutely by Bari's wounds and the physical evidence of the Subaru's floorboards and seats, the FBI would not drop that version for almost two months, until July, when the Oakland district attorney declined to make any formal charges against Bari and Cherney and essentially dropped the case and any further investigation.

The only real information that had been developed by the FBI during that two months was from its laboratory analysis of the bomb site remnants and the wreckage of the Subaru. The lab concluded that there was no question the explosive device had been inside the passenger compartment, directly under the driver's seat. In fact it had all been attached to a piece of plywood that fit quite snugly in that space, so it wouldn't move around. Whoever put it there had covered it from view with a blue cotton material, bits of which were found embedded in Judi Bari. The bomb itself was a pipe, eleven inches long and two inches across and wrapped in finishing nails to create a shrapnel effect. Its triggering device began with an arming switch and a wind-up pocket watch whose minute hand had been broken off. When the hour hand completed its circuit of anywhere from one to twelve hours, it made contact with a screw and completed an electrical circuit, thereby fully arming the bomb but not detonating it. Actual detonation was the function of a half-inch-diameter ball bearing that had to receive sufficient impetus to roll into place and close the circuit completely. The lab described this as a "motion device" and these kinds of devices were usually referred to as "booby traps" rather than bombs. This was a bomb built to blow up a car on the move, most likely exactly the one it did.

Who put it there still remains a mystery, to the FBI and everyone else.

It was twelve days after the bombing before Darryl and Judi saw each other again. The reunion was possible because Judi's police guard was removed and, still being held only on suspicion rather than indictment, she was officially released from custody and eligible to receive visits in her hospital room from other than attorneys or family members. Darryl could have come in to see her a day earlier, but it took him a day to screw up his courage. The sight of her lying there maimed sent his heart into his throat. They talked for an hour.

She was angry at the press coverage they'd been getting and terrified that the FBI would succeed in railroading them.

Darryl cried and said he would do everything he possibly could to get the truth out. He told her he loved her and that everything would be all right. He also told her that Redwood Summer would go ahead without them, as others picked up their roles and continued the fight.

63

Two weeks earlier, Darryl would have assumed that Greg King would have been the first to step in and carry on but, by the time Darryl saw Judi, Greg had become what Darryl later described as the bombing's third victim.

At the time the bomb went off, Greg King was addressing a meeting of the public relations directors of all the Bay Area electronic media, convened at the studios of San Francisco's NBC-TV affiliate. He told the group they should be covering not only the fate of the redwoods but also the crackdown by the government on environmental activists. That, he argued, was the story of the future. Afterward, he drove up to his parents' home in Sonoma County, where he first received a garbled message from one of his friends that made it sound as though Darryl and Judi had been in an automobile accident. Greg called for some clarification.

Darryl and Judi were in a wreck? he asked.

No, his friend answered. It was a bomb.

Greg was dumbstruck.

Greg spent the next two days at his parents' and then, very much against their wishes, drove down to Berkeley to participate in a vigil for Darryl and Judi outside of the Oakland Police Department. It was here that his incapacitation began.

That evening, he was hanging around smoking dope and talking with several other Earth Firsters in their house when he was designated to go to the nearby store for candles to use in the vigil and they found him a ride with the activist at whose house Judi had stayed the night before the bombing. The activist was headed over to Oakland and would drop Greg at the grocery several blocks away. Greg could walk back.

Greg had never met the man he was riding with before and it was only after they were under way that he learned who he was. That freaked Greg immediately. He had been concocting scenarios in his mind for the bombing and one was that the owner of the house in front of which Judi's car had been parked had planted the bomb. Greg would later identify the man as someone who was likely a government agent. Still, that evening right after the bombing, they chatted as they drove, but the gradual change in the man's voice from jovial to firm escalated Greg's fears. Then the man stopped his car at a light in back of a car with a shiny new bumper sticker that said "CAR BOMB." The driver read it out loud and commented that that wasn't a very funny bumper sticker. Greg thought his tone of voice was menacing and that the sticker was a threat. He demanded to be let out immediately and then walked back to the house where the other Earth Firsters were.

When he told them about the bumper sticker and his suspicions of the man who'd given him a ride, the others were sympathetic—they were all very fond of Greg—but they also said he was being paranoid. He'd smoked too much. Greg said he wasn't at all, but, in any case, he was leaving for the North Coast right away.

As soon as Greg left, however, things only escalated for him, congealing into a pattern he would later remember as "sick" and "very, very weird."

It started when he turned the ignition on his car. In that instant, he was convinced it was about to explode. It didn't, but Greg's fears kept escalating as he headed toward the freeway. Driving without a sense of much more than the general direction in which he was headed, he was soon lost in the myriad streets blocked by concrete barriers that the city of Berkeley used to keep through traffic out of its residential neighborhoods. Every few blocks a new barrier appeared, forcing another turn to find a new path. At one point, he kept turning this way and that, and every time, he ended up in front of the same modest one-story cinderblock bungalow. Finally, feeling like a fly caught in a spider's web, Greg just pulled over to the curb. As he sat there, his head swirling, he concluded that he had been drugged, that one of Earth First!'s enemies had somehow slipped him a powerful hallucinogen. Greg would maintain that conclusion forever after.

As he was parked by the Berkeley curb, he thought he was dying. It was hard to breathe and he had to tell himself to continue doing so, even though it was easier just to forget about it and deny himself oxygen. His breath was all he had left, he reminded himself. He had to suck it in no matter how hard it hurt. Rain was falling heavily now, clattering on the car roof, and he was so cold he thought maybe he was just hallucinating being in a car and was really outside dying of hypothermia. He banged his feet on the floorboards and slapped his hands together to keep warm. Eventually, that slapping became a rhythmic pounding that got slower and slower, like a clock winding down. A woman in a bright blue parka walked past outside, then walked past again, and again. A white sedan drove by, then drove by again, then again. On its final cruise past, a hand came out of the window and silently waved goodbye. By then, Greg was convinced that when the slapping rhythm of his hands wore down and finally stopped, a bomb hidden somewhere in his car would detonate. He tried to keep clapping but his hands felt like lead and he couldn't maintain. Finally, he just stopped, called out a series of plaintive goodbyes to his mother and his father and everyone else he cared about, and waited for the explosion.

No explosion was forthcoming and, once the sense of relief at its absence passed, Greg noticed that his body was getting increasingly numb and decided that he had better get out of the car so someone could take him to the hospital. There was no one outside to rescue him, so he began walking and came to a big north-south street where all the northbound lanes were blocked off for a street repair that wasn't happening. From the lack of any real road building activity, he concluded that the blocked street was part of a plot to drive him south, into Oakland where he could be easily dealt with, as Judi and Darryl had been. Remembering that he needed help, he then went up to a strange house but abandoned the effort when a hostile voice shouted from behind the door and demanded to know just what he wanted. At a loss for anything else to do, Greg began wandering on foot. For several minutes, two black men followed him with their hands in the pockets of their raincoats, but, when he turned to face them, they fled. Greg then kept walking—wondering if he would be doomed to wander these streets for eternity—until suddenly he saw Darryl's van drive past. He couldn't see who was driving it, but he was sure it was Darryl's van.

By then all the walking had left him feeling a little less wobbly and he returned to his car to attempt to drive out of town again. This time he stumbled onto a main traffic artery and knew he'd at least escaped Berkeley. Along the road to the freeway, he passed a white mini-van identical to one that had followed him up in Humboldt two weeks earlier and had been seen parked outside the motel where he and the other climbers had rendezvoused before the Golden Gate Bridge action. They might not let him go, he told himself, but he was going anyway.

At the off ramp for Interstate 80, Greg turned north and decided to take the Richmond Bridge over to U.S. 101 and drive to his parents' house in the Sonoma County town of Guerneville. For the entire duration of the two-hour trip, he watched the same car in his rearview mirror, following him at the same discreet distance no matter how slow or fast Greg went. When he reached Sonoma County, Greg decided to avoid his parents' for the moment, thinking someone would probably be waiting for him there, and ended up sleeping in an abandoned barn he knew of outside of the town of Occidental. In the morning, he drove on to Guerneville, again discerning surveillance behind him for most of the trip. He stopped along the way at Armstrong Woods, one of his favorite hiking spots, and in the parking lot, he saw four men in suits get out of an American-made sedan and walk across his path, each one staring at him as they went. When he walked toward them, they got back in their car and drove off. Fifteen minutes later, the men cruised by again, staring at Greg all the way. He thought their message was clear: they were not about to let him alone. Not now, not ever.

At his parents', Greg tried to sleep again but all the symptoms he'd felt sitting in his car the day before returned. His breathing became difficult, his body numb. When he dozed, he woke suddenly with a racing heart. He thought it might be a relapse but his strongest suspicion was that he had been dosed a second time, probably by a man out walking a pit bull who had passed him several miles back.

Eventually Greg King got enough hold on himself to write in his journal. "I am a victim of chemical and/or biological *and* psychological warfare by the heinous industrial thought police," he noted. "In order to censure me, the beast had to show its ugly side."

By the time Greg made his way back up to Humboldt a week later, to the tiny cabin where he was living in the Mattole watershed off Briceland Road, he realized that he was through. He couldn't stand up to these kinds of forces anymore and he couldn't go through that kind of assault again. He made one visit to the Redwood Summer base camp out near Whitethorn, where volunteers had begun arriving, but that was it. Mostly, he just hung out at his cabin until the middle of July, when he moved down to his parents' home, sitting with his mother daily until the first week of August, when she finally died.

Sometimes at night Greg King dreamed of derring-do, of the Eel and the Van Duzen, of All Species Grove and Little Rainbow Ridge, but he would never organize around there again. It was over and he was done.

64

By August, of course, Redwood Summer was in full swing and, though far short of the national spectacular Darryl Cherney had once imagined, it was a summer like none other for Humboldt County. Utilizing a full-time hard core of some two hundred long-hairs mostly from around California, the effort managed a spate of headlines, also mostly around California, but those headlines moved farther and farther back in the newspapers as the summer progressed and for long stretches disappeared entirely outside of coverage on the North Coast. Close to fifteen hundred attended rallies in front of the Louisiana Pacific Pulp Mill on Humboldt Bay and in front of the Georgia Pacific Mill in Mendocino. Much smaller groups managed to disrupt a dozen or so logging shows, mostly in August when things were their craziest. August's dementia was magnified by two other events that turned Humboldt on its ear. The first was a decision by a federal drug task force to use a National Guard unit on two weeks of training exercises to attack southern Humboldt's cannabis farms. As a consequence, soldiers in full battle gear, their weapons loaded, were being choppered into clearings in the second growth overlooking the Mattole, east of the Eel, and out toward the Lost Coast. They were accompanied by a freak set of thunderstorms that ignited several forest fires so that the air was often thick with smoke and the roads were full of firefighters and gear being ferried about to stanch the conflagration.

John Campbell mostly watched from a distance with his mouth shut except to make a public complaint that a Redwood Summer task force had chained themselves to fire-fighting equipment out at one of the company's logging shows. The equipment in question included a D-8 Cat and a logging truck. When a demonstration came to Scotia, hoisting signs lauding the Ancient Forest and attacking Charles Hurwitz, John watched from his office as they were greeted by sheriffs arrayed in brand-new riot gear.

Campbell's closest personal encounter with Redwood Summer came on August 17 out at the Simpson Timber Company in Korbel. Campbell was there to participate in an industry symposium and Redwood Summer's troops were picketing outside. John was his usual hail-fellow-well-met self and engaged in the small talk about all these hippies. John was always quick to point out that he had no idea what happened to those two down in Oakland with the bomb and all, but it sure looked like they got caught with their hand in the cookie jar and got it blown off.

When it came time for John to leave, picketers were blocking the entrance to Simpson's parking lot and some of them recognized Campbell, so the yelling stepped up. The Highway Patrol made an opening in the line and waved Campbell through. The farther he got from the lot gate, though, the closer the crowd edged until, without warning, several longhairs began climbing up on his fenders and jumping on the trunk. Sheriff's deputies pulled them off, then one of the sheriffs told Campbell to keep driving and get the hell out of there. As he cleared the crowd, however, another protester came flying out of nowhere and landed on his hood. Campbell drove about seventy yards down the road before he stopped and told the hippie to get the bloody hell off his car.

The hippie yelled back through the window: No way, no fucking way.

At this point, John could see more demonstrators running down the road toward him, so he punched the accelerator for another quarter mile, stopped again, and again demanded this idiot get the bloody hell off his hood.

No way, he said. His friends were coming and when they got here, Campbell would be captured.

Campbell saw he was still being pursued and so did the hippie. The man on the hood grinned almost as wide as the windshield. Bad press, he laughed at Campbell, very bad press.

John snorted. Bad press, my ass. He hit the gas again, pressing the hippie up against the safety glass, and accelerated for another quarter mile and then slammed on the brakes. The hippie managed to hang on by his fingertips.

At that point a sheriff's car pulled up and the hippie was arrested and eventually sentenced to four months in jail.

Redwood Summer kept accelerating to its grand finale on Labor Day: a march through Fortuna to the Pacific Lumber second-growth mill and back. It was one of the few of the Redwood Summer events that Darryl Cherney managed to make. He'd been kicking back and playing music at a friend's house down in San Francisco's East Bay, letting his eye recover, occasionally visiting Judi who was now out of the hospital and back in Mendocino, and occasionally giving press interviews, but he figured this march was not something he could miss. The city of Fortuna had passed a local ordinance to prevent it, but the ordinance had been overturned in court several days earlier and the city ordered to allow the event. At 10:00 A.M., some five hundred marchers started up from a campsite along the Eel River at Fernbridge and moved along U.S. 101 with a Highway Patrol escort until they reached the Fortuna Boulevard exit and, at 1:00 P.M., they turned off and headed into town.

Fortuna was waiting with as ugly a display as Darryl Cherney had ever seen. All along the several-mile-long route of the march, locals lined the road. Some had been waiting for the hippies since that morning, sipping beer from Styrofoam coolers. More than a few brought along baseball bats and golf clubs in case anything serious broke out. The timber crowd was serenaded by a loudspeaker system blasting at full volume, playing a recording of "It Don't Pay to Be an Earth Firster," a big hit on Humboldt County juke boxes all summer long. In every verse, Earth Firsters were cut out of trees, run over by trucks, or just plain shot.

"It don't pay to be an Earth Firster," the chorus went,
"It will only get you hurt real fast,

It don't pay to be an Earth Firster,
Cause if you join Earth First!, you will have a blast."

When the hippies finally showed up, some of the locals threw eggs, some threw tomatoes, some threw balloons filled with yellow paint, and some threw rocks. Even more flipped the bird and screamed for Earth First! to go home and crawl back in the goddamn hole they came out of. In response to one passing banner extolling Mother Earth, a portion of the local crowd began shouting "Jobs First!" More than a hundred police were on duty, called in from as far away as San Francisco, and at several points along Fortuna Boulevard, uniformed officers had to physically separate shouting groups of longhairs and millworkers. Sheriffs detained two Fortuna residents carrying rifles in the vicinity.

Darryl shuddered and walked along with the others. He was scared and knew full well that there was probably no single person the lumberjacks carrying golf clubs would rather tee off on than Darryl Cherney. To protect himself, he relied on several members of the event's security contingent, who surrounded him in a phalanx. He also relied on camouflage. In preparation for the march, Darryl cut his hair short and shaved his beard and, in that condition, even most members of Earth First! didn't recognize him. As he walked along, he heard several groups of Timber People shout out that they wanted Darryl Cherney so they could finish what had been started in Oakland, but obviously they had no idea where he was, even when he was walking right past them. To vent their anger, they flung produce at the flatbed truck carrying portable toilets for the marchers, laughing that the slimy little son of a bitch was probably hiding in one of those.

When the march reached the PL mill, there was a short rally. Ordinarily Darryl would have been one of the featured speakers—his guitar hanging off his neck, singing "Where You Gonna Go When the Trees Are Gone?" or "You Can't Clearcut Your Way to Heaven"—but, today, he considered it far too dangerous even to identify himself.

Following the rally, the intrepid five hundred marched back down the gauntlet through which they'd come. More fruit and vegetables flew through the air, more taunts, and more rocks. A few chain saws were revved for the marchers' benefit. Then, at last, Fortuna was behind them and Redwood Summer was over.

65

In Humboldt County, among the little towns along the Eel, the Mad, the Mattole, and the Van Duzen, more than a few people would use that moment on Labor Day, 1990, when the last hippie crossed back over the Fortuna city limits, to date when the war ended.

By September everybody in the county, one side or another, was spent, sapped by the pitch and frequency of all that had gone on and on and on. Then, the first Tuesday in November, the state of California voted and stalemate settled in for an extended stay. The Forests Forever initiative, authored in large part by The Man Who Walks In The Woods, lost 48 percent to 52 percent. The initiative sponsored by the timber industry lost 29 percent to 71 percent. The timber-law *status quo* satisfactory to neither side would continue unrevised and it was now obvious that neither side was going to get an upper hand sufficient to seize control of the issue anytime soon—and that no one could continue to fight at this pace. So the issue slipped into the doldrums, with sporadic conflict, but to small advantage, usually before one judge or another. The Redwood Action Team was defunct by the time Redwood Summer ended and its direct action campaign shut down, so few logging shows would be stormed anymore. But the courts would continue to keep Pacific Lumber out of Headwaters while PL continued to cut the other pockets of its old growth, its residuals, and its second growth at the same pace Charles Hurwitz had always wanted. Both he and Earth First! would continue to villify each other, but almost no one would stage any frontal assaults for a while.

It had been two years of pitched battle and, now, the war was over and nobody'd won.

Epilogue

1

None of what happened to Humboldt County could ever have been set in motion without Michael Milken, and Michael Milken reached his nadir on April 20, 1990, standing in a New York criminal court room, when he pled guilty to six felony counts: conspiracy to violate the laws of the United States, aiding and abetting the failure to file a truthful and accurate Schedule 13 D with the Securities and Exchange Commission, securities fraud, aiding and abetting the violation by a registered broker-dealer of the SEC's reporting requirements, mail fraud, and assisting the filing of a false tax return. None of the six pertained to his backing of Charles Hurwitz in the takeover of the Pacific Lumber Company. As part of the deal, Milken would pay $600 million in penalties and agree to cooperate with federal prosecutors. "I am sorry," he told the court. "I did break our nation's laws. I allowed myself to get too caught up in what I was doing to consider the consequences or to stop myself from doing what I knew was wrong. For that I am truly sorry and ashamed."

Milken was sentenced to ten years in prison and entered a minimum-security federal facility in California in March, 1991. His sentence was eventually reduced and he served twenty-two months in a minimum-security federal prison before being released to a federal halfway house and then paroled. After his release, he was diagnosed with prostate cancer and underwent chemotherapy. Despite his fine, Milken was still reputed to be worth more than $1 billion.

2

The investment bankers Drexel Burnham Lambert, who provided Milken with his roost, filed for bankruptcy in February 1990, shortly after settling criminal charges with the SEC.

3

Charles Hurwitz's original strategy to cut Headwaters Forest continued to come to naught. Because EPIC continued to block PL access in the courts, Hurwitz and John Campbell had to find a cash flow elsewhere and did. In the meantime, other efforts to save the forest were mustered. The Headwaters Forest Act was submitted to the U.S. Congress in August 1993 and finally voted upon in 1994. The bill called for immediately purchasing the 3,000 acres of Headwaters proper and eventually purchasing another 41,000 acres surrounding it, including the last remains of All Species Grove. Pacific Lumber objected to selling any of its lands, but made it clear that if it must sell, it would insist on fair market value and it considered the fair market value of Headwaters Forest to be in the neighborhood of $600 million—three-quarters of what Hurwitz paid for the entire company in 1985. Pacific Lumber reversed its position on the bill, becoming an advocate for the proposal shortly before it was taken up by the House of Representatives for a vote. The bill then passed the House but died in the Senate.

In March 1995, Pacific Lumber announced that it was dropping its voluntary moratorium on Headwaters THPs and would recommence making every attempt to cut there as soon as possible. In September 1995, the California Department of Forestry granted Pacific Lumber a "salvage logging" permit for Headwaters Forest that would allow them to take out all down, dying, or damaged trees. Earth First!, led again by Judi Bari and Darryl Cherney, greeted this new threat with a demonstration of 2,000 people in front of PL's

Carlotta mill. Three hundred demonstrators were arrested. Shortly afterwards, Pacific Lumber announced a new one-year moratorium on its plans to salvage logs in Headwaters Forest and indicated that it hoped the public would use this breathing space to negotiate a purchase.

The possibility of Headwaters' sale increased as the deadline on the moratorium neared and the Clinton administration, hoping to score some visible environmental successes, added the redwood grove to its immediate agenda. The president himself encountered Charles Hurwitz at a 1996 fund raiser in Houston. The subject of Headwaters reportedly came up between them, and Clinton mentioned the asking price and remarked that Hurwitz couldn't really be serious about selling the old-growth stand. Apparently Hurwitz indicated that he indeed wanted to sell, because the pace of negotiations between a deputy secretary of the Interior and the chairman of Maxxam soon quickened. The formula eventually constructed by the negotiators involved trading surplus federal property to Maxxam for Headwaters. At one point, one of the properties being discussed was a portion of the now vacant naval base on Treasure Island in San Francisco Bay. A deal was finally struck in September 1996 as the end of the voluntary moratorium approached and Earth First! again massed several thousand demonstrators at PL's Carlotta log decks. The agreement included Headwaters Forest plus another smaller old-growth grove and several thousand acres of second-growth buffer around the two, a total of some 7,500 acres to be exchanged for some $380 million worth of either property or cash, two-thirds of which would be put up by the federal government and one-third by the state of California, subject to legislative approval. In addition, the deal allowed Hurwitz ten months in which to draw up a Habitat Conservation Plan for PL's entire acreage to be submitted for approval to the U.S. Fish and Wildlife Service. PL had drawn up two such plans previously, both of which had already been judged inadequate by Fish and Wildlife. Should he fail to design an acceptable plan during this ten month window, Hurwitz retained the right to void the entire deal, returning negotiations to square one. An approved plan would free Hurwitz from further enforcement of the Endangered Species Act—an option EPIC would likely fight in court—and the agreement commits the federal government to join with Maxxam in defending any legal challenge to the arrangement.

4

The principal purchaser of Drexel's 1986 Pacific Lumber issue, the Executive Life Insurance Company, was gutted by the 1990 collapse of the junk bond market. Executive Life also held the annuity upon which the PL Pension Fund covering all the years preceding the takeover depended. It had, of course, long since been stripped of its surplus to pay off Charles Hurwitz's bridge financing. In April 1991, the prospects of Executive Life Insurance became so dire that the California insurance commissioner stepped in and seized control of the company. Its collapse amounted to the largest insurance failure in United States history. Under the operational system set up by the insurance commissioner, the Pacific Lumber annuity continued to pay retirement benefits, but only at seventy cents on the dollar. Saying Executive Life's failure had caught him by surprise, John Campbell was quick to reassure his workforce. Charles Hurwitz, Maxxam, and Pacific Lumber would make up the difference so no pensioners would be shorted on their checks. So far, Hurwitz, Maxxam, and PL have lived up to Campbell's promise.

Hurwitz, Maxxam, and PL were also the defendants in a suit over that same pension fund. The group Bertain helped out in 1990 eventually retained a firm of pension law specialists and, in 1991, they were joined in that suit by the U.S. Department of Labor. The Department of Labor's legal filing characterized Maxxam's decision to purchase its annuity from Executive Life as a violation of federal law and also sought an order prohibiting Charles Hurwitz from ever serving as the fiduciary of a pension plan again.

That suit was settled in the summer of 1996 with a payment of $7 million cash, to be distributed among the company's pensioners.

5

In March 1993, Charles Hurwitz succeeded in refinancing the 1986 Pacific Lumber bonds and avoiding the balloon payments due at the issues' approach of maturity. He also reorganized the company and, in doing so, ensured that Bill Bertain's goal of forced "takeback"— in which Pacific Lumber would be returned to the stockholders who owned it prior to Hurwitz's tender offer—was now impossible.

After March 1993, what had been the Pacific Lumber Company was now broken into separate pieces. Pacific Lumber itself became just the sawmills and several thousand acres of forest. The new PL issued $235 million worth of new junk bonds with the assistance of Salomon Brothers, the investment bankers who had been hired by the old PL in 1985 to defend it against Hurwitz's takeover. A subsidiary of PL, Salmon Creek Corporation, was formed to hold the 6,000 acres of old growth that included Headwaters Forest free and clear of any debt. And a separate, third, company—Scotia Pacific Holding Company—was established to hold ownership of the company's remaining 179,000 acres of timberlands. Scotia Pacific's timber was in turn used to collateralize a $385 million issue of investment-grade, relatively low-interest bonds, whose sale was used to pay off Pacific Lumber's former debt. This new issue of investment-grade bonds also ensured that even if Bill Bertain's former stockholders won a judgment calling for the Pacific Lumber Company's return, the holders of that collateralized debt would still have legal priority over them, making return impossible.

Nonetheless, Bertain continued to pursue his lawsuits against the original perpetrators of the takeover. Eventually he won settlements from the fund set aside by Drexel as part of settling the charges filed in late 1989 by the SEC, from a similar fund set aside by Ivan Boesky, from yet another fund set aside as part of Michael Milken's eventual plea bargain, and from Maxxam, its insurance company, and the insurer of the old Pacific Lumber board of directors. The total awards to the previous shareholders won by Bertain and the big-time law firms with whom he'd allied his cause was some $150 million. Bertain's cut of the award allowed him enough to pay off the more than $600,000 in debts he had accumulated since beginning his quest, and little else.

By the time of the award, Bill had moved his office out to the home he'd built for Rebecca back when this was all first starting. His old office overlooking the waterbed showroom was demolished after being condemned by Humboldt County in order to make room for expansion of the jail across the street. In May 1996, Bertain revived a suit against Maxxam he'd first filed ten years earlier and resumed his legal pursuit of Hurwitz. That suit is awaiting trial.

6

Two of Hurwitz and Milken's collaborators in the Pacific Lumber Company takeover served criminal penalties.

Ivan Boesky, whose secret arrangement with Milken covered Hurwitz's flanks, pled guilty to conspiracy to file a false statement with the Securities and Exchange Commission and served two years of a three-year sentence—eighteen months in a minimum-security prison and six months in a halfway house.

Boyd Jeffries, who held some 2.5 percent of Pacific Lumber's outstanding shares for Hurwitz until after the market took off and then sold them to him at a cut-rate price, pled guilty to aiding and abetting a record-keeping violation and violating legal margin requirements, and became a government witness in several securities cases. He never went to jail and served a brief sentence doing community service, teaching young people the game of golf in Aspen, Colorado.

7

None of the members of the Pacific Lumber board that sold Charles Hurwitz the company remained on the board after its merger into Maxxam.

Gene Elam, Pacific Lumber's president, went on to a job at Pacific Gas and Electric and then, from there, to a position as chief financial officer at the Homestake Mining Corporation, where he is currently employed.

Bob Hoover, PL's chairman of the board, returned to retirement in San Clemente, California.

Ed Carpenter—Stan Murphy's best friend, John Campbell's former father-in-law, and the director on the PL board whose judgment Suzanne Beaver relied on most—died of heart failure in January 1992 at the age of eighty.

Suzanne Beaver—widow of Stan Murphy, mother of Warren and Woody—ceased having any active involvement in business after the takeover, dividing her year between a house in San Francisco, one in Napa County, and the Murphy family ranch on Larabee Creek.

8

Woody Murphy, the first member of his family ever to be fired by the Pacific Lumber Company, returned to public view very briefly after Hurwitz had swallowed PL when he appeared on Humboldt County's local TV news in 1989. Earth First! staged a seaborne demonstration on Humboldt Bay to protest the export of raw logs and, in the course of the demonstration, several Earth Firsters landed their boat on the beach at Woody's Fields Landing log deck. Tracked by a video crew, Woody ran down to where the sheriffs were containing the invasion and demanded that the demonstrators be arrested. One of the Earth Firsters began screaming at Woody that he was an exploiter of the forest and Woody began screaming back that he'd never seen such a dumb bitch in all his life and she'd better get the hell off his beach or he was going to arrest her himself. To shut Woody up, the sheriffs finally had to tell him to back off or they were going to arrest him, too.

9

Warren Murphy—Stan's younger son and the last member of his family to aspire to the Pacific Lumber c.e.o.'s chair—moved to San Diego in the immediate aftermath of Hurwitz's takeover but continued to return to Humboldt County regularly, monitoring his business interests in a Eureka bank and vacationing out at the family ranch on Larabee Creek.

That ranch was the subject of Warren's only interaction with Pacific Lumber Company after it became Charles Hurwitz's. It also provided his only interaction with his former friend, John Campbell. The Larabee Creek ranch had always had hunting rights on the Pacific Lumber timberlands around it but, in September 1986, when Warren stopped by the office to pick up the keys to the logging road gates as was the family's custom, PL refused to release them and Warren was informed that the Murphys' hunting privileges had been revoked. That led to a court fight and a state of continuous friction, in which PL log trucks passing through Murphy land on the company's right of way left pasture gates open, scattering cattle, and a PL security person intimated that the Murphys were involved in drugs. Warren considered it all Campbell's "personal vendetta," undertaken to show, yet one more time, that he was the guy in charge.

10

Contrary to all his fellow workers' expectations, it was not Kelly Bettiga's penchant for mouthing off at company meetings or even his joining Bill Bertain's suit against Maxxam, Hurwitz, Milken, and Drexel that ended his career at Pacific Lumber. Rather, it was the rigors of standing at a chop saw, constantly pulling boards from left to right.

In 1989, Kelly's back began giving him significant trouble and he went to the doctor, who diagnosed him as suffering from a bulging disk. For the next two years, he continued working with the aid of two back braces, pain pills, two knee braces, a brace on his left arm, elastic supports on both calves, and braces and tape on both wrists. Throughout that time, he repeatedly requested that the company transfer him to a job that put less strain on his body, but no transfer was forthcoming. His one connection left in the front office told him quite simply that because the company would just as soon he pulled up stakes and went on down the road, they were never going to find him another job. Finally, in November 1991, when shooting pains began running up and down his legs, Bettiga filed for job-related disability with PL's workman's compensation insurance program. After several months of examination and rehabilitation, he was diagnosed as suffering from a rotated hip and a herniated disk exacerbated by extensive hip slippage. Kelly Bettiga spent most of the next three years in physical rehabilitation, drawing two-thirds pay from PL.

In 1994, Bettiga began retraining for new employment by enrolling in Humboldt State University as a graduate student in history. PL sought to cut his retraining benefits when he did so but a Workman's Compensation judge ordered the benefits reinstated until Bettiga completed work on his master's degree.

11

At 11:06 A.M. on Saturday, April 25, 1992, Scotia was rocked by the eighth most powerful earthquake recorded in the United States during this century.

The initial quake—6.9 on the Richter scale and centered near Petrolia out in the Lost Coast—did no significant damage in Scotia but a 6.0 aftershock at 12:42 A.M. on Sunday snapped the town's gas and water mains. A fire then started in the general store and spread throughout the Main Street business district. The Scotia Volunteer Fire Department turned out to fight the blaze and in the midst of its efforts, a third quake hit—6.5 on the Richter scale—dooming any chance of saving the coffee shop. Eventually the pharmacy, the lumber yard, the variety store, and the hardware store were destroyed as well. Total damages were estimated at $16 million. The Winema Theatre up the block, site of Charles Hurwitz's legendary golden-rule speech, survived unharmed. Some sixty homes in Scotia, the new power plant, and Mills A and B suffered some structural damage, but the mills were back on line within two weeks.

John Campbell announced almost immediately that Charles Hurwitz was committed to rebuilding the charred end of his downtown and, within two years, it was indeed rebuilt.

12

John Campbell also pursued Charles Hurwitz's commitment to squeeze maximum cash flow out of Pacific Lumber. After the earthquake, Campbell moved the start of the day shift at Mills A and B to 5:00 A.M. That meant the shift finished an hour earlier in the afternoon and the resulting surplus electricity from the company's new power plant could be sold to the North Coast's utility grid during peak hours, when the scale paid by the utilities was its highest.

It was the kind of move his detractors had long expected from John. Several days before Christmas 1990, not long after the stalemate settled in, Darryl Cherney led a demonstration to Campbell's house in Redway, to leave him a gift-wrapped present of coal, the traditional Christmas gift to those who had done bad things during the previous year.

Campbell called the sheriffs to force the demonstration off his property, but the demonstration only retreated over the property line and continued. Then Candy Boak and a platoon of Timber People arrived to heckle Darryl's crowd and the two groups faced off at each other for half an hour.

The hippies were singing a song Darryl had composed in honor of Campbell, to the tune of "Hang Down Your Head, Tom Dooley":

"You came from Australia
You married one of the Murphys
They owned Pacific Lumber and all of the redwood trees
As soon as you hit it big time
You made good your life
You didn't need the Murphys, so you divorced your wife.
Hand down your head, John Campbell
Hand down your head and cry
Hand down your head, John Campbell
You made the forest die."

John listened to the racket outside and didn't flinch. If he'd been worried about what those bloody freeloaders thought of him, he pointed out, he'd have been in the nuthouse a long time ago.

13

Patrick Shannon—the peddler of Humbold County's ESOP dreams —reappeared briefly during Redwood Summer, announced that he had no choice but to support the hippies, and marched with them through downtown Fortuna. At the gates to PL's second-growth mill, he was asked by several of the march's organizers to say a few words and gave a rousing speech through the bullhorn. Darryl Cherney freaked out when he learned Shannon was to speak but was unable to prevent it. Darryl told the organizers who unwittingly issued the invitation that they had managed to select perhaps the only person whom the rabid crowd of Fortuna onlookers despised more than Darryl himself.

14

Pete Kayes—who'd helped Patrick Shannon rent the Hydesville fire house for his first ESOP meetings—believes he pretty much guaranteed that he would lose his blacksmith's job when he lost his complaint against Charles Hurwitz and Pacific Lumber at the NLRB. After that, it was all over the grapevine that the company was going to get rid of Kayes by eliminating his job as soon as the opportunity arose.

The axe finally fell on a Friday afternoon in early February 1991. Word was sent for Pete to report immediately to his supervisor's office. When he got there the foreman and a personnel guy from the front office were waiting. The man from the front office said the company no longer needed a full-time blacksmith so Kayes was being "terminated for departmental reorganization." Kaye's supervisor added that with all the trouble the company was having getting its THPs approved, there just wasn't enough work to go around.

Kayes said that was bullshit and they all knew it. This had nothing to do with the lack of work. He was getting fired because of all that he'd done with ESOP and as payback for him going to the NLRB.

The personnel man denied it, but said nothing that changed Kayes's mind.

Eventually, Pete was told he could clean his stuff out of the shop now or come back and do it later.

Pete chose now.

It took him half an hour and while he was packing, a few people stopped in to have a last cigarette and say goodbye, but most stayed away, as though Pete had a communicable disease.

15

Lester Reynolds, another ESOP diehard and a named plaintiff in the lawsuit over the pension plan, testified before the Senate Subcommittee on Labor chaired by Senator Howard Metzenbaum of Ohio during the summer of 1990, when Redwood Summer was swarming over Humboldt. Lester had barely graduated from high school in rural Oregon some four decades before, but he wrote his own testimony. The testimony filled one page, single-spaced, and did little more than describe how their previous pension fund had been discarded for an Executive Life annuity. It took Lester a week to compose and some three minutes to read in front of the senators.

No one at PL had any idea what Lester was up to until the *San Francisco Chronicle* ran a story about the committee's hearings and Lester's expected testimony. When requesting time off in order to travel to Washington, Lester had only said that he had personal business to which he had to attend. Shortly after the *Chronicle* article, Lester's supervisor came running into the shop and began pressuring the rest of the monorail crew if they knew anything about Lester's going to Washington. No one did. Reynolds was back at work the next day, having flown home immediately after his testimony, and he could see that the shit had hit the fan. His supervisor wouldn't even look him in the face, but Lester had no apology. He just said he figured the trip was his own business, not PL's.

Shortly after Lester's testimony, the rules for requesting personal leave from work were changed to require those requesting it to explain what they were going to do with their time off.

16

In the fall of 1990, the author of Charles Hurwitz's other ongoing legal challenge, The Man Who Walks In The Woods, a.k.a Robert Sutherland, a.k.a. T.M.W.W.I.T.W., accompanied an American delegation invited to the town of Severobaikalsk on Lake Baikal to advise local officials on the pitfalls of developing their resources. Woods told the Siberians they should keep a wary eye on American timber companies, who were known to be eyeing the area's forests. That initial trip led to several more and among the projects he advised the Siberians to resist was one involving Charles Hurwitz's Kaiser Aluminum Corporation.

Since then, The Man Who Walks In The Woods has continued his work as EPIC's litigation director. He still lives in the house built by the deranged veteran off the Ettersburg Road and dreams of one day going completely native and living out on the side of King's Peak, near the atomic center where the universal soul wells up out of the planet.

Woods's principal collaborator, Cecilia Lanman, continued to be perhaps the Pacific Lumber Company's most dogged foe. In a fight over one PL THP filed out on Owl Creek near Headwaters, she addressed a 1992 meeting of the state Board of Forestry in Sacramento. Her speech came after PL had spent three hours making its case for being allowed to harvest the grove in question and she was told she would be limited to five minutes' worth of comments. She announced that those limits were grossly unfair and that she would refuse to be bound by them. To shut her up, the board eventually had her physically removed from the room and threatened her with arrest.

17

Judi Bari's wounds healed but she never regained full use of her right leg and continued to suffer from the damage to her internal organs. She resumed her activism and continued to be a leading figure in the Mendocino County environmental movement and California radical circles. She and Darryl Cherney eventually sued the FBI, the Oakland Police, and eight specific individuals from those agencies, charging that they had been falsely arrested in a manner solely designed to discredit Earth First!, subjected to illegal search and seizure, and that their rights to equal protection had been violated when they were singled out for investigation and no genuine investigation for the real bomber was conducted.

In response to discovery motions by the plaintiffs, the Oakland District Attorney's Office claimed to have accidentally destroyed all of its records on the bombing, but the FBI recently released some 5,000 pages of documents and both FBI and Oakland Police Department officers have been deposed by Bari and Cherney's legal team. The documents revealed that, among other things, the bureau used the bombing as an opportunity to conduct illegal surveillance on a number of environmental activists, apparently with the direct approval of then FBI Director William Sessions. The Oakland P.D. admitted not even considering these previous threats against Bari and Cherney in their investigation, dismissing them as a "publicity ploy" that was "insincerely made." When asked whether the FBI's characterization of Bari and Cherney had influenced the decision to arrest the two Earth First! activists and charge them with bombing themselves, the supervising police lieutenant testified that "this wasn't a carload of nuns who were carrying the bomb."

In late 1996, as this edition was being readied for press, Judi Bari was diagnosed with terminal breast cancer. She informed friends that she had less than a year to live.

18

Candy Boak's phone calls to Judi Bari stopped after the bombing and Candy threw herself into Mothers Watch, a pro-timber organization she founded along with several other women. Candy said Mothers Watch was necessary to put the Earth Firsters on notice that there were a lot of Timber People who were fed up and were going to stand up and fight back. During Redwood Summer, Mothers Watch mustered some two hundred Timber People to march on the Earth First! office in Arcata. Most carried signs saying such things as "Earth First! Is The Problem, Not The Solution" and "Would You Trust Your Children's Future To Earth First!?" They met beforehand in a rally at the Arcata baseball park, decorated with tombstones, representing families that would die if Earth First! succeeded in getting Forests Forever passed. Candy was later questioned by police in connection with a phony bomb placed in Redwood Summer headquarters and an accompanying phony bomb threat, but no action was taken against her.

19

Greg King returned to his job reporting for the Sonoma County *Weekly* and then moved on to a reporter's job in Lake County. Within several months of the incident in Berkeley that drove him out of Earth First!, he experienced a mysterious permanent loss of capacity in his lungs, despite being in the best shape of his life. Two years after that, he was diagnosed with testicular cancer, which is now in a state of remission. He eventually left Lake County and now works in a Whole Foods Market in Mill Valley, California, and has begun acting as EPIC's press contact for the San Francisco media.

20

Darryl Cherney continued to be a leading figure in Earth First! and
the North Coast environmental movement but without the wider
public visibility of the old Redwood Action Team days. In 1992, he
ran into John Campbell in the Garberville supermarket.

Hi, John, he said.

Hi, Darryl.

How's it goin'?

Great, just great. How about you?

Couldn't be better, John, couldn't be better.

With that, the two headed down different aisles—John for the
meat section, Darryl to purchase zucchini.

Darryl thought about calling after him to inquire how old Charlie
was doing, but he thought better of it.

21

To no one's surprise, Charles Hurwitz was doing fine.

Aside from the pension fund suit, the only remnant of his high-
flying collaborations with Michael Milken that continued to dog Hurwitz was the 1988 collapse of the United Savings Association of Texas
and its subsequent $1.3 billion public bailout. In 1992, the Federal
Deposit Insurance Corporation informed the United Financial Group
—the holding company controlled by Hurwitz and his allies at Drexel
Burnham Lambert—that UFG was "liable . . . for breach of their fiduciary duties . . . for wrongfully causing USAT to pay dividends to
[UFG], for wrongfully failing to maintain the net worth of USAT, and
for failing to remit tax refunds to USAT." In all, the FDIC then estimated its claim against United Financial Group in the neighborhood
of $548 million, but filed no formal legal action until August 1995.
At that point, the FDIC finally filed suit against him for $250 million.
Eventually the federal Office of Thrift Supervision filed a $900 million
claim against Hurwitz as well. The FDIC case is still awaiting trial, and
the one brought by the Office of Thrift Supervision is scheduled to
be heard by an administrative law judge in the spring of 1997. In negotiations over the sale of Headwaters Forest, Hurwitz would seek unsuccessfully to have both cases dropped as part of the sales agreement.

Otherwise, Charles Hurwitz maintained relative invisibility, continuing Maxxam's run in the Fortune 500 but surfacing in the national press only when he made a lowball bid on Continental Airlines that was rejected, and then again when his name was brought up in speculation of who might buy his hometown Houston Rockets basketball franchise.

Charles was last known to have visited Humboldt in June 1991, to attend a reception for John Campbell after the PL president's second marriage. The reception was held at the Benbow Inn resort south of Garberville, along a wide, meandering stretch of the Eel lined with sandy beaches. The occasion was all fun, no business, and Charles wore a sports shirt rather than his usual dark suit. Otherwise, he looked just the same.

Hurwitz's invisibility resumed until November 1994, when *The Wall Street Journal* ran a story claiming that the Texas takeover artist had retained Salomon Brothers to help him shop the Pacific Lumber Company. The *Journal* claimed Hurwitz was seeking $1 billion for all of the company's assets, minus Headwaters Forest. Maxxam issued a statement the following day, saying that it had indeed retained Salomon to help it consider the parent company's options regarding PL, but that it had decided not to pursue any of those at the present time. Timber industry insiders speculated that Hurwitz was unable to find anyone willing to pay his price, largely because the company was heavily leveraged and faced with ongoing environmentalist opposition to its cutting practices. "But Charlie is a good horse trader," one unnamed timber executive observed, "and I expect we'll see some other [possible deals] down the line."

That timber executive was far from the only one with such expectations. In all that had happened around Pacific Lumber since he showed up, Charles Hurwitz remained the only obvious winner and there was little reason to think that was about to change.

22

Still, it was left to Hurwitz's old collaborator, Michael Milken, to supply the last word. By 1993, Milken had been elevated as the living symbol of the eighties and, after a news item that he was doing a series of guest lectures at the UCLA business school, was even accorded a character in a week's worth of the comic strip "Doonesbury." In that character's inaugural strip, Milken lectures at a biz school.

"I know a lot of you have been asking yourself 'Who is this Professor Milken,'" he says to his class, "'this genius who created a new world of financial instruments.' Well, I'm many things, of course, but most of all, I'm a survivor. After a 98-count indictment and a 6-count plea bargain, I'm still here—and with $1 billion to show for it. Why? Because I never wavered from the three principles of the Milken Code! And what's the code? All together now . . ."

With that the class begins to shout the Milken Code in unison: "GREED WORKS! CRIME PAYS! EVERYBODY DOES IT!"

"And again," Milken intones.

Greed works, crime pays, everybody . . .

A Note on Sources

The foundation of this story is some one hundred and twenty hours of interviews, both on-the-record and confidential, conducted between 1990 and 1995 with this story's participants. Of all the major characters, only Gene Elam, Charles Hurwitz, and Michael Milken declined to speak with me. Charles Hurwitz did, however, respond briefly in writing to a long written interrogatory. I also interviewed a number of other individuals who did not become characters in this book but were significant players in the events that overtook the Humboldt County timber industry during and after the takeover of the Pacific Lumber Company.

Those eyewitness accounts were buttressed by a considerable body of information in the public and legal domain, culled from the archives of the Stanford University Libraries, the University of California Libraries, the Securities and Exchange Commission, the *San Francisco Chronicle*, *The San Francisco Examiner*, *The New York Times*, the California State Assembly, the California Department of Forestry, Hill & Knowlton, the Pacific Lumber Company, Humboldt County Earth First!, the Environmental Protection Information Center, the Data Center in Oakland, the Oakland Police Department, the Federal Bureau of Investigation, the Subcommittee on Oversight and Investigations of the Committee on Energy and Commerce of the U.S. House of Representatives, and the Federal Courts for the Northern District of California and the Southern District of New York, as well as several dozen private individuals in Humboldt and Mendocino Counties.

In addition, I hiked extensively along the watersheds of the Mattole and Eel Rivers to examine the Humboldt redwood forest at ground level, including trips into Headwaters Forest.

I was assisted in portions of this research by Naomi Steinberg, Leslie Weiss, Sophie Harris, Stephan DuVal, Susan Reiner, Gabriel Harris, Dr. Cheri Joy Forrester, Elizabeth Vitelli, the City Center Motel, and PKG Systems.

Index